W9-BVD-746

WITHDRAWN
UNIVERSITY LIBRARY
THE UNIVERSITY OF TEXAS RIO GRANDE VALLEY

PAN AMERICAN UNIVERSITY LIBRARY
BROWNSVILLE, TEXAS 78520

WILKIE COLLINS: WOMEN, PROPERTY AND PROPRIETY

Wilkie Collins: Women, Property and Propriety

Philip O'Neill

BARNES & NOBLE BOOKS
TOTOWA, NEW JERSEY

© Philip O'Neill 1988

First published in the USA 1988 by
BARNES & NOBLE BOOKS
81 ADAMS DRIVE
TOTOWA, NEW JERSEY, 07512

ISBN: 0–389–20771–3

Library of Congress Cataloging-in-Publication Data
O'Neill, Philip.
Wilkie Collins: women, property, and propriety.
Bibliography: p.
1. Collins, Wilkie, 1824–1889—Criticism and
interpretation. 2. Women in literature. 3. Sex role
in literature. 4. Property in literature. 5. Manners
and customs in literature. I. Title.
PR4498.W6054   1988   823'.8   87–27554
ISBN 0–389–20771–3

For My Parents

Contents

Acknowledgements

My special thanks go to Dr Vic Sage in the School of English and American Studies at the University of East Anglia who first introduced me to the novels of Wilkie Collins. I must also thank Dr Roger Sales and Dr Thomas Elsaesser also of the University of East Anglia.

The scene opens on a bedroom — and discloses, in broad daylight a lady in bed.

Persons with an irritable sense of propriety, whose self-appointed duty it is to be always crying out, are warned to pause before they cry out on this occasion. The lady now presented to view being no less a person than Lady Lundie herself, it follows, as a matter of course, that the utmost demands of propriety are, by the mere assertion of that fact, abundantly and indisputably satisfied. To say that anything short of direct moral advantage could, by any possibility, accrue to any living creature by the presentation of her ladyship in a horizontal, instead of a perpendicular position, is to assert that Virtue is a question of posture, and that Respectability ceases to assert itself when it ceases to appear in morning or evening dress. Will anybody be bold enough to say that? Let nobody cry out, then, on the present occasion.

Man and Wife, p. 167

Introduction

The novels of Wilkie Collins occupy a marginal space in the history of English letters. Some critical attention has been paid to *The Moonstone* and *The Woman in White* but even this appropriation is not given the academy's full seal of approval. Rather *The Moonstone* is seen to be the first detective novel and *The Woman in White* is identified as one of the better examples of the sensational genre, a popular literary form which flourished for a brief while in the 1860s. Collins has been widely identified as a writer of 'middle-brow' fiction and condemned by inconsequent praise; as a result, his large and varied fictional output has been allowed to slip into oblivion.

This process began to operate during the writer's own life-time and Collins was himself often a witness to it, certainly when he read Forster's biography of Dickens. Forster had been keen to play up his own relationship with Dickens and underemphasise the Collins connection. Seeing himself belittled in this fashion irritated Collins to speak of the biography as 'The Life of John Forster, with occasional anecdotes of Dickens.'[1] While Forster almost completely edits Collins out of this work on Dickens, it is a Dickens shadow which haunts more recent appreciation of Collins. T. S. Eliot merely compounds this approach in his essay, written in 1927, 'Wilkie Collins and Dickens'.[2] Eliot is nostalgic for a more literary culture and the essay is as involved with a critique of the cinema as it is with a sustained appraisal of Collins. Eliot identifies 'the replacement of dramatic melodrama by cinematographic melodrama, and the dissociation of the elements of the old three-volume melodramatic novel into the various types of the modern 300 page novel'.[3] This dissociation of sensibility is deplored and Eliot recalls a 'golden age' when

> The best novels *were* thrilling; the distinction of genre between such-and-such a profound 'psychological' novel of today and such-and-such a masterly 'detective' novel of today is greater than the distinction of genre between *Wuthering Heights*, or even *The Mill on the Floss*, and *East Lynne*, the last of which 'achieved an enormous and instantaneous success, and was

1

translated into every known language, including Parsee and Hindustani.'[4]

To appreciate Wilkie Collins, Eliot argues, it is necessary to 'reassemble the elements which have been dissociated in the modern novel'. In the nineteenth-century novel, drama had coexisted with melodrama and a comparative study of the novels of Collins and Dickens does much 'to illuminate the question of the difference between the dramatic and the melodramatic in fiction'.[5] All of this, at first, appears very favourable to Collins, but, in the opposition he constructs, Eliot privileges drama. To a large extent this dramatic quality is the preserve of the Dickensian novel and it is the work of Dickens which is used as a cultural yardstick with which to measure Collins. The 'greatest novels' will always be read but, Eliot concedes, that 'it is not pretended that the novels of Wilkie Collins have this permanence.'[6] As far as Eliot is concerned, Collins' melodramatic novels are of value really only as an antidote to the melodrama of the cinema and he is grudging in his praise of Collins.

> And in *The Moonstone* Collins succeeds in bringing into play those aids of 'atmosphere' in which Dickens (and the Brontës) exhibited such genius, and in which Collins has everything except their genius. For his purpose, he does not come off badly. Compare the description of the discovery of Rosanna's death in the Shivering Sands – and notice how carefully, beforehand, the *mis-en-scène* of the Shivering Sands is prepared for us – with the shipwreck of Steerforth in *David Copperfield*. We may say 'There is no comparison!' but there *is* a comparison; and however unfavourable to Collins, it must increase our estimation of his skill.[7]

Eliot is really a poor ally of Collins and the faint praise may have done more to condemn Collins to the critical twilight than would a sustained and polemical dismissal of his novels. Nor is this the only example in the essay where the tenuous nature of Eliot's criticism becomes visible. I would suggest that there is a certain desperation in the attempt to draw up the coordinates identifying drama and melodrama.

You cannot define Drama and Melodrama so that they shall be

reciprocally exclusive; great drama has something melodramatic in it, and the best melodrama partakes of the greatness of drama.[8]

In the context of this essay the dialectic is suspect; Eliot is trying desperately to curtail the popularity of the cinema by advertising the melodramatic qualities of the Collins novels. His appreciation of these novels is rather flimsy and its distant nature is signalled by Eliot's misspelling of the name of Mrs Lecount, a character in *No Name*. Characteristically, however, the essay is not merely ephemeral: Eliot mentions astutely, but in passing, the important operations of Fate and Chance in the novels. In this work, I look in considerable detail at the compound subtleties associated with the workings of Chance, Fate and Providence. Collins places great importance on Chance and his plots and characters are governed more by Chance than any benign Providence or by the operation of Fate.

Eliot also does not miss the opportunity to describe *The Moonstone* as 'the first and greatest of English detective novels'.[9] It is just this critical strait-jacketing which I think it is important to qualify because it misses much of the substance of the novel as a whole. Eliot is not the first, however, to make this claim: G. K. Chesterton had written in 1912 that *The Moonstone* is 'probably the best detective tale in the world.'[10] Dorothy L. Sayers supports this reading of the novel in a discussion of *The Moonstone* first published in 1929, two years after Eliot.[11] This, after Eliot, is orthodox but Sayers saw further and in another introduction, published in 1944, she suggests that Collins is 'genuinely feminist in his treatment of women'.[12]

This is an interesting question but it reiterates and reverses some problems first described by Mrs Oliphant and is connected with Collins' reputation as a sensation novelist. Categorising Collins as a sensational novelist did little to assist any serious reading of his works. A short passage from an anonymous review of *Armadale* will give some idea of the *Westminster Review*'s reception of this genre.

There is no accounting for tastes, blubber for the Esquimaux, half-hatched eggs for the Chinese, and Sensational novels for the English. Everything must now be sensational. Professor Kingsley sensationalizes History, and Mr. Wilkie Collins daily life. One set of writers wear the sensational buskin, another the sensational sock. Just as in the Middle Ages people were afflicted with the Dancing Mania and Lycanthropy, sometimes barking like dogs, and sometimes mewing like cats, so now we have a Sensational Mania. Just, too, as those diseases always occurred in seasons of dearth and poverty, and attacked only the poor, so does the Sensational Mania in Literature burst out only in times of mental poverty, and afflict only the most poverty-striken minds.[13]

The Westminster Review was one of the more liberal of the Victorian journals, and yet it is Mrs Oliphant, writing in the more conservative *Blackwood's*, who qualifies this approach to the sensational novel and argues that Collins is one of the more sophisticated practitioners in the genre. She is discussing *The Woman in White*.

We cannot object to the means by which he startles and thrills his readers; everything is legitimate, natural, and possible; all the exaggerations of excitement are carefully eschewed, and there is almost as little that is objectionable in this highly-wrought sensation novel, as if it had been a domestic history of the most gentle and unexiting kind.[14]

However, what Mrs Oliphant does object to in this essay is Collins' treatment of women. Surprisingly, she almost totally ignores Marian but identifies a 'radical defect' in the conception of Laura.

Yet Mr. Wilkie Collins drives his sensitive and delicate heroine, without any reason in the world for the sacrifice, into a marriage which she regards with horror; makes her drive away her love, and half-kill herself in the effort to give him up, and rather holds her up as the victim of an elevated sense of duty, when, at the cost of all these agonies, she fulfils her engagement, and becomes the unhappy wife of Sir Percival Glyde. Bad morals under any explanation; but when no real reason exists, absolute folly as well, and an ineffaceable blot upon a character meant to be everything that is womanly and tender and pure. It was necessary to marry the two for the exigencies of the story; but the author of the story has shown himself too much a master of the arts of fiction to be tolerated in such a slovenly piece of work as this. A little more care in the arrangement of the marriage – a little less voluntary action on the part of Laura – nay, even the hackneyed expedient of a solemn deathbed charge from her father, or obligation on his part to the undesirable bridegroom – would have given the heroine a much greater hold on the sympathies of the reader, which, we are sorry to say, she loses entirely after the very first scenes.[15]

Mrs Oliphant fails to recognise that Collins is deliberately subverting the popular literary representation of women. She is unaware that Collins' description and treatment of women is not because of the demands of sensationalism, but is an articulation of a very basic objection to the common representation of women in literature. Collins had already published two essays on this very subject in *Household Words*. Mrs Oliphant's attempts to read Collins as a highly skilled sensation novelist blinds her to what is happening in some of these works. The whole question of Collins' treatment of women is worthy of attention. It cannot easily be explained away. Collins sees the situation of women as both symptomatic of, and supportive to, bourgeois patriarchy. Women cannot be discussed in Collins in isolation from the authority exercised by property and mediated through the sense of propriety.

I begin with a discussion of *The Moonstone* and *Armadale*. The detective work in *The Moonstone* parallels the work of the literary critic and it is possible to argue that the novel tests the validity of the process of interpretation for the reader. Popular expectation of the detective genre has set up certain assumptions about *The Moonstone* but the paradox is that this first detective story itself disrupts the reader's expectation about the genre it is commonly taken to have established. While the traditional detective stories may be experienced as essentially reassuring because they project the image of a cosmos subject to the operation of familiar laws, *The Moonstone* disrupts and subverts this very process. Despite Collins' attention to scientific accuracy in the novel any faith in the ability of a dominant rational code to order our awareness of the world is questioned. There is little satisfaction for the reader who believes in the idea of a hidden logic in the world; rather the world is revealed to be governed by Chance. No particular rational order is exposed as privileged; instead, the novel demonstrates the inadequacy of rational explanations in an uncertain universe. Christian Providence is as incompetent as theories of social Darwinism, for example, in this random and indeterminate world. I discuss *The Moonstone* first because it is, as I have implied above the novel which establishes an oversimplified view of the Collins *oeuvre*. However, both *The Moonstone* and *Armadale* also strikingly dramatise the struggles between the competing values of Providence, Fate and Chance. In the juxtaposition of the various accounts of Armadale's dream, Collins again examines the possibility of maintaining a firm, monopolised purchase on reality. The very nature of reality is questioned in *Armadale* and the probability of a transparent world where all is as it appears on the surface becomes, at best, a possibility and, at worst, an illusion. In Collins' fiction there often appears to be little to prevent the successful manipulation of all social codes so that they operate, finally, in the interests of scoundrels. If roguery can keep up a good social appearance, it is allowed to flourish, inhabiting a realm of appearance in which, as Collins shows, society musters its moral codes. These 'rational' codes are interrogated in *Armadale* and this is worked in such a way as to include an illumination of the disjunction between appearance and reality. In particular, Collins' representation of Lydia Gwilt condenses some of these themes into a discussion of the problematic nature of gender stereotyping.

These themes are corroborated in *The Fallen Leaves*, the Collins novel, I would argue, which is currently most worthy of revival. It is a text which has a great deal to say about the representation of women and comes nearest to justifying the 'feminist' label of Sayers. *The Fallen Leaves* is a concentrated text of social criticism containing cogent and sustained comment on contemporary attitudes to politics, business and religion. The content of this novel probably exemplifies Collins at his most eclectic, but this is successfully integrated into a work which focuses these themes around a discussion of the representation of women. Contemporary and more recent reception of this novel is negative and this is not simply because of its apparent assertiveness. There is indeed a rhetorical shift in the novel when it seems that the social and public criticism gives way to the private world of romance. However, I take issue with the view that sees the novel as a work of Dickensian social criticism concluding with a love story. Rather the same criticism is extended from the public to the private sphere and the sexual status-quo is shown to support the public corruption of contemporary England.

Basil is one of Collins' earliest novels and I include discussion of it at this rather anachronistic point because it is important to move away from the idea that *Basil* is merely a work of Collins' literary apprenticeship. Even in this early work Collins is disrupting genre expectation and it is important to consider *Basil* in the context of the more famous novels. As in *The Woman in White*, for example, Collins is already reworking stereotypes in this early work.

The Woman in White must still remain a central text in the Collins canon and it is of pivotal importance in my argument. This novel continues an examination of the relations of property and propriety, linked with the stereotypical representations of gender, and does so in terms of appearance and reality. The word 'propriety' recurs so frequently in this novel that it is impossible to ignore it. Significantly too, it is often linked with appearance and contrasted with that reality which is dictated and circumscribed by the world of property. It is implicit in *The Woman in White* that propriety is a lived practice, an ideology with a material basis which encourages and reproduces an attitude to the world. An ironic pattern of gender ambiguity distributed throughout the characters in the novel demonstrates that for Collins, this attitude belongs to culture rather than nature.

The more explicit social and political nature of Collins' work is indicated by the fact that *Man and Wife* (1870) discusses the state of the Marriage Laws in the light of the report of the Royal Commissioners on the Laws of Marriage published in 1868. Collins also works into this novel a discussion of Athleticism and utilises journalistic reports, in the style of Charles Reade, on the effects of this cult on the universities. This obsession with the topical is commonly understood to mark a change of direction in Collins and to be a sign of his aesthetic decline. However, the situation of wedlock is of central importance, not merely because of a narrow topical interest on Collins' part, but because the patriarchal nature of the marriage laws are more broadly exposed in the terms of the hardship they cause to women. Women are imaged as commodities to be exchanged between men in the interests of property. And while this may not be an altogether new departure, Collins succeeds in showing in unprecedented detail how the law operates to maintain this structure and the subordination of women in the interests of property.

The importance of gender in the organisation of society is also at the heart of *No Name*. With the death of her father, the heroine of this novel finds that she is no longer a legal subject and has no rights in the eyes of the law. Her property is confiscated and the novel follows her attempts to regain her father's estate. Collins develops, to a more tragic degree, further conflicts between sincere feeling and social manipulation and, while moral justice may be on the heroine's side, it is only when she satisfies the interests of legal propriety that she is rewarded with any material success. Again Collins emphasises the social construction of reality and, in its particular form in this novel, it is a masculine construction which serves and protects the rights of property. There is also a dominant theatrical motif in this novel which emphasises the idea of society as spectacle. This is an expansion of the author's concern with the play of illusion and reality which he has developed in other contexts. *No Name* also emphasises the functioning of Chance and it is suggested that life, rather than being determined by a Providential order, is founded on the random machinations of Chance.

Many of the concerns outlined above are clustered around the question of the representation of women and more general questions of gender. My final chapter encapsulates these emergent themes in several of Collins' novels from different periods in his career. Stereotypical representation of women is often the observable symptom of a too easy, and therefore necessarily limited view of reality. The 'objective' and 'impartial' legal system, together with an entire regime of decorum and propriety, serves the factional interest of property. For Collins the organisation of society is not neutral but is a cultural and historical construction. Propriety is a nebulous, but powerful system of ideas and social practices which attempts to dehistoricise society and conceal the fact that these practices have a material base.

1

The Moonstone and *Armadale*

The importance of interpretation cannot be emphasised enough in any discussion of Wilkie Collins. There is a telling passage in the significantly named *The Dead Secret* which underlines and emphasises this point.

> The letter was read again and again; was critically dissected paragraph by paragraph; was carefully annotated by the doctor, for the purpose of extricating all the facts that it contained from the mass of unmeaning words in which Mr. Munder had artfully and lengthily involved them; and was finally pronounced, after all the pains that had been taken to render it intelligible, to be the most mysterious and bewildering document that mortal pen had ever produced.[1]

In many ways this passage may be read as symptomatic of the entire Collins canon and also has implications which may influence that appropriation of Collins which sees him as nothing more than the writer of *The Moonstone*, one of the earliest and most effective of detective stories. The quest for meaning and the search for clues to interpret events are all common aspects of the work of the detective, the literary critic and the general reader. Of course *The Moonstone* is a detective story but it is also a text which rehearses and reworks the business of the literary critic. In parallel with the efforts to discover the villain in the novel run the reader's and critic's attempts to understand the plot and gain a full appreciation of the story. It is just as important to read *The Moonstone* as a novel which interrogates the process of reading itself as it is to see it as an early example of a new genre. And this approach to the text has the further advantage that, if it is kept in mind, the relationship between *The Moonstone* and other Collins fiction becomes less problematic and more of a piece. If *The Moonstone* is seen less as the first detective story and more as a novel which offers a caveat about easy interpretation, Collins' work may be seen as more consistent in its concerns. It then becomes more difficult to caricature him as merely the writer of *The Moonstone* and *The Woman in White* whose talent then went off the boil and who became all too involved in writing didactic fiction.

The Moonstone asks to be read as a detective story, but a detective story which acts as a metaphor for the activity of reading itself. There is a passage in the novel which is a miniature of the work as a whole. This is Ezra Jennings' transcription of Mr Candy's disjointed mutterings as the old doctor suffered the effects of his fever. Ezra Jennings attempts to penetrate through the obstacle of the disconnected expression to the thought which is underlying it, to find the coherent mind behind the inarticulate babbling. From a mere outline of several sentences, Jennings seeks to clarify the voice of his employer. A short example will give some idea of the extent of Jennings' task:

> . . . Mr. Franklin Blake . . . and agreeable . . . down a peg . . . medicine . . . confesses . . . sleep at night . . . tell him . . . out of order . . . medicine . . . he tells me . . . and groping in the dark mean one and the same thing . . . all the company at the dinner-table . . . I say . . . groping after sleep . . . nothing but medicine . . . he says . . . leading the blind . . . know what it means . . . witty . . . . a night's rest in spite of his teeth.[2]

Building on this Jennings constructs the following narrative:

> . . . Mr. Franklin Blake is clever and agreeable, but he wants taking down a peg or two when he talks of medicine. He confesses that he has been suffering from want of sleep at night. I tell him that his nerves are out of order and that he ought to take medicine. He tells me that taking medicine and groping in the dark mean one and the same thing. This before all the company at the dinner-table. I say to him, you are groping after sleep, and nothing but medicine can help you find it. He says to me, I have heard of the blind leading the blind, and now I know what it means. Witty – but I can give him a night's rest in spite of his teeth.[3]

The reader of *The Moonstone* is faced with a similar task to that of

Ezra Jennings. The reader must connect together the various narratives into a coherent whole, and must 'weave a smooth and finished texture out of the ravelled skein'.[4]

Rather than offer an immediately perceptible and transparent purchase on reality *The Moonstone* must be continually read and re-read, written and re-written. This becomes clear very early in the novel when the local policeman, Superintendent Seegrave, reads the clues leading up to the disappearance of the diamond in one way only to have his opinion shattered and our trust in him destroyed when the great Sergeant Cuff reinterprets the same clues in a completely different way. Gabriel Betteredge describes events leading up to the mystery of the vanishing diamond; this is one half of the novel and the final section of the work simply questions Betteredge's account of these events. Collins never suggests that Betteredge is an omniscient narrator and the fact that he is also a character in the story calls his assumptions and interpretations into doubt. The case does not merely rest here however. There are a selection of incidents in the text where it is made abundantly clear that the Betteredge version of events is far from definitive. Perhaps the most colourful of these involves the old retainer in his favourite role as mentor to Franklin Blake. Betteredge is holding forth on marriage, his opinions based on his own experiences with his wife Selina. All women have their faults, their way of riding the high horse, Betteredge explains and he details an example of how he handled his wife when she refused to cook for him. Betteredge placed her in the parlour, cooked his own meal, then left the kitchen spick and span. He concludes this homily with a glorious non-sequitur for Franklin Blake's edification.

> "For the rest of that woman's life, Mr. Franklin, I never had to cook my dinner again! Moral: You have put up with Miss Rachel in London; don't put up with her in Yorkshire. Come back into the house." Quite unanswerable! I could only assure my good friend that even *his* powers of persuasion were, in this case, thrown away on me.[5]

Betteredge had hoped to instruct Franklin Blake about women but this should serve as a warning to the reader to be on guard against accepting, too easily, any of Betteredge's interpretations of the events he recounts. And it is easy to make the case that it is not simply a matter of refusing Betteredge's individual opinion but an entire system of thought. Betteredge himself makes much of, and mocks, Franklin Blake's European education and continental habits of thought and Blake, himself, identifies Betteredge's opinions as 'redolent of the most positive philosophy I know – the philosophy of the Betteredge school.'[6] Accordingly, in the lighthearted exchanges between Franklin Blake and Betteredge, as they quarrel about the missing diamond, there is a testing of the validity of various philosophical speculations. What is at stake is the validity of philosophical premise and the ability to provide interpretations of our world.

Even in Betteredge's own narrative, there are many examples of his inconsistencies and the general emphasis on interpretation should warn the reader to be chary about all interpretation. Betteredge's own pyrrhonistic dictum 'Many men, many opinions'[7] has a peculiar resonance when it is placed in this context and it gains momentum, yet again, when it is pointed out to be a recurrent motif in this first section of the text. Here Betteredge is commenting on Franklin Blake's and Godfrey Ablewhite's reactions to Superintendent Seegrave. ' "That man will be of no earthly use to us. Superintendent Seegrave is an ass." Released in his turn, Mr. Godfrey whispered to me, – "Evidently a most competent person. Betteredge, I have the greatest faith in him!" '[8] And this is not the first example in the novel where an array of contrary opinions about the same thing is set in front of us. After the Indians' visit to Frizinghall, there is a difference of opinion expressed about these suspect jugglers and their nation.

> In the country those men came from, they care just as much about killing a man, as you care about emptying the ashes out of your pipe. If a thousand lives stood between them and the getting back of their Diamond – and if they thought they could destroy those lives without discovery – they would take them all. The sacrifice of caste is a serious thing in India, if you like. The sacrifice of life is nothing at all.
>
> I expressed my opinion, upon this, that they were a set of murdering thieves. Mr. Murthwaite expressed *his* opinion that they were a wonderful people. Mr. Franklin, expressing no opinion at all, brought us back to the matter in hand.[9]

A little earlier in the novel Betteredge and Franklin Blake discuss the Colonel's motivation for bequeathing the diamond to his niece.

'I can see,' says Mr. Franklin, 'that the Colonel's object may, quite possibly, have been – not to benefit his niece, whom he had never even seen – but to prove to his sister that he had died forgiving her, and to prove it very prettily by means of a present made to her child. There is a totally different explanation from yours, Betteredge, taking its rise in a Subjective-Objective point of view. From all I can see, one interpretation is just as likely to be right as the other.'[10]

The reference to the 'Subjective–Objective' point of view is interesting because in the contrasting views of Betteredge and Franklin Blake, as has been mentioned, there is a rehearsal of the debate between a peculiar and individual version of British positivism and Blake's 'foreign varnish'[11] as Betteredge describes his training. The mention of varnish is important here. It denotes Betteredge's derogatory view of Franklin's approach to life and suggests that his foreign training and foreign education is a veneer and a surface which may be actually corrupting and subverting a more honest, and essentially more English grasp of reality. Blake explains that he is 'an imaginative man; and the butcher, the baker, and the tax-gatherer, are not the only credible realities in existence to *my* mind'.[12] He cautions Betteredge that

'There is a curious want of system, Betteredge, in the English mind; and your question, my old friend, is an instance of it. When we are not occupied in making machinery, we are (mentally speaking) the most slovenly people in the universe.'[13]

But Betteredge is completely impervious to this advice and explains that 'It is one of my rules in life, never to notice what I don't understand',[14] and, in his turn, advises the reader to 'Cultivate a superiority to reason, and see how you pare the claws of all sensible people when they try to scratch you for your own good!'[15] Betteredge looks toward *Robinson Crusoe* almost as a secular Bible and depends on it for guidance when he is confronted with difficulty. Betteredge and Franklin hold contrasting views yet Collins seems unwilling to delineate them precisely. This substantiates my interpretation of the novel which argues, that what are at issue, are the difficulties involved in all interpretation rather than the relative merits of any particularised philosophy. For example, Betteredge's insistence on the centrality of *Robinson Crusoe* implies both empiricism and faith. It is difficult to separate one from the other.

Betteredge and Franklin Blake are probably contrasted most keenly in their interpretation of Rachel's behaviour after the theft. The text makes clear all that is involved in this opposition.

'Your sherry is waiting for you, sir,' I said to him. I might as well have addressed myself to one of the four corners of the room; he was down in the bottomless deep of his own meditations, past all pulling up. 'How do you explain Rachel's conduct, Betteredge?' was the only answer I received. Not being ready with the needful reply, I produced *Robinson Crusoe*, in which I am firmly persuaded some explanation might have been found, if we had only searched long enough for it. Mr. Franklin shut up *Robinson Crusoe*, and floundered into his German-English gibberish on the spot. 'Why not look into it?' he said, as if I had personally objected to looking into it, 'Why the devil lose your patience, Betteredge, when patience is all that's wanted to arrive at the truth? Don't interrupt me, Rachel's conduct is perfectly intelligible, if you will only do her the common justice to take the Objective view first, and the Subjective view next, and the Objective-Subjective view to wind up with. What do we know? We know that the loss of the Moonstone on Thursday morning last, threw her into a state of nervous excitement, from which she has not recovered yet. Do you mean to deny the Objective view, so far? Very well, then – don't interrupt me. Now, being in a state of nervous excitement, how are we to expect that she should behave as she might otherwise have behaved to any of the people about her? Arguing in this way, from within-outwards, what do we reach? We reach the subjective view. I defy you to controvert the Subjective view. Very well then – what follows? Good Heavens! the Objective-Subjective explanation follows, of course! Rachel, properly speaking is *not* Rachel, but Somebody Else? You are unreasonable enough, Betteredge; but you can hardly accuse me of that. Then how does it end? It ends, in spite of your confounded English narrowness and prejudice, in my being perfectly happy and comfortable. Where's the sherry?'[16]

Betteredge's philosophy is now identified as 'English narrowness and prejudice' and his faith in the prophetic powers of *Robinson Crusoe*, akin to the non-conformist use of the Bible, is dismissed as superstition. Yet, throughout the novel, ambiguity and ambivalence are stressed and it is emphasised that it is difficult to be confident in any opinion. Cuff has an argument with Mr Begbie the gardener about horticulture and it is explained that 'In the matter of the moss rose there is a great deal to be said on both sides!'[17] When Godfrey Ablewhite is eventually unveiled as the villain in this work, Sergeant Cuff explains that 'With regard to the subject now in hand, I may state, at the outset, that Mr. Godfrey Ablewhite's life had two sides to it.'[18] And in the course of *The Moonstone* there are often more than two sides to a problem as when Rosanna promises Franklin that the diamond thief will never be found. Betteredge advances three possibilities which could explain this and her immediate behaviour. It may be to advance her own self-importance; it may be because she is ill or again because she is 'breaking her heart about Mr. Franklin Blake'.[19]

Sometimes this difficulty in reading through the confusions in the text rests on the predisposition to accept all too quickly appearance for reality. Betteredge falls into this trap in his initial reactions to Superintendent Seegrave and Sergeant Cuff.

For a family in our situation, the Superintendent of the Frizinghall police was the most comforting officer you could wish to see. Mr. Seegrave was tall and portly, and military in his manners. He had a fine commanding voice, and a mighty resolute eye, and a grand frock-coat which buttoned beautifully up to his leather stock. 'I'm the man you want!' was written all over his face; and he ordered his two inferior policemen about with a severity which convinced us all that there was no trifling with *him*.[20]

Seegrave looks authoritative and efficient so Betteredge is prepared to trust him in his professional capacity. This contrasts with Betteredge's initial description of Cuff.

A fly from the railway drove up as I reached the lodge; and out got a grizzled, elderly man, so miserably lean that he looked as if he had not got an ounce of flesh on his bones in any part of him. He was dressed all in decent black, with a white cravat round his neck. His face was as sharp as a hatchet, and the skin of it was as yellow and dry and withered as an autumn leaf. His eyes, of a steely light grey, had a very disconcerting trick, when they encountered your eyes, of looking as if they expected more of you than you were aware of yourself. His walk was soft; his voice was melancholy; his long lanky fingers were hooked like claws. He might have been a parson, or an undertaker – or anything else you like, except what he really was. A more complete opposite to Superintendent Seegrave than Sergeant Cuff, and a less comforting officer to look at, for a family in distress, I defy you to discover, search where you may.[21]

Of course, Betteredge's faith in appearance is ill-founded and Seegrave proves to be a very inferior officer in comparison with the unlikely Cuff. But then popular expectation is overturned on a variety of levels in *The Moonstone*. The coordinates separating good and bad, light and dark fluctuate and fuse and popular prejudice is parodied and turned against itself.[22] Many of these common biases are focused in the figure of Ezra Jennings. Betteredge makes the assertion 'that the appearance of Ezra Jennings, speaking from the popular point of view, was against him', and even his name is 'as ugly as a name need be'.[23] But in a novel which deals so much with dualities and ambivalence it is appropriate that Jennings should combine so many apparently opposite qualities into his nature and appearance.

The door opened, and there entered to us, quietly, the most remarkable-looking man that I have ever seen. Judging him by his figure and his movements, he was still young. Judging him by his face, and comparing him with Betteredge, he looked the elder of the two. His complexion was of a gypsy darkness; his fleshless cheeks had fallen into deep hollows, over which the bone projected like a pent-house. . . . From this strange face, eyes, stranger still, of the softest brown – eyes dreamy and mournful, and deeply sunk in their orbits – looked out at you, and (in my case at least) took your attention captive at their will. Add to this a quantity of thick closely-curling hair, which by some freak of Nature, had lost its colour in the most startlingly partial and capricious manner. Over the top of his head it was still of the deep black which was its natural colour. Round the sides of his head – without the slightest gradation of grey to break the force of the extraordinary contrast – it had turned completely white.[24]

Jennings is a man of contrasts; his figure and face clash, his eyes look out of place and his piebald hair is an irregular growth of black and white. He is an enigma designed to confuse stereotypes and show the inadequacy of 'the popular point of view'.

As someone on the margins of society, a 'gypsy', Ezra Jennings has a certain contempt for the social graces. He reports, with a degree of wry humour, the fact that Mrs Merridew doubts the 'propriety' of allowing Rachel to stay alone in a house full of men. 'Mrs. Merridew stands in mortal fear of the opinion of the world. She has unfortunately appealed to the very last man in existence who has any reason to regard that opinion with respect.'[25] Such is the extent of Jenning's isolation that he even finds himself in dispute with his medical colleagues in Frizinghall about the medical treatment which would best serve Mr Candy's recovery.

> The two doctors were for keeping him on gruel, lemonade, barley-water, and so on, I was for giving him champagne, or brandy, ammonia, and quinine. A serious difference of opinion, as you see! a difference between two physicians of established local repute, and a stranger who was only an assistant in the house.[26]

Jennings is on the other side of polite society and his vision is other and different. His father was English but 'there was the mixture of some foreign race in his English blood'.[27] He explains that he has a strong empathy with Franklin Blake because 'You have youth, health, riches, a place in the world, a prospect before you. You, and such as you, show me the sunny-side of human life, and reconcile me with the world I am leaving, before I go.'[28] Jennings even transgresses gender stereotypes. 'Physiology says, and says truly, that some men are born with female constitutions – and I am one of them!'[29]

Ultimately it is Jennings who supplies the answer to the

PAN AMERICAN UNIVERSITY LIBRARY
BROWNSVILLE, TEXAS 78520

mystery of the disappearing diamond. However, it would be a mistake to read this success as a vindication of Jennings' scientific method. The situation is more complicated than this and there are grounds to suggest that his triumph is as much a matter of chance as it is the result of sustained and rigorous thought. There is a certain tentativeness, which is more than just tactical, in one of the first explanations of his hypothesis which he gives to Blake. He is sceptical of the legal version of events as they have been elaborated by Bruff, but, also modest about his own proposals.

'With all deference to you,' he said, 'and with all deference to your legal advisor, I maintain the opinion which I expressed just now. It rests, I am well aware, on a mere assumption. Pardon me for reminding you, that your opinion also rests on a mere assumption as well.' The view he took of the matter was entirely new to me. I waited anxiously to hear how he would defend it.

'I assume,' pursued Ezra Jennings, 'that the influence of the opium – after impelling you to possess yourself of the Diamond, with the purpose of securing its safety – might also impel you, acting under the same influence and the same motive, to hide it somewhere in your own room. *You* assume that the Hindoo conspirators could by no possibility commit a mistake. The Indians went to Mr. Luker's house after the Diamond – and, therefore, in Mr. Luker's possession the Diamond must be! Have you any evidence to prove that the Moonstone was taken to London at all? You can't even guess how, or by whom, it was removed from Lady Verinder's house! Have you any evidence that the jewel was pledged to Mr. Luker? He declares that he never heard of the Moonstone; and his banker's receipt acknowledges nothing but the deposit of a valuable of great price. The Indians assume that Mr. Luker is lying – and you assume that the Indians are right. All I say, in differing with you, is – that my view is possible. What more, Mr. Blake, either logically or legally, can be said of yours?'[30]

At the most, Jennings will only argue his view is possible and so probability and chance are inserted implicitly into the debate. It is only a possibility that Jennings holds the key to the mystery. And the chance that this possible interpretation is correct is

PAN AMERICAN UNIVERSITY LIBRARY
BROWNSVILLE, TEXAS, 78520

emphasised at another point in the novel. Although Jennings is researching a respectable medical subject, the brain and the nervous system, his own academic pedigree is not as impeccable as it might appear. To reinforce and lend credibility to his case, Jennings shows Franklin Blake two scientific treatises, one by a Dr Carpenter, the other written by a Dr Elliotson. The success of Jennings' explanation is reduced even more to a matter of chance if it is known that while Carpenter was a respectable scholar and genuine scientist, Elliotson on the other hand, was a suspect character and had something of the reputation of a quack.[31] As Hutter suggests the medical authority is actually contradictory so the possibility of the success of the Jennings experiment does seem to be a matter of chance. Once again no interpretation is privileged and the entire matter of making sense of the world is left to the meanderings of chance.

Armadale is not a detective novel and yet it shares many of the concerns and themes of *The Moonstone*. *Armadale* also interrogates the process by which meaning is given to events, but it never satisfactorily convinces that there is simply one meaning and one answer or that the novel can resolve contradiction. Collins is aware of the result of this. His readers will be made uneasy because the novel does not satisfy the desire to confirm the reader in the comforts of bourgeois existence. Instead, *Armadale* has an equivocal end. Contradictions are maintained and sustained. The appendix makes this clear.

> NOTE: – My readers will perceive that I have purposely left them, with reference to the Dream in this story, in the position they would occupy in the case of a dream in real life – they are free to interpret it by the natural or supernatural theory, as the bent of their own minds may incline them.[32]

In the body of the novel a supernatural and a rational explanation compete for credibility. There is the desperate hope that some rational view will satisfy all the riddles of the story, but the reader is still uneasy and the supernatural can never be dismissed for any length of time. There is always contradiction and it is impossible to rest contented with one single version of events. There is a conflict between the internal unfinalised nature of the events and the external completedness of the novel itself. The story does come to an end but little is resolved. This is an unusual way to end a Victorian novel and Collins may be seen as going some way to curtail and limit this dissatisfaction by writing an appendix – a supplement which will make things right and answer all conundrums. But once again Collins frustrates the reader as again supernatural and rational incidents are given equal prominence. He writes of the strange events aboard the ship 'Armadale' while that vessel lay in the Huskisson Dock at Liverpool in November 1865, 'that is to say when thirteen monthly parts of *Armadale* had been published'.[33] Apparently three men had been poisoned mysteriously while sleeping on the ship, suffocated by poisoned air. Collins refers the reader to the relevant issues of *The Times* and *Daily News* to confirm these facts. The novelist is underlining the inexplicable, by invoking the facts of a contemporary case. The scepticism of the fiction is supported by the inexplicability of real facts. How else could events on the ship, a ship with the same name as the novel, parallel the plot of the novel itself?

No sooner has this been said, however, before Collins then emphasises the rationality and scientific accuracy of *Armadale*. The Norfolk Broads are described in the novel only 'after personal investigation of them' and on this, like other matters, the author explains that he has spared no effort 'to instruct myself on matters of fact'.[34] Like *The Moonstone*, *Armadale* is marked by appeals to authority and quotation from legal and scientific text books. Wilkie Collins has Armadale and Miss Milroy study a legal tome together and the Appendix concludes with a statement defending the accuracy of the description of Dr Le Doux's medical equipment.

> Wherever the story touches on questions connected with Law, Medicine, or Chemistry, it has been submitted before publication, to the experience of professional men. The kindness of a friend supplied me with a plan of the Doctor's Apparatus – and I saw the chemical ingredients at work, before I ventured on describing the action of them in the closing scenes of this book.[35]

But even this appeal to medical authority is dubious if the suspect medical authority for *The Moonstone* is recalled.

Throughout *Armadale* there is the simultaneous presentation of contradictory explanation and exposition. It is as if the author is playing with the need of the nineteenth-century reader to have some rational, scientific gloss on the world. Collins goes some way towards satisfying this desire but then pulls up short and also foregrounds the terrible and the irrational in life. One explanation will not hold for long. Events are counter and contrary and apparently will not accommodate themselves to any settled view of things. As in the appendix, as much importance is given to the rational and scientific in man as is given to the supernatural aspects of life. One incident undermines the other just as a scientifically verifiable description is juxtaposed with mention of the uncanny coincidence aboard the Liverpool boat.

Armadale has as its theme the problem of interpretation, in particular the interpretation of the mysterious dream of Allan Armadale. As the novel develops, the reader is left in a quandary as to whether or not events may be explained in any rational manner or whether they have their origin in a fateful intervention over which people have no control. Collins will not satisfy the reader either way on this question and even at the close of the novel, there is little indication that one interpretation is more accurate than another. Midwinter makes a copy of Armadale's dream and, at one point, agrees to show it to Mr Hawbury, the local doctor with whom he is breakfasting. Hawbury has been told the significance Midwinter places on the dream, the dream as a warning of things to avoid in the future, but the doctor immediately reinterprets it from an 'essentially practical point of view'.

> After reading the narrative attentively to the last line (under which appeared Allan's signature) the doctor looked across the breakfast-table at Midwinter, and tapped his fingers on the manuscript with a satirical smile.
>
> "Many men, many opinions," he said. "I don't agree with either of you about this dream. Your theory," he added, looking at Allan, with a smile, "we have disposed of already: the supper that *you* can't digest, is a supper which has yet to be discovered. My theory we will come to presently; your friend's theory claims attention first."[36]

Allan's dream took place upon the 'confounded timbership *La Grace de Dieu*', the very ship, significantly named, upon which Midwinter's father killed Allan's father. This is one of the first strange coincidences in the novel. Mr Hawbury reads Midwinter's

account of the dream over the breakfast table the next morning.
Midwinter believes the dream is a supernatural warning to Allan
who accounts for the dream as a symptom of indigestion. The doctor
disagrees with both young men and volunteers his own reading of
the dream. Midwinter suggests that the doctor's account is suspect
because the view of a medical man 'seldom ranges beyond the point
of his dissecting knife'.[37] So in the contrasting views of Hawbury,
Armadale and Midwinter, we have in miniature a problem which
dominates the entire novel. The doctor is an advocate of rationality,
Armadale a trifle naive, and Midwinter believes in the supernatural.
Collins will not deny or support either view although Armadale's
innocence is censured.

> "There it is in a nutshell! – Permit me to hand you back the
> manuscript, with my best thanks for your very complete and
> striking confirmation of the rational theory of dreams." Saying
> these words, Mr. Hawbury returned the written paper to
> Midwinter, with the pitiless politeness of a conquering man.
> "Wonderful! not a point missed anywhere from beginning to end!
> By Jupiter!" cried Allan, with the ready reverence of intense
> ignorance. "What a thing science is!" "Not a point missed, as you
> say," remarked the doctor, complacently. "And yet I doubt if we
> have succeeded in convincing your friend." "You have *not*
> convinced me," said Midwinter. "But I don't presume on that
> account to say that you are wrong."
>   He spoke quietly, almost sadly. The terrible conviction of the
> supernatural origin of the dream, from which he had tried to
> escape, had possessed itself of him again.[38]

The author warns us to be on our guard against accepting too readily
the doctor's interpretation. It is not for nothing that he describes
Allan's outburst as 'the ready reverence of intense ignorance'. By
such means Allan's naive rationality is made suspect and shown to
lack any of the sophistication of the competing ideas of Midwinter
and the doctor. Collins makes little effort to conceal the
contradictions which divide these two. There is no attempt to hide
these differences and suggest that, in actual fact, there is a
consensus and that any disagreement is simply one of emphasis.
The doctor realises this.

> The doctor rose – laid aside his moral dissecting-knife –
> considered for a moment – and took it up again.

"One last question," he said. "Have you any reason to give for going out of your way to adopt such a mystical view as this when an unanswerably rational explanation of the dream lies straight before you?"

"No reason," replied Midwinter, "that I can give, either to you or to my friend."

The doctor looked at his watch with the air of a man who is suddenly reminded that he has been wasting his time. "We have no common ground to start from," he said; "and if we talked to doomsday, we should not agree."[39]

Midwinter is not convinced by the doctor, and when Armadale offers to tear up his copy of the dream, Midwinter explains that he will stick to his guns and will not consider a change of opinion until they reach Thorpe-Ambrose. The point is that while Collins appears to be indicating an authorially sanctioned reading, this interpretation is constantly negated and disrupted. One explanation follows another in quick succession and each one contradicts what has gone before.

Further evidence of the supernatural view of things, is given by Midwinter's interpretation of the dream, when Collins as omniscient narrator, again and again undermines our confidence in Armadale's judgement. We are told that 'Allan's essentially superficial observation had not mislaid him for once' when the young man is examining his recently inherited manor-house.[40] That his opinion is normally superficial should put readers on their guard. Again when Allan is introduced to Major Milroy, the author remarks that a man 'with a larger experience of the world, and a finer observation of humanity than Allan possessed, would have seen the story of Major Milroy's life written in Major Milroy's face'.[41] Allan is socially gauche as he takes tea with the Major and is too insistent in his concern for Mrs Milroy. 'A closer observer than Allan might have suspected that their conversation was displeasing to the retired officer.'[42] But there are also times when Collins conforms to and confirms stereotype. While, at one stage, as above he is determined to warn against a too easy acceptance of the obvious, he will, at another time confirm and build upon predominant prejudice and opinion. This is the case when Allan first visits the Milroy's in their cottage. A stereotype from popular illustration is invoked.

Before Allan could reply, they turned the corner of the plantation, and came in sight of the cottage. Description of it is needless; the civilized universe knows it already. It was the typical cottage of the drawing-master's early lessons in the neat shading and the broad pencil touch – with the trim thatch, the luxurient creepers, the modest lattice-windows, the rustic porch, and the wicker birdcage, all complete.[43]

This received opinion is again voiced, or better double-voiced, in the description of Dr Downward but in this passage there is a distancing which signals Collins' recognition of the dangers of the too-easy acceptance of appearance.

The doctor bowed. If the expression may be pardoned, he was one of those carefully-constructed physicians, in whom the public – especially the female public – implicitly trust. He had the necessary bald head, the necessary double eyeglass, the necessary black clothes, and the necessary blandness of manner, all complete. His voice was soothing, his ways were deliberate, his smile was confidential. What particular branch of his profession Doctor Downward followed, was not indicated on his door-plate – but he had utterly mistaken his vocation, if he was not a ladies' medical man.[44]

Armadale's dream has a double front and is open to different interpretation. It is not an easy matter to interpret it with any degree of certitude. While Collins acts as omniscient narrator the impression is that Midwinter's reading of events may be a true description of the state of play. However, in other passages, in the correspondence between Miss Gwilt and Mrs Oldershaw, it is certainly the case that a plot is underway to injure Allan. The machinations of these two women explain so much which otherwise would appear as strange and eerie coincidence. The doctor's rational view may not be correct but an equally rational view may explain events in the dream as a foreshadowing of the Gwilt–Oldershaw conspiracy. The situation can, at times, be very confused because this conspiracy to defraud Allan is not recognised by Midwinter and is often understood by him in terms of supernatural intervention.

The supernatural view is again predominant when, in his exploration of the house at Thorpe-Ambrose, Midwinter recognises the room which Armadale describes in his dream. Midwinter asks himself if it is simply chance which allows for such coincidence.

"Here in the country-house, or there on board the Wreck," he said bitterly, "the traces of my father's crime follow me, go where I may." He advanced towards the window – stopped and looked back into the lonely neglected little room. "Is *this* chance?" he asked himself. "The place where his mother suffered is the place he sees in the Dream; and the first morning in the new house is the morning that reveals it, not to *him*, but to *me*, Oh, Allan! Allan! how will it end?"[45]

Midwinter has been made sensitive to the operation of chance, Fate and Providence and their competing and potentially divergent implications and connotations. In his confession to Mr Brock he asks 'Which am I – now that the two Allan Armadale's have met again in the second generation – an instrument in the hands of Fate, or an instrument in the hands of Providence?'[46] Unaware of Miss Gwilt's plot to secure for herself the Armadale fortune, Midwinter sees all the evidence indicate support for a supernatural interpretation of the dream. When Miss Gwilt arrives at Thorpe-Ambrose she dashes off to join the picnic set on the Broads. Midwinter and Allan discover her standing at the water's edge in a pose very similar to that prophesied in the dream.[47] Simultaneous to this, Mr Brock the priest who educated Allan has become aware of Mrs Oldershaw. Brock suspects correctly that she is plotting against Allan and in the attempt to protect his former pupil sends Midwinter a description of the woman he has been tricked into believing is Miss Gwilt. Midwinter now apparently has the evidence to satisfy his suspicion that the woman in the dream is the governess, the Miss Gwilt who conspired with Mrs Oldershaw in Kensington. Midwinter spies on Miss Gwilt and discovers that she does not answer the description provided by Brock. The evidence of his own eyes convinces Midwinter that the dream warning is false on this count at least. Miss Gwilt is not part of a fatal conspiracy working against Allan, but what, in fact, she claims to be, the innocent governess of the Milroy family. Midwinter concludes that, to date, his entire reading of the events had been wrong and that the dream did not have any special significance. It may, after all, have even been a symptom of Armadale's indigestion.

The entire change wrought in his convictions by the memorable event that had brought him face to face with Miss Gwilt, was a change which it was not in his nature to hide from Allan's knowledge. . . . The merit of conquering his superstition was a merit which he shrunk from claiming, until he had first unsparingly exposed that superstition in its worst and weakest aspects to view. . . . The glaring self-contradictions betrayed in accepting the Dream as the revelation of a fatality, and in attempting to escape that fatality by an exertion of free will – in toiling to store up knowlege of the steward's duties for the future, and in shrinking from letting the future find him in Allan's house – were, in their turn, unsparingly exposed.[48]

The rational appears to have triumphed, but it is obviously not the end of the matter because the author quickly points out that it was just Midwinter's victory over his fatalism that actually favoured the 'fulfilment of the Second Vision of the Dream'.[49] When Allan discovers that the room in question had been specially considered by his mother, he immediately turns it into his own personal quarters. Eventually the two men argue and then realise immediately that they are merely fulfilling the prophecies of the dream once again.

The rain drove slanting over flower-bed and lawn, and pattered heavily against the glass; and the two Armadale's stood by the window, as the two Shadows had stood in the second Vision of the Dream, with the wreck of the image between them. Allan stooped over the fragments of the little figure, and lifted them one by one from the floor. "Leave me," he said, without looking up, "or we shall both repent it."
    Without a word, Midwinter moved back slowly. He stood for the second time with his hand on the door, and looked his last at the room. The horror of the night on the Wreck had got him once more, and the flame of his passion was quenched in an instant. "The Dream!" he whispered under his breath. "The Dream again!"[50]

Not for long is the reader allowed to rest in the certainty that some rational approach to events in the novel hold the monopoly on truth.

Armadale is a novel which deliberately confronts its readers with the suggestion that nothing is as it appears on the surface and that there is usually more than one explanation for events. Rather than conceal these facts Collins creates the impression that contradictions will always be with us. It is an unsettling idea and the reader's faith in the power of the rational mind and any sense of complacency takes quite a shaking. In *Armadale* the supernatural appears to have the upper hand and ironically it is the villains of the piece who seem to exemplify rationality. It is Miss Gwilt and Mrs Oldershaw, who with Dr Downward/Le Doux live on their wits, plot and plan and expect their calculations to pay dividends. This is a peculiar statement of the work ethic. But even here all is not well as Miss Gwilt increasingly falls under the influence of Midwinter's superstition about the dream.

Can I say I believe in it, too? I have better reasons for doing so than he knows of. I am not only the person who helped Mrs. Armadale's marriage by helping her to impose on her own father, – I am the woman who tried to drown herself; the woman who started the series of accidents which put young Armadale in possession of his fortune; the woman who has come to Thorpe-Ambrose to marry him for his fortune now he has got it; and more extraordinary still, the woman who stood in the Shadow's place at the pool! These may be coincidences, but they are strange coincidences. I declare I begin to fancy that *I* believe in the Dream too![51]

The consequence of this confession is that any rational explanation suffers from a loss of credibility when Miss Gwilt expresses her misgivings and tends to see things as does Midwinter. Throughout the narrative Midwinter's view is only partially privileged: the reader is held back from the conviction that Midwinter is right because it is clear from the Oldershaw–Gwilt correspondence that there is evidence of conspiracy to defraud Armadale. Rather than any supernatural agency, events have an all to human source. Ultimately the threats to rationality may be seen as a convenient gloss to conceal the scheme working against Allan Armadale. So when the human agents themselves, in this case Miss Gwilt, describe a lack of confidence in their own autonomy, the case for the supernatural is very strong.

Armadale is a novel which describes contradiction and warns against the tendency to limit one's vision of the world. It now only remains to list several occasions where this theme percolates through the text to affect isolated incidents in the course of the novel. It marks Collins' success in this work that crucial themes in the narrative as an integral whole manage to colour certain details of an almost imperceptible nature. Minor detail becomes important only in this context. For example, it is Mrs Milroy's false supposition that her husband is having an affair with Miss Gwilt that instigates the investigation of the new governess. Her jealousy blinds her perception of the world but this incident, based on misapprehension, is important for the development of the plot. Again, Miss Gwilt notes how the logic of rational thought, as pursued by Brock and Midwinter, proves that she is not herself. '*I have been proved not to be myself.*'[52] This blatant illogicality is the basis for the critique of positivism in *The Moonstone* where the evidence points to Franklin Blake as the thief. Collins takes this form of apprehension to its limit and shows that, in fact, it does not have any unique purchase on the truth. This knowledge that appearance and reality can differ is known by some of the characters. Mrs Milroy warns Allan that 'the most innocent actions are liable, in this wicked world, to the worst possible interpretation'.[53] Pedgift Senior makes a similar point to Allan.

> You and my son are young men; and I don't deny that the circumstances, on the surface appear to justify the interpretation which, as young men, you have placed on them. I am an old man – I know that circumstances are not always to be taken as they appear on the surface – and I possess the great advantage, in the present case, of having had years of professional experience among some of the wickedest women who ever walked this earth.[54]

Miss Gwilt, one of the most calculating characters in the novel, seldom rests with a surface reading of things, and, in her dealings with Midwinter, is constantly asking herself if 'he was what he appeared to be'.[55] In this world, where nothing is as it appears to be, official documents conspire against the truth. Miss Gwilt's comments on her wedding certificate are significant.

> There, in black and white, was the registered evidence of the marriage, which was at once a truth in itself, and a lie in the conclusion to which it led![56]

The certificate was true in that the named parties did marry, but false, if the assumptions were made, that the Allan Armadale on the certificate was the master of Thorpe-Ambrose. Not even buildings can be trusted.

> Buildings have their physiognomy – especially buildings in great cities – and the face of this house was essentially furtive in its expression. The front windows were all shut, and the front blinds were all drawn down. It looked no larger than the other houses in the street, seen in front; but it ran back deceitfully, and gained its greater accommodation by means of its greater depth. It affected to be a shop on the ground floor – but it exhibited absolutely nothing in the space that intervened between the window and an inner row of red curtains, which hid the interior entirely from view. At one side was the shop-door, having more red curtains behind the glazed part of it, inscribed with the name of "Oldershaw." On the other side was the private door, with a bell marked Professional; and another brass plate, indicating a medical occupant on this side of the house, for the name on it was "Doctor Downward." If ever brick and mortar spoke yet, the brick and mortar here said plainly, "We have got our secrets inside, and we mean to keep them."[57]

Appearance is not to be trusted. Mrs Oldershaw turns to religion towards the end of the novel and Miss Gwilt is far from convinced by the conversion.

> "It was easy to see, by this time, that the circumstances (whatever they might have been) which had obliged Mother Oldershaw to keep in hiding, on the occasion of my former visit to London, had been sufficiently serious to force her into giving up, or appearing to give up her old business. And it was hardly less plain that she had found it to her advantage – everybody in England finds it to their advantage, in some way, – to cover the outer side of her character carefully with a smooth varnish of Cant."[58]

This 'varnish of Cant' operates to the ultimate in the characters of Bashwood's son and in Dr Downward. While the older Bashwood's attempts to hide his inadequacies are all too obvious – he has a 'cheap brown wig, which made the pretence of being his own natural hair' and 'The one attractive feature in his clean-shaven, weary old face, was a neat set of teeth – teeth (as honest as his wig), which said plainly to all inquiring eyes, "We pass our nights on his looking-glass, and our days in his mouth," ' – the son is described in completely different terms.[59]

No ordinary observation, applying the ordinary rules of analysis, would have detected the character of Bashwood the younger in his face. His youthful look, aided by his light hair, and his plump beardless cheeks; his easy manner, and his ever ready smile; his eyes which met unshrinkingly the eyes of everyone whom he addressed, all combined to make the impression of him a favourable impression in the general mind. No eye for reading character, but such an eye as belongs to one person, perhaps, in ten thousand, could have penetrated the smoothly-deceptive surface of this man, and have seen him for what he really was – the vile creature whom the viler need of Society has fashioned for its own use. There he sat – the Confidential spy of modern times, whose business is steadily enlarging, whose Private Inquiry Offices are steadily on the increase. There he sat – the necessary Detective attendant on the progress of our national civilization; a man who was in this instance at least the legitimate and intelligible product of the vocation that employed him; a man professionally ready on the merest suspicion (if the merest suspicion paid him) to get under our beds, and to look through gimlet-holes in our door.[60]

Bashwood is the necessary detective who looks under our beds and beneath the surface of things because increasingly in modern times appearance can no longer be trusted. Ironically, in the passage above, he himself is presented to us as pure appearance. Dr Downward manages to keep up appearances and apparently escapes unscathed from events described in the novel. Miss Gwilt whose eventual sincere feelings for Midwinter contribute to her end, is appalled by the doctor's duplicity and his concentrated effort to conceal his real nature. It is part of his art to be able to say something and mean another. While ostensibly talking of something completely other, he manages to convince Miss Gwilt that she must poison Midwinter. Miss Gwilt records his reaction when she actually dares put this proposition into words.

" 'Kill him!' repeated the doctor in a paroxysm of virtuous alarm.

'Violence – murderous violence – in My Sanatorium! You take my breath away!'"

I caught his eye, while he was expressing himself in this elaborately indignant manner, scrutinizing me with a searching curiosity which was, to say the least of it, a little at variance with the vehemence of his language and the warmth of his tone. He laughed uneasily, when our eyes met, and recovered his smoothly confidential manner in the instant that elapsed before he spoke again.[61]

The novel warns against those who take an 'entirely superficial investigation of the circumstances'.[62] They inevitably arrive at the wrong conclusion. Appearance should be scrutinised closely for the reality which lies behind it. It is an unfortunate aspect of Victorian society that appearance and reality can no longer be seen as one. Pedgift Senior makes this point in a letter to his son concluding the business of the novel. He is speaking in particular of Dr Downward/Le Doux.

We live, Augustus, in an age eminently favourable to the growth of all roguery which is careful to keep up appearances. In this unlightened nineteenth century, I look upon the doctor as one of our rising men.[63]

2

The Fallen Leaves

The Fallen Leaves is Wilkie Collins' least successful book.[1] This is the opinion of standard criticism, but it is a view much disputed by the more perspicacious readers. In his anthology of Collins' criticism, Norman Page finds this dismissive view of *The Fallen Leaves* a 'judgement endorsed by Swinburne (who found it "ludicrously loathesome") and Sadleir, as well as by most of the contemporary reviewers'.[2] And while this may have been the dominant reading of the novel, it is not the only one. Page cites reviews in *The Athanaeum* and in the *British Quarterly Review* which are positive in their appreciation.[3] This view is supported by Robert Ashley who claims that Collins' work did not decline as much in quality as some critics say, but that of Collins' novels, 'Not even the worst of them. *The Fallen Leaves* is wretched, and the best, such as *Heart and Science* possesses considerable merit.'[4] It is a matter of speculation why the negative reading has held sway for so long because an examination of *The Fallen Leaves* would show it to be overwhelmingly partial and one-sided. Against this barrage of abuse it is necessary to recall that the *Spectator* found the novel 'capital entertainment', admittedly with the rider that its didactic purpose should not be taken too seriously.[5] All of this falls within the contours of a scholarly debate which Collins refused and it is my intention to describe the parameters of this furore, signal the aesthetic and indeed moral and political arguments which substantiate it, and attempt to come to terms with the text itself. The themes and concerns of the novel are explicit and sometimes, are recognised by the critics. Yet they fail to take them seriously. Collins has mapped a reading route through the novel, but it is a path which reviewers refused. In his comments on the reception of the work, Collins writes that the reviewers appear to be reading *The Fallen Leaves* in a way which is counter to his intentions.[6] That they failed to appreciate his project or treat it as a work of ideas is best exemplified by the writer who can ignore the speech on socialism, and yet take exception to the description of a woman chewing tobacco.[7]

Once again it is important to give full attention to what Collins wrote in the preface to his novels. In the particular case of *The Fallen Leaves* Collins carries discussion of this work on into *Jezabel's Daughter* and takes advantage of this space in the dedication to a novel published immediately after *The Fallen Leaves* to explain its predecessor. These prefaces are of crucial interest. They are directed more at the general reader than reviewers, but Collins never underestimated the importance of book reviews. Dickens had argued against Collins' habit of introducing his work, but in *The Fallen Leaves* the 1879 preface is remarkably non-controversial, almost an apology for itself rather than the more usual attempt at an explanation of aesthetic principle.

> Experience of the reception of *The Fallen Leaves* by intelligent readers, who have followed the course of the periodical publication at home and abroad, has satisifed me that the design of the work speaks for itself, and that the scrupulous delicacy of treatment, in certain portions of the story, has been as justly appreciated as I could wish. Having nothing to explain, and (as far as my choice of subject is concerned) nothing to excuse, I leave my book, without any prefatory pleading for it, to make its appeal to the reading public on such merits as it may possess.[8]

Collins is allowing his novel to speak for itself although he is manipulating matters, just a little, in his appeal to 'intelligent readers', and the reference to 'scrupulous delicacy' could be seen as an attempt to flatter the reader. Those with a sophisticated critical appreciation, Collins is suggesting, will be sympathetic to the novel. These are the really intelligent readers. As for those who would take umbrage at the work, in reserving judgement, Collins implies a rather eloquent comment.

The preface is also significant for the fact that it attests to Collins' faith in the reading public. The professional reviewer is reminded, perhaps none too subtly, that the author has already published the work as a serial and that the general public appeared to be well pleased. Therefore to fault the novel is to cross swords with the general public. 'Intelligent readers' fuse with 'the reading public' in Collins' rhetoric and the thrust of this articulation is directed against the professional readers hired by the literary journals to publish their views and opinions. Collins had long held the idea of an extended democracy of readers. In an article for *Household Words* in 1858 he identified an immense public of readers, – 'the universal public of the penny-novel – Journals'.[9] He was very prepared to take this group seriously.

Collins replied to some of the criticism made against *The Fallen Leaves* in the dedication to *Jezabel's Daughter*. He mentions that one of the characters offended that sort of propriety 'felt by Tartuffe, when he took out his handkerchief, and requested Dorine to cover her bosom'.[10] As an example of this offended sensibility it is worth looking at an article in the *Saturday Review* of August 1879. The anonymous reviewer grants that Collins is 'low' in his choice of subject matter in *The Fallen Leaves* and that in the treatment of his theme, he is sustained in his 'unwholesomeness'. The preface to the novel had made little impression on the reviewer and Collins is criticised severely.

> Certainly there is nothing of 'prefatory pleading' in what the author says here. He does not plead, but attests, and attests roundly. Like Clive he is astonished at his own moderation. He has had to deal with a set of degraded wretches. He has had to take his readers among the lowest outcasts, and has not been for one moment indelicate. On the contrary, there is, as he tells us, 'scrupulous delicacy of treatment in certains portions of the story.' / . . . / Is he, we might ask him, scrupulously delicate when he describes the open mouth of the quartermaster of an American steamer, 'from which the unspat tobacco-juice trickled in little brown streams'? Where in these days of word-painting, as it is called, are we to draw the line? Sailors too often have nasty habits; but that does not justify an author in disgusting his readers with nasty descriptions. Does Mr. Collins display this scrupulous delicacy for which he is so famed, in the account he gives of an infamous hag, who is suffering under an attack of delirium tremens in the kitchen of a thieves' lodging house? . . .[11]

Victorian prejudice is confirmed in this quotation. Nothing, it is suggested, should be included in art which could possibly offend respectable opinion. This is a view which Thackeray supported when he was a young man: 'I am thankful to live in times when men no longer have the temptation to write so as to call blushes on women's cheeks, and would shame to whisper wicked allusions to honest boys.'[12] Yet opinion was by no means as univocal as this. Thackeray himself was inconsistent and Bulwer-Lytton advanced a contrary view. After the publication of *Lucretia* the latter was condemned for his choice of subject and, in response to this criticism, wrote the pamphlet 'A Word to the Public' which he published in an appendix to the 1853 edition of his novel.

> It is the treatment that ennobles not the subject. Grant that the characters are what convention calls *low* – in birth, station, instruction; born in a cellar, dying on a gibbet, they are not one jot, for these reasons, made *necessarily* low to art. Art can, with Fielding, weave an epic from adventures with game-keepers and barbers. Art can, with Goethe, convert into poetry, the most lofty, the homely image of a girl condemned for infanticide.[13]

The argument about the proper subject matter for literature and art continued through the Victorian period with both the novelists and reviewers wavering in their opinions. Collins is generally consistent in his views on this topic and may be understood to have advocated artistic freedom for writers. He is at the very centre of this debate from *Basil* to his latest novel in 1879.[14]

Against this backcloth it is worth while considering Collins' comments on the reception of *The Fallen Leaves* in the dedication to *Jezebel's Daughter*. He explains to his Italian translator, Alberto Caccia, that the new novel is not the promised sequel to *The Fallen Leaves*. The first part of this story has 'through circumstances connected with the various forms of publications adopted this far, addressed itself to a comparatively limited class of readers in England'.[15] The dedication continues with yet another statement of Collins' trust in the public reader as opposed to the professional critic. He takes the view that when *The Fallen Leaves* is eventually published in a cheap edition it will meet with the reception it deserves. This, in turn, will encourage him to write the sequel. Collins expresses a great faith in the general reader, but, more significantly, suggests that the reviewers behave as a kind of cultural sieve. They sift through various novels accepting some and rejecting others. The reviewers act as a cultural-literary police force who attempt to protect the general reader and, in effect, censor the available material. Collins rehearses these points to Caccia.

> Your knowledge of English Literature – to which I am indebted for the first faithful and intelligent translation of my novel into the Italian language – has since informed you, that there are certain important social topics which are held to be forbidden to the English novelist (no matter how seriously and how delicately he may treat them), by a narrow-minded minority of readers, and by the critics who flatter their prejudices. You also know, having done me the honour to read my books, that I respect my art far too seriously to permit limits to be wantonly assigned to it, which are imposed on no other civilised country on the face of the earth. When my work is undertaken with a pure purpose, I claim the same liberty which is accorded to a writer in a newspaper, or to a clergyman in a pulpit; knowing by previous experience, that the increase of readers and the lapse of time will assuredly do me justice, if I have only written well enough to deserve it.[16]

Here Collins is roundly repeating Bulwer-Lyttons point that 'it is the treatment that ennobles, not the subject'. No topic should be refused discussion in a novel provided that it is handled with artistic competence and verve. Collins is correct to see that the reviewers' attempts at censorship are historically bound and will certainly change over time. Collins' mention of an increased readership seems to equate popularity with literary or moral rectitude. Is it possible that he is suggesting that an increase in popularity is a measure of sincerity and integrity? Whatever the case might be, what must be recognised is that, at the base of Collins' aesthetic, there is a contempt and ill-feeling for the literary establishment which Collins identifies with the literary reviews. It is this seeming disregard for the literary journals which must be emphasised rather than the naive credo that popularity, *per se*, may be taken to indicate artistic worth. The purchase of the polemic forces him into this corner rather than any firm faith in the righteousness of popular belief.

Elsewhere, in this dedication, Collins repeats views given expression by other novelists who also suffered from this stifling **artistic** morality. Charles Reade had pointed to the particular standards which allowed journalists greater elasticity of approach than that granted to the novelist. He wrote a letter to *The Times*, 26 August 1871, entitled 'Facts must be Faced'.

That a journalist has the right to put into his headed type and to amplify, discuss and dwell upon any subject whatever, and that the poet or novelist has not an equal right to deal with that subject in fiction, this is monstrous and the mere delusion of a rabid egotism.[17]

In this letter Reade considered it the task of the novelist 'to weave the recorded facts / . . . / of this great age into the forms of Art'. What were these facts as reported in the press? Reade offers a summary of the contents of contemporary newspapers. 'Lunacy, Prisons, Trade Unions, Divorce, Murder, Anonyma'.[18] Like Collins, Reade is aggrieved that what is fine matter for the journalist should be forbidden the novelist and poet.

Collins is also echoing contemporary debate when he alludes, by implication, to the greater freedom enjoyed by writers in other countries. For example, in his essay on Balzac, Collins praises the Frenchman 'as a writer who sternly insists on presenting the dreary aspects of human life, literally, exactly, nakedly as he finds them'.[19] It is to literature's advantage that its subject matter should be extended in this way. However, this is not an opinion shared by the essayist in *Fraser's* who complained that with contemporary literature 'We are losing, if not our modesty, at least refinement; not so much refinement of expression, though that is often wanting, but refinement of thought and mind. The faults of the French school are creeping into our literature and threaten to flourish there.'[20] Evidently the welcome extended by Collins to Balzac and the French was not universally echoed in England.[21]

Collins refuses to defend his choice of subject matter in *The Fallen Leaves* in the face of overt Grundyism but rather simply states that he has

never asserted a truer claim to the best and noblest sympathies of Christian readers than in presenting them, in my last novel (*The Fallen Leaves*), the character of the innocent victim of infamy, rescued and purified from the contamination of the streets. I remember what the nasty posterity of Tartuffe, in this

country, said of "Basil", of "Armadale", of "The New
Magdalen", and I know that the wholesome audience of the
nation at large has done liberal justice to those books. For this
reason, I wait to write the second part of "The Fallen Leaves",
until the first part of the story has found its way to the
people.[22]

Again Collins is circumventing the professional reception of his
novels and placing his trust with the general reader. Collins'
attitude to literary journalism is at one with the view he takes of
so much of the cant and convention of Victorian society, a society
whose proprietorial rules are so often exposed in the novels. It
can be supposed that, for Collins, the literary journals signal yet
another insidious brand of propriety in society. The appeal to 'the
people' is a challenging attempt to break out of the literary
strait-jacket and discuss real issues in a disinterested fashion. This
gesture is itself contained by some of the ideologies of the time. In
particular, Collins does not feel any discomfort in claiming to
write for 'Christian readers'. Rather it actually appears to be the
case, for Collins, that Christianity is a worthwhile and benevolent
popular force in society and is the preserve of the people as a
mass. This must be countered with the fact that Collins is also
prepared to write disfavourably of certain versions of
Christianity.[23] For example, Miss Clack's rampant evangelicism is
censured, whereas in *The Fallen Leaves* the project seems to be to
differentiate between the Christian religion as a progressive force
and the appropriation of religion as a form of expediency which
can conceal a mass of hypocrisy. Collins has an equally finely
tuned approach to religion in *The Black Robe* which, at first
reading, may appear to be an attack on the Jesuits, but, more
accurately is a novel which only condemns certain practices of the
Jesuits. The machiavellianism of one priest, Father Benwell, is
eclipsed by the charity and concern of another, Father Penrose.
Collins usually nuances his work in this fashion and he excercises
the ability to describe problems in a far more subtle fashion than
that which would identify him as a mere polemicist or author of
purpose novels. The advantages and disadvantages of Christian
socialism are investigated in *The Fallen Leaves* in a way which is far
from simple-minded advocacy and the relationships of this
doctrine with commercial London life are fused with the story of

'the innocent victim of infamy, rescued and purified from the contamination of the street' – the rescue of a prostitute.

The Fallen Leaves may then be seen as a controversial book in 1879 because of its implicit and explicit attacks and criticisms of contemporary business ethics, the established Church and the institution of Parliament. Society's treatment of the fallen woman is explored and social hypocrisy towards the Magdalen figure is placed in sharp relief. This is given added sustenance by a series of motifs which undermine society's views on gender and relationships between the sexes. All this is given apparently real historical reference by mention of various forms of Christian socialism as they were known to Collins. What this means, in effect, is that Collins created an imaginative amalgam of various Christian socialist doctrines in a very individual way. He emphasises certain aspects of the doctrine while ignoring other Christian socialist teachings.

It is Collins' peculiar and individual version of Christian socialism that lies at the heart of this text. It is difficult to isolate his themes for individual attention but, to a large extent, his subject matter is all discussed from a perspective which is informed by various versions of Christian socialism. The history of this movement has been well documented. In England it developed as a prophylactic against what was seen, by some members of the Church of England, as the excesses of the Chartists and it flourished for a while in the period 1848–54. It underwent a revival in 1877 and this time survived as a distinct movement until about 1914 when its membership had all but collapsed or drifted into the Fabian and Labour movements. It is important to bear in mind that at no time in either period could the English Christian socialists be seen as a radical force in society but rather they were social reformers whose main intention was to emphasise class cooperation rather than class confrontation. 'Christian Socialism', said Marx in The Communist Manifesto, 'is but the holy-water with which the priest consecrates the heart-burnings of the artistocrat'.[24] Marx may well be oversimplifying a more composite case as the relationship of the Christian socialists to the Labour movement was often vexed and contradictory. If it is to be seen at all as a movement with even a minimal radical intent it is difficult to explain the behaviour and attitudes of some of its leading members. They were sympathetic to the more moderate Chartists but when, at the National Convention of Chartists in London on 4 April 1848, it was decided to petition Parliament six days later, opinion amongst leading Christian socialists was divided. There was a general fear of violence and, to protect property, the government decided to recruit 150 000 special constables. Frederick Maurice, the intellectual leader of the Christian socialists, applied to join but was refused because he was a clergyman. However, while his colleague Thomas Hughes was accepted, J. M. Ludlow, another leader of the movement, decided that the government was over-reacting and went to work as usual on the morning of 10 April, the day Parliament was to be petitioned. It was differences such as these which would eventually result in the dissolution of Christian socialism as a coherent movement in 1854.

There is no evidence that Collins had any interest in this first flowering of Christian socialism and while its regeneration in 1877 predates publication of *The Fallen Leaves* by two years I have only been able to establish the most tenuous of connections with Collins. The Pre-Raphaelite painters G. Lowes Dickinson and Dante G. Rossetti became involved in the Working Men's College founded in December 1852 and Collins may have been aware of this because of his friendship with the Pre-Raphaelites in particular Millais and Holman Hunt. However, because of the lack of more substantial documentary evidence, it is necessary to look elsewhere to explain Collins' fascination with Christian socialism. In the autumn of 1873 Collins went on a reading tour of the United States and there is some speculation that he may have found time to visit a Christian socialist community at Brocton on Lake Erie calling itself the Brotherhood of the New Life. His letters from America are particularly unhelpful on the subject but he does indicate an interest in such religious groups in a letter to Frederick Lehmann dated 2 January 1874. 'I am going "Out West" from this, and I *may* get as far as the Mormons.'[25] So again Collins' actual contact with these communities must stand as a matter of speculation but what has been documented is the fact that Collins did own a copy of Charles Nordhoff's *The Communistic Societies of the United States* first published in 1875. Nordhoff does not mention the Brocton community but since its corrupt leader Thomas Lake Harris advocated celibacy it is obviously not the model for Tadmor in *The Fallen Leaves*.[26] I believe that a much more substantial case can be made by suggesting that Collins' information about Christian socialist communities and Tadmor in particular comes from Nordhoff's book. Rather than base Tadmor on one particular community it is an imaginary reconstruction of the best features of these communities as Collins saw them. A reading of Nordhoff suggests that there is no one model for Tadmor. The rules and regulations of these communities varied from one to the other, particularly their regularisation of sexuality, marriage and the treatment of women. While some, as at Brocton, advocated celibacy in marriage, others, such as the Oneida community founded by J. H. Noyes, the author of *History of American Socialism*, supported polygamy and communal living. It is from his understanding of the life-style of the Oneida community that Collins may have found support for his critique of the situation of women in *The Fallen Leaves*. But certainly he would have found in Nordhoff evidence to support his view that contemporary Christianity in England had become a degenerated form of an ideal. This ideal was the Christianity taught by Christ in the New Testament and this was working to a much greater extent in these American communities than in mainstream society.

The Fallen Leaves opens with a Prologue which highlights corruption in contemporary business life and what it serves to demonstrate is this idea of degenerated form. Implicit in the Prologue is a Christian socialist critique of the English business world. A porter in a stationery shop, John Farnaby makes his employer's daughter pregnant as part of an overall plan to become a partner in the business. This is an apt beginning to the novel because it encapsulates the two major shortcomings of society which, Collins suggests, Christian socialism can ameliorate. These are the degenerated Christian morality which is wholly held in sway by the dictates of finance and property and the situation of women in this society. We are made aware of this in the reaction of the stationer, Benjamin Ronald, and his wife to their daughter's predicament. It is difficult to distinguish between Mrs Ronald's feelings of disgrace and disappointment that her daughter has become pregnant and her horror that this event has been worked to guarantee Farnaby's advance into the stationery business. She is equally appalled by both aspects of the affair; one is fused with the other and her daughter's private fate is seen in terms of the effect on the family business. Defending her actions in taking her daughter to Ramsgate, Mrs Ronald insists that she was not operating solely with the intention of protecting the girl's reputation.

"But I had a harder trial still to face," she said, "I had to save her, in spite of herself, from the wretch who had brought this infamy on us. He has acted throughout in cold blood; it is his interest to marry her, and from first to last he has plotted to force the marriage on us. For God's sake, don't speak loud! She is in the room above us; if she hears you it will be the death of her. Don't suppose I am talking at random; I have looked at his letters to her; I have got the confession of the servant girl. Such a confession! Emma is his victim body and soul. I know it! I know that she has sent him money (*my* money) from this place. I know that the servant (at her instigation) informed him by telegraph of the birth of the child. Oh, Benjamin, don't curse the poor helpless infant – such a sweet little girl! Don't think of it! Show me the letter that brought you here. Ah, I can tell you who wrote it! *He* wrote it. In his own interests: always with his own interests in view. Don't you see it for yourself? If I succeed in keeping this shame and misery a secret from everybody – if I take Emma away, to some place abroad, on pretence of her health – there is an end of his hope of becoming your son-in-law; there is an end of his being taken into the business. Yes! he, the low-lived vagabond who puts up the shop-shutters, *he* looks forward to being taken into partnership, and succeeding you when you die! Isn't his object in writing that letter as plain to you now as the heaven above us? His one chance is to set your temper in a flame, to provoke the scandal of a discovery – and to force the marriage on us as the only remedy left."[27]

There is a confusion of motives apparent in Mrs Ronald's speech. The heart-felt response of the outraged mother and loyal wife is compounded with the indignation of the business-woman who is horrified that the vagabond servant should use this particular route to gain a partnership in the firm. Farnaby took advantage of their daughter but the full clout of their wrath concentrates on the effects of his action on their business rather than on their self-respect as parents. Ronald's unawareness, and blind patriarchal morality is contrasted with his wife's unconventional, but loyal, tactical grasp of the situation. Further there is a disjunction and an articulation of the old family morality and the ideology of commerce. It is a degenerated form of Christianity which allows for this equivocation of motives and for the private world of the family to be governed by the public world of finance. In this prologue Collins is describing a world without Christian socialism. It is a world where the public sphere of money and property has a far-reaching effect on and relationship to the private world of individual relationships. Just what especial effect this has on the situation of women is a large concern of *The Fallen Leaves.*

The apparently redundant prologue does not function purely in terms of plot but is a picture of a world which has developed without Christian socialism. The first chapter introduces us to the hero of the novel, the appropriately named Amelius Goldenheart. Inscribed in this name is the idea of amelioration and the association of Goldenheart situates us right in the centre of Christian socialist ideas. One of the first Christian socialist documents written by Maurice and first published in 1851 argued that the kingdom of God could be founded on earth if sufficient attention was paid to the Bible.

> "Socialists who are not seeking to inform the world according to a scheme of their own, but to discuss the actual laws which govern it, should be prepared to examine all manner of facts that bear upon the life and destinies of mankind. Christians should be prepared to prove that they have not imputed their doctrines to the Bible but have found them there."[28]

The Sermon on the Mount was always seen as a political manifesto by the Christian socialists which would allow them to build the kingdom of God on earth. From it they drew ideas of brotherhood, equality and cooperation (cooperation, not conflict), and it allowed them to formulate this Golden Rule. This Golden Rule, the belief in self-sacrifice rather than self-interest, contrasted the Golden Rule to the rule of gold and was a central tenet of Christian socialists in both its periods of strength, from the early theorists who stressed cooperation to its renaissance in the Knights of the Golden Rule, the American reformers who were at their peak in the 1890's.[29] Whatever its source, Collins' hero Amelius Goldenheart obviously fits into this trajectory.

Amelius Goldenheart is on his way to London 'to see life'.[30] He has a letter of introduction to Mr John Farnaby, a stationer of the firm of Ronald and Farnaby. Amelius describes him as an example to us all, a man who has risen 'by dint of integrity and perseverance from the position of a poor porter in a shop to be one of the most respected mercantile characters in the City of London'.[31] From this heavily dramatic irony it becomes clear that Goldenheart's function in the text is to expose the corruptions in a society which would recognise Farnaby as a paragon of virtue. And while it is true that *The Fallen Leaves* is a critique of English society it is a critique which measures the advantages and disadvantages of contemporary London Life against those of an imagined Christian socialist community, Tadmor in Illinois.[32]

The doctrines of this community are explained in some detail in these opening pages of the novel. Goldenheart falls into conversation with an English clergyman who is rather dubious about the virtues of Christian socialism. Mr Hethcote, to whom Goldenheart is speaking, supposes that as a young boy Goldenheart had been bribed by the Christian socialists. Again highlighting the prejudices of the day, Mr Hethcote imagines there to be little Christianity in the Tadmor doctrine.

> "A sermon?" Mr. Hethcote repeated. "Very little religion in it, I suspect."
>
> "Very little indeed, sir," Amelius answered. "Only as much religion as there is in the New Testament. I was not quite old enough to understand him easily – so he wrote down his discourse on the fly-leaf of a story-book I had with me, and gave it to me to read when I was tired of the stories. . . . 'My dear little boy, *the Christian religion as Christ taught it, has long ceased to be the religion of the Christian world. A selfish and cruel Pretence is set up in its place.* Your own father is one example of the truth of this saying of mine. He has fulfilled the first and foremost duty of a true Christian – the duty of forgiving an injury. For this he stands disgraced in the estimation of his friends: they have renounced and abandoned him.'"[33]

The essential point here is clear. Christianity has itself become a charade and the spirit of religion has become so diluted in the material world that it is now nothing more than a degenerated form. This division between Christianity, as Christ taught it and the Church of England is at the forefront of Christian socialist doctrine as Christensen explains:

Maurice regarded the Established Church as being the perfect embodiment of God's revelations to man. But from this did not in any way follow that he sanctioned the actual religious teachings and practices of the Church of England. On the contrary its clergy and laity has hardly ever had a more severe critic than Maurice. To his mind all the religious parties in the Church had denied the true principles of the Church and, instead of giving witness to the world of the good tidings from God, had set up their own religious opinions and systems. They were possessed by an exclusive and self-satisfied spirit which puts up barriers between themselves and the rest of mankind – and in so doing they denied the Divine Order established by God in Christ. As Maurice saw it, his calling must be to bear witness to this fact, in fierce opposition to the religious world of his day.[34]

What Christensen is emphasising about Maurice's doctrine is the distinction between the ideal Christianity taught by Christ in the New Testament and the degenerated form of Christianity which, Maurice believes, is the current practice of the Church of England.

There then follows an explanation of economic distribution in the community. Goldenheart counters Hethcote's charge – 'Nobody has a right to be rich among you, of course?' – with the forceful retort that 'All men have a right to be rich – provided they don't make others poor.'[35] Again this is orthodox and the account Goldenheart gives of the economic organisation of Tadmor is nothing more than a summary of Nordhoff's documentary account right down to a listing of the typical occupations of the Tadmor members.

We don't trouble ourselves much about money; that's the truth. We are farmers, carpenters, weavers, and painters; and what we earn (ask our neighbours if we don't earn it honestly) goes into the common fund, and so makes things easy for the next man, who comes with empty pockets. While they are with us, they all live in the same comfort, and have their equal share in the same profits – deducting the sum in reserve for sudden calls and bad times. If they leave us, the man who has brought money with him has his undisputed right to take it away again; and the man who has brought none bids us good-bye, all the richer for his equal share in the profits which he has personally earned.[36]

This is a markedly vague statement and does not really elucidate many of the details of economic organisation at Tadmor but again this is orthodox Christian socialism as Peter d'A. Jones explains in his account of the revival of the Christian socialist movement.

> . . . despite their unusual vanity and fascinating qualities as individuals, and despite the moral courage they revealed in opposing the conventional wisdom and morality of their epoch, many Christian socialists were curiously naive in matters of theory. Certainly no startling advances or breakthrough in the evolution of socialist thought came as a result of their work.[37]

This vagueness at the centre of Christian socialism may have attracted Collins and he further complicates the picture by selecting just those aspects of the teachings which appeal to him and rejecting other facets of the movement which have little interest for him. Maurice also had an eclectic philosophy and dogma was relatively unimportant for him except for pragmatic reasons. This vagueness was also a good strategy at this time because it allowed the Christian socialists to negotiate freely with contemporary Biblical exegesis, the discoveries of science and comparative religion. Goldenheart uses this argument when he explains that the Tadmore community are more interested in guiding their lives according to the spirit of the New Testament rather than in living under the sway of hard and fast religious dogma.[38]

Throughout the novel Collins uses Goldenheart to point at an array of social abuses and double-dealing in contemporary society. Sometimes these abuses can be very trivial, for example lack of punctuality at dinner, and at other times they are much more serious. It is difficult to encapsulate these criticisms in one theoretical rubric so the vagaries of Christian socialism itself allow Collins to extrapolate from many of its doctrines and add to it some of his more idiosyncratic views. However, in a key section of the novel, Collins has Goldenheart enumerate in considerable detail a Christian socialist critique of social ills. This speech is important in that it is both a statement of Collins' version of Christian socialism and an interesting gloss on the political complexities of England in the 1870s. It fuses together many of the issues which divided the early Christian socialists and is a curious juxtaposition of these views, which are historical, and the imagined politics of Tadmor as Collins gleaned them from his reading of Nordhoff. The speech recognises the necessity for and inevitability of change in contemporary, degenerated society but it attempts to channel this change in the direction of Christian socialism. As Collins sees it, Christian socialism can either prevent change or, in the aftermath of revolution, guide society in a positive and acceptable direction. Goldenheart talks about the imminence of revolution

> – in England, as well as in Europe generally – [which is] beyond the reach of that lawful and bloodless reform which has served us so well in past years. Whether I am mistaken in this view (and I hope with all my heart it may be so), or whether events yet in the future will prove that I am right, the remedy in either case, the one sure foundation on which a permanent, complete, and worthy reformation can be built – whether it prevents a convulsion or whether it follows a convulsion – is only to be found within the covers of this book.[39]

The book is the New Testament and orthodox Christian socialism as alluded to in this passage must be seen by the reader as an attempt to contain change within recognised parameters and ultimately to defeat the forces which lead to socialist revolution. The emphasis is very much on individual change. Maurice, for example, believed that too much concentration on the world only detracts from the more important communion with the spiritual order. Maurice's choice of title for this movement – 'Christian Socialism' – was no accident as he explains in a letter to Ludlow.

> *Tracts on Christian Socialism* is, it seems to me, the only title which will define our object, and will commit us at once to the conflict we must engage in sooner or later with the unsocial Christians and the unChristian socialists.[40]

It is evident here that Maurice is as anxious to curb the excesses of the 'UnChristian socialists' as he is to reform, never mind transform, capitalism in England. There were, of course, more radical Christian socialists, notably Ludlow, Neale and Thomas Hughes and Goldenheart's speech echoes some of these conflicting voices as if they spoke in unison. Historically, Christian socialism cannot be seen as a radical movement but this does not detract from its contemporary shock value.

Ladies and Gentlemen, thoughtful people accustomed to watch

the signs of the times in this country, and among other nations of Europe, are (so far as I know) agreed in the conclusion, that serious changes are likely to take place in present forms of government, and in existing systems of society, before the century in which we live has reached its end. In plain words, the next revolution is not so unlikely, and not so far off, as it pleases the higher and wealthier classes among European populations to suppose. I am one of those who believe that the coming convulsion will take the form, this time, of a social revolution, and that the man at the head of it will not be a military or a political man – but a Great Citizen, sprung from the people, and devoted heart and soul to the people's cause. . . . All that I can now attempt to do is (first) to point out some of the causes which are paving the way for a coming change in the social and political conditions of this country; and (secondly) to satisfy you that the only trustworthy remedy for existing abuses is to be found in the system which Christian Socialism extracts from this little book on my table – the book which you all know under the name of The New Testament.[41]

It should be apparent from the above that Goldenheart is representing Christian socialism as reform and not as revolution. He appears to be in Maurice's camp and the contemporary reader has little to fear from this vision of society. But it is possible that when many readers meet the term Christian socialism it is the noun which makes most impression on them and the moderating and qualifying adjective is all but ignored. Goldenheart is right to stress the fear of radical change at this time because the 1870s marks a period when the government was making express legislation to answer discontent and by such means contain it. For example 1867 marked an important enfranchisement act which gave the vote to urban workers. 1874 was the first year of Disraeli's six year Tory social reform ministry which produced a mass of legislation. In 1875 there was the first working-class housing act of the century, codification of factory measures and a public health act both in 1878, labour reforms, including in 1875 acts legalising peaceful picketing and very significantly the 'Master and Servant Act' was retitled the 'Employers and Workmen Act'.

Goldenheart focuses his speech around the Church, business and the Houses of Parliament.

What is the public aspect of this thing called Christianity, in the England of our day? A hundred different sects all at variance with each other. An established church, rent in every direction by incessant wrangling – disputes about black gowns or white; about having candlesticks on tables, or off tables; and about bowing to the east or bowing to the west; about which doctrine collects the most respectable support and possesses the largest sum of money, the doctrine in my church, or the doctrine in your church, or the doctrine of the church over the way. Look up, if you like, from the multitudinous and incessant squabbling among the rank and file, to the high region in which the right reverend representatives of state religion sit apart. Are they Christians? If they are, show me the Bishop who dares assert his Christianity in the House of Lords, when the ministry of the day happens to see its advantage in engaging in a war! Where is that Bishop, and how many supporters does he count among his own order?[42]

There is some rumbling against religion in other Collins' novels but here it is given explicit statement. The argument is that the Church is the handmaiden of government, guaranteeing and sustaining the powers that be and offering support for official policy. Goldenheart is attacking that coupling of Altar and Throne which Jervy, a renegade Irish man in the audience, boasts is at the core of his conservative politics. Through Goldenheart, it is suggested that it is the function of the Church to aid the establishment of social consensus. This task now determines received Christianity and the Church ignores the real meaning of the New Testament. Here Collins anticipates some of the criticism levelled against the Anglican church by the second generation of Christian socialists.

Maurician socialists fought a losing battle against the placid indifference of the main body of the Established Church, / . . . / The Church of England remained an upper-class social organisation – "The Tory party at prayer," in the words of one wag. Christian socialists in the later Victorian period were less inhibited about attacking the Establishment itself than the Mauricians were. Men like Stewart Headlam, C. L. Marson, and Thomas Hancock were more alive to the need of eradicating class consciousness, snobbery and elitism, and for smashing the upper-class Tory image of Anglicanism.[43]

Goldenheart's indictment of contemporary ills is a moral critique of individual human failing. Rather than criticise the organisation of society, his tirade is directed more at the failings of the Church to produce people, in the spirit of the New Testament, who are 'true, humane, gentle, modest, strictly scrupulous and strictly considerate with their neighbours'.[44] If the Churches did produce such people, it is inferred, all would be right with the country. The fault, Goldenheart suggests, is in man's heart and not at all to do with an unjust division of wealth and exploitative capitalism. The language of his critique is that of a moral attack on British public life.

Look at our commerce. What is its social aspect, judged by the morality which is in this book in my hand? Let those organized systems of *importance, masquerading under the disguise* of banks and companies, answer the question – there is no need for me to answer it. You know what respectable names are associated, year after year, with the shameless falsification of accounts, and the merciless ruin of thousands on thousands of victims. You know how our poor Indian customer finds his cotton-print dress a sham that falls to pieces; how the savage who deals honestly with us for his weapons finds his gun a *delusion* that bursts; how the half-starved needlewoman who buys her reel of thread finds printed on the label a false statement of the number of yards that she buys; you know that in the markets of Europe, foreign goods are fast taking the place of English goods, because the foreigner is the more honest manufacturer of the two – and lastly, you know, what is worse than all, that these cruel and wicked deceptions, and many more like them, are regarded, on the highest commercial authority, as 'forms of competition' and justifiable proceedings in trade. Do you believe in the honourable accumulation of wealth by men who hold such opinions and perpetrate such impostures as these? . . . my business is with the present, public aspect of the religion, morals and politics of this country; and, again I say it, that aspect presents one wide field of corruption and abuse, and reveals a callous and shocking insensibility on the part of the nation at large to the *spectacle* of its own demoralization and disgrace.[45] (my italics)

The language of this moral stricture is worthy of note. Victorian business is identified in terms of 'imposture', 'masquerade' and 'spectacle'. Again society is seen in terms of the dichotomy between appearance and reality. 'Forms of competition' and free enterprise are so many veils and gauzes which conceal, immorally conceal, a vast process of expropriation and exploitation. Competition was a constant target of the Christian socialists and they argued that competition in society should be replaced by cooperation and brotherhood. They believed that 'if the competitive spirit and the profit motive, so important to the new middle classes could be abolished, the objects of the movement would be achieved. They were more troubled by the spirit of the age – of the rich and poor alike – than by the conditions of the age'.[46] Goldenheart confirms this interpretation of the reasons for social injustice when he suggests that it is because of greater honesty on the behalf of foreign manufacturers that they are overtaking English manufacturers in the competition for foreign markets. He completely ignores the argument that explains the slump in English trade by the fact that foreign manufacturers, most notably Germany and the United States, were overtaking England because their industrial and economic base was more modern and more efficient.

Goldenheart spends little time in his dismissal of the House of Lords.

In the first place, that assembly is not elected by the people, and it has therefore no right to existence in a really free country. In the second place, out of its four hundred and eighty-five members, no less than one hundred and eighty-four directly profit from the expenditure of the public money; being in the annual receipt, under one pretence or another, of more than half a million sterling. In the third place, if the Assembly of the Commons has in it the will, as well as the capacity, to lead the way in the needful reforms, the assembly of the Lords has no alternative but to follow or to raise the revolution which it only escaped by a hair's-breadth, some forty years since.[47]

Here Goldenheart seems to be moving to the left of the Christian socialist political spectrum. It was a broad church of political opinion and while some of its members may have supported a call for the dismissal of the House of Lords, its patron, Maurice, was much more circumspect and even expressed doubts about the advantages of full democracy. Ludlow and Neale were all in favour of treating the workers as equals but Maurice's concept and ideal of a reformed church, which would transcend class difference, made him see class difference as an irrelevance. He appears to have been in favour of government and social leadership dominated by his own class, the upper-middle class. He even had doubts about the merits of the Reform Bill of 1867 which gave the vote to industrial workers. Maurice is on record as having commented on the 1867 reforms – 'I do not mean to follow the will of a majority.'[48]

Goldenheart has little time for a House of Lords and is almost equally dismissive of the House of Commons. While the House of Commons may have the power to change things, it lacks the will.

> The number of members is a little over six hundred and fifty. Out of this muster, one fifth only represent (or pretend to represent) the trading interests of the country. As for the members charged with the interests of the working class, they are more easily counted still – they are two in number! Then in Heaven's name (you will ask) what interest does the majority of members in this assembly represent? There is but one answer – the military and aristocratic interests. In these days of the decay of representative institutions, the House of Commons has become a complete misnomer. The Commons are not represented; modern members belong to classes of the community which have really no interest in providing for popular needs and lightening popular burdens.[49]

This could be read as a radical critique going well beyond Maurice and the Christian socialist call for reform but Goldenheart concludes his speech with an emphasis on the efficacy of Christian socialism as a system of doctrines which can actually reform society without recourse to fundamental change. He draws attention to the existence of 'cooperative shops' but it is unclear whether these are retail shops or workshops. Cooperative shops were an innovation whole-heartedly endorsed by the Christian socialists but there is no mention in this speech of the debate within the Christian socialist movement between those who advocated consumer controlled, retail outlets and the more radical contingent around Ludlow who wanted to see producers' associations.

Goldenheart concludes with the suggestion that the Tadmor model which, he argues, is already working well for a small community should be emulated by society at large. The final suggestion is that it is the hearts of the people that are at fault – people are just not good Christians – and that Christian socialism is a means to overcome class antagonism and to build the Kingdom of God on earth.

> Why, my good friends, the people in this country, who are unworthy of the great trust which the wise and generous English constitution places in their hands, are so numerous that they can be divided into distinct classes! There is the highly educated class which despairs and holds aloof. There is the class beneath – without self-respect, and therefore without public-spirit – which can be bribed indirectly, by the gift of a place, by the concession of a lease, even by an invitation to a party at a great house which includes the wives and daughters. And there is the lower class still – mercenary, corrupt, shameless to the marrow of its bones – which sells itself and its liberties for money and drink.[50]

Goldenheart's speech is ultimately a moral critique. Individual members of each class are guilty of individual failing and if they were only to reform themselves and become better people all would be well with society. Christian socialism, with its emphasis on the teaching of the New Testament, provides the wherewithal for this to be done. Warning against those 'UnChristian socialists' of whom Maurice was so wary, Goldenheart explains the relevance of Christianity.

> Do not, I entreat you, suffer yourselves to be persuaded by those purblind philosophers who assert that the divine virtue of Christianity is wearing out – as all falsities and all impostures must and do wear out. Never, since Christ and his apostles first showed men the way to be better and happier, have the nations stood in sorer need of a return to that teaching in its pristine purity and simplicity than now![51]

Society needs Christianity even more than ever at this crisis point in its development and the organisation of the Primitive Christian socialist community at Tadmor provides a model, which, Goldenheart argues, should be adopted by society at large if a cataclysmic change is to be avoided. In this regard Goldenheart is an orthodox disciple of Maurice who was originally encouraged to enter the social arena in the attempt to harness and contain the challenge offered by the Chartists.

Reference to Tadmor and the specific American translations of Christian socialism has been kept to a minimum so far in my reading of *The Fallen Leaves*. I argue that Tadmor does not have a foundation in any one particular American community but is an imaginary society which Collins put together from a reading of Nordhoff's book. Some of these communities, described by Nordhoff, feature strongly in *The Fallen Leaves* and their implicit articulation in the novel provides the second and more substantial reason why *The Fallen Leaves* was so badly misunderstood and why Collins should have found it necessary to answer these criticisms in the dedication to *Jezabel's Daughter*. While the advocation of Christian socialism in the public sphere can be seen from a modern perspective as conservative, the application of Collins' understanding of Christian socialism in the private sphere marks a genuinely radical proposal.

Goldenheart gives explicit statement to his theories about social organisation but throughout the novel he comes into contact with several women and in these experiences a version of Christian socialism is alluded to in so far as it has effect on the position and situation of women. Goldenheart explains how women are treated, indeed how sexuality is managed at Tadmor in the opening pages of the novel.

Our community becomes a despotism, gentlemen, in dealing with love and marriage. For example, it positively prohibits any member afflicted with hereditary disease from marrying at all; and it reserves to itself, in the case of every proposed marriage among us, the right of permitting or forbidding it, in council. We can't even fall in love with each other, without being bound, under penalties, to report it to the Elder Brother; who in his turn, communicates it to the monthly council; who, in their turn, decide whether the courtship may go on or not. That's not the worst of it yet! In some cases – when we haven't the slightest intention of falling in love with each other – the governing body takes the initiative. 'You two will do well to marry; we see, it if you don't. Just think of it will you?' You may laugh; some of our happiest marriages have been made in that way. Our governors in council act on an established principle: here it is in a nutshell. The results of experience in the matter of marriage, all over the world, show that a really wise choice of husband or wife is an exception to the rule; and that husbands and wives in general would be happier together if their marriages were managed for them by competent advisers on either side. Laws laid down on such lines as these, and others equally strict, which I have not mentioned yet, were not put into force. Mr. Hethcote, as you suppose, without serious difficulties – difficulties which threatened the very existence of the Community. But that was before my time. When I grew up, I found the husbands and wives about me content to acknowledge that the Rules fulfilled the purpose with which they had been made – the greatest happiness of the greatest number. It all looks very absurd, I dare say, from your point of view. But these queer regulations of ours answer the Christian test – by their fruits ye shall know them. Our married people don't live on separate sides of the house; our children are all healthy; wife-beating is unknown among us; and the practice in our divorce court wouldn't keep the most moderate lawyers on bread and cheese. Can you say as much for the success of the marriage laws in Europe? I leave you, gentlemen, to form your own opinions.[52]

Here Collins is making Goldenheart a spokesperson for an alternative sexual code and this is not the only reference to the management of sexuality at Tadmor. We also see how it works in practice. A certain Miss Millicent falls in love with Goldenheart and the Tadmor laws are put to the test in adjudicating in the instance when a woman falls in love with a man almost young enough to be her son. The difference between nature and culture is highlighted here. Many of our habits, attitudes and ideas are the results of particular historical moments but it is the business of ideology to make these cultural assumptions and prejudices appear natural. In this particular instance Collins describes the masculine parameters of culture, of a cultural regime which presents itself as the natural order and conceals its own specific historical formation.

"You can't expect to persuade us that a laughable thing is not a thing to be laughed at. A woman close on forty who falls in love with a young fellow of twenty one – " "Is a laughable circumstance," Rufus interposed. "Whereas a man of forty who fancies a young woman of twenty-one is still in the order of Nature. The men have settled it so. But why the women are to give up so much sooner than the men is a question, sir, on which I have long wished to hear the sentiments of the women themselves."[53]

Collins is modest enough not to attempt to give the female angle on this problem but he is perspicacious enough and courageous enough to suggest that it is a question worthy of study. A different perspective is given to the problem already in that the speaker is American, Rufus Dingwell, the man from the New World and he sees things differently from Mr Hethcote, the English vicar, who is all too ready to laugh at the idea of a young man with an older woman.

The situation in the anecdote at this point is that Goldenheart has captured the affections of the older woman. And while Tadmor may make some allowances for this liaison – certainly it may regard it with more tolerance than would be granted it in mainstream society – still there are inadequacies too, even in the socialist society. Returning to an old theme, Collins makes clear for the reader that, despite their very best intentions, Goldenheart and Miss Millicent may have their behaviour misinterpreted. They ignore the importance of appearance and how the community may interpret their actions. They go out together in a rowing boat forgetting that 'appearances on the lake might lead to false conclusions on shore'.[54] Throughout his novels, Collins investigates the disjunction between appearance and reality and the fact that the truth of the matter is not always what first meets the eye. Here it seems that this is also the case in the community and its members too are only too quick to read appearance for reality. Evidently Tadmor has not cleansed itself of all the faults of society at large and Collins here distances himself from the Christian socialist community on this point. He is prepared to point up the shortcomings of both camps. It is interesting that spying at Tadmor should be condemned in this way because, while there is no one model for this community in Illinois, it was spying on each other, encouraged by its founder Cabet, which contributed to the downfall of the Nauvoo community.[55] Goldenheart and Miss Millicent are spied upon and their actions are completely misunderstood.

Goldenheart listens to the woman's story. She is the victim of a man who cheated her out of four thousand pounds and then abandoned her. Her situation is tragic but our sympathy is equally directed towards the 'poor middle classes' in England. Miss Millicent is allowed to expand on the miserable and pathetic lives of this group, the class who suffer most from the dialectic of property and propriety.

I don't think there are such miserable lives anywhere as the lives led by the poor middle classes in England. From year's end to year's end, *the one dreadful struggle to keep up appearances*, and the heart-breaking monotony of an existence without change. We lived in the back street of a cheap suburb. I declare to you we had but one amusement in the whole long weary year – the annual concert the clergyman got up, in aid of his schools. The rest of the year it was all teaching for the first half of the day, and needlework for the young family for the other half. My father had religious scruples; he prohibited theatres, he prohibited dancing and light reading; he even prohibited looking in at the shop-windows, because we had no money to spare and they tempted us to buy. He went to business in the morning, and came back at night, and fell asleep after dinner, and woke up and read prayers – and next day to business and back, and sleeping and waking and reading prayers – and no break in it, week after week, month after month, except on Sunday, which was always the same Sunday; the same church, the same service, the same dinner, the same book of sermons in the evening. Even when we had a fortnight once a year at the seaside, we always went to the same place and lodged in the same cheap hotel. The few friends we had led just the same lives, and were beaten down flat by just the same monotony. All the women seemed to submit to it contentedly except my miserable self.[56]

Where Dickens would tend to concentrate on grotesque caricature in his presentation of class, Collins gives a picture of the robotic, ritualistic nature of an entire class's thoughts and habits. In the passage above the attack on Sabbatarianism may be traced back to the opening chapter of *Hide and Seek* and combines with the ridicule of Evangelicism in *The Moonstone*. The attack on rational recreation is similar in theme to the social criticism found in *A Rogue's Life*. Interestingly, it is a female character who has this insight into the void of petty-bourgeois ritual. Women exhibit the contradictions of role more clearly than men and it is a feature of Collins' writing that he creates particularly strong women characters. These women can be seen as being aggressively masculine but it is more to the point to see them as figures who challenge accepted and natural, that is, masculine, notions of gender and push to the limits the social space traditionally allowed to women. There, it is Miss Millicent who challenges and condemns the monotony of lower middle class life, and later the relationship between women and their role in society is investigated in the novel in the figures of Mrs Farnaby, Regina and Sally.

The English Christian socialists, in both periods of their activity, did not discuss questions of gender, marriage or the situation of women. And, according to Nordhoff, the majority of the American communities were conventional in their attitudes to the family and the management of sexuality. Indeed women are often the victims of prejudice in these communities and are made to suffer even more than they would be in society at large. Such were the religious scruples of some of the communities that women were seen as a constant threat to the moral wholesomeness of the men. Nordhoff writes of the Amana community's treatment of women.

> The sex, I believe, is not highly esteemed by these people, who think it dangerous to the Christian's peace of mind. One of the most esteemed writers advises men to "fly from intercourse with women, as a very highly dangerous magnet and magical fire." Their women work hard and dress soberly; all ornaments are forbidden. To wear the hair loose is prohibited. Great care is taken to keep the sexes apart. In their evening and other meetings, women not only sit apart from men, but they leave the room before the men break ranks.[57]

Collins obviously read his Nordhoff very selectively if he found in these accounts of American communities signposts for a better and fairer treatment of women. The Amana community is not atypical; others such as the Shakers advocated celibacy, a celibacy, however, which was associated with a qualified equality between the sexes.

> They hold strongly to the equality of women with men, and look forward to the day when women shall, in the outer world as in their own societies, hold office as well as men. "Here we find the women just as able as men in all business affairs, and far more spiritual." "Suppose a woman wanted, in your family, to be a blacksmith, would you consent?" I asked; and he replied, "No, because this would bring men and women into relations which we do not think wise." In fact, while they call men and women equally to the rulership, they very sensibly hold that in general life the woman's work is in the house, the man's out of doors, and there is no offer to confuse the two.[58]

However Nordhoff's study would not have been without interest for Collins. The followers of J. H. Noyes, the Perfectionists of Oneida, were bound to have appealed to him as they appear to have had a much more enlightened attitude to women and supported this with a theory which equated the situation of women in the outside world with all the iniquities of private property.

> The community system, which they thus hold to have been divinely commanded, they extend beyond property – to persons; and thus they justify their extraordinary social system, in which there is no marriage; or, as they put it "complex marriage takes the place of simple." They surround this singular and, so far as I know, unprecedented combination of polygamy and polyandry with certain religious and social restraints; but affirm that there is "no intrinsic difference between property in persons and property in things; and that the same spirit which abolished exclusiveness in regard to money would abolish, if circumstances allowed full scope to it, exclusiveness in regard to women and children.[59]

Nordhoff may be right to see these ideas as 'unprecedented' but in many of the Collins novels the situation of women with regard to property is problematic and Collins often equates the situation of women with the laws defending property. In *The Fallen Leaves* he may not argue for polygamy and polyandry, but he is anxious to demonstrate how society discriminates against women and how this is often justified in terms of the laws of property. Rufus Dingwell comes to this conclusion towards the end of the novel.

> Left alone in the library, Rufus walked restlessly to and fro, driven by a troubled mind. "I was bound to do it," he thought; "and I ought to be satisfied by myself. I'm not satisfied. *The world is hard on women – and the rights of property is a damned bad reason, for it.*"[60] (my italics)

Again it is Dingwell, the man from the New World, who is allowed this insight into the situation of women. Society may be 'damned hard' on women but this comes to the reader as homespun philosophy rather than with the full force of authorial authority. Significantly, it is not Goldenheart, the Christian socialist, who makes this statement.

Thus rather than emphasise fixity of perspective, *The Fallen Leaves* describes alternative Christian socialist philosophies with some ambiguity. Christian socialism was an alternative world view which in its manifest versions informs Goldenheart's approach to life in the novel. In his first encounter with Mr Farnaby, Goldenheart jumps to the defence of American culture and criticises Farnaby whose insular view makes him see English society as the social norm and all others as inferior derivations.

> "Excuse me for noticing it," he said. "Your manners are perfectly gentlemanlike, and you speak English without any accent. And yet you have been brought up in America. What does it mean?"
> I grew worse and worse – I got downright sulky now. "I suppose it means," I answered, "that some of us, in America cultivate ourselves as well as our land. We have our books and music, though you seem to think we only have our axes and spades. Englishmen don't claim a monopoly of good manners at Tadmor. We see no difference between an American gentleman and an English gentleman. And as for speaking English with an accent, the Americans accuse *us* of doing that."[61]

The effect of this exchange is to emphasise the relativity of notions of culture and good manners. English society is not the social norm by which other nations and societies may be judged. Rather it is merely one colour in a social and political spectrum. And it is not only geographical space which creates different manners and allows both Goldenheart and Dingwell to make criticisms of England. Values and manners also change over time and this temporal aspect is brought into play in the novel with the introduction of Toff, Goldenheart's French butler. Toff represents the old values which are contrasted with both the American's straightforwardness, Goldenheart's Christian socialism, and the popular perceptions of the day.

Goldenheart accepts Farnaby's invitation to visit him at home and meets Mrs Farnaby and her niece, Regina. He is strongly impressed by Mrs Farnaby.

> I never before saw such a woman; I never expect to see such a woman again. There was nothing in her figure, or in her way of moving that produced this impression on me – she is little and fat, and walks with a firm, heavy step, like the step of a man.[62]

Although Goldenheart continues, in his description of Mrs Farnaby, to ascribe the strange impression she made on him to her eyes – 'the soul in torment that looks at you all the while out of her eyes' – it is worthy of note that she has 'the step of man', a man's walk and also a particular 'muscular handshake'. Again Collins is disrupting traditional gender attributes and Mrs Farnaby is seen as an interesting character by Goldenheart and, to a lesser extent, by Dingwell because she refuses the recognised paradigms of gender stereotyping. This is further emphasised during the private conversation with Goldenheart concerning her lost daughter, an incident the reader is familiar with from the prologue to the novel. In the privacy of her own room, Mrs Farnaby offers Goldenheart a cigar and smokes one herself. Goldenheart describes her 'den'.

> The room bore no resemblance to a boudoir. A faded old Turkey carpet was spread on the floor. The common mahogany table had no covering; the chintz on the chairs was of a truly venerable age. Some of the furniture made the place look like a room occupied by a man. Dumbbells and clubs of the sort used in athletic exercises hung over the bare mantelpiece; a large ugly oaken structure with closed doors, something between a cabinet and a wardrobe, rose on one side to the ceiling; a turning lathe stood against the opposite wall. / . . . / No traces of books or music were visible; no needlework of any sort was to be seen; no elegant trifles; no china or flowers or delicate lace-work or sparkling jewelry – nothing, absolutely nothing, suggestive of a woman's presence appeared in any part of Mrs. Farnaby's room.[63]

Mrs Farnaby has masculine attributes and surrounds herself with masculine accessories. She is obviously not a stereotypical representative of the Victorian wife. Collins further complicates this picture of her by refusing to place her in some other stereotypical role which would account for her behaviour. The male accessories in her room contrast, almost inexplicably, with the illustrations on her walls which relate to an obsession with motherhood, that most basic of female roles. Mrs Farnaby rides uneasily between these contrasting representations of women. She combines masculine gender characteristics with a fixation on the female role of mothering.

Several humorous scenes illustrate the limitations of middle class behaviour and manners. Mrs Farnaby has dreamed that

Goldenheart will find her abandoned daughter, the child deserted by her husband in his attempt to inherit the stationery business. Mrs Farnaby is Mr Ronald's daughter. Goldenheart will recognise this child by means of a membrane or web connecting the third and fourth toes of the left foot. Mrs Farnaby's own foot is similarly marked and she exposes her foot to Goldenheart so he will know exactly what he is looking for. In *Man and Wife* Collins plays with the reader's sense of propriety and, in an ironic twist, argues that morality is a matter of posture.[64] Something of the same logic informs Mrs Farnaby's defence of her action.

> "When a woman has a pretty hand," Mrs. Farnaby proceeded, "she is ready enough to show it. When she goes out to a ball, she favours you with a view of her bosom, and a part of her back. Now tell me! If there is no impropriety in a naked bosom – where is the impropriety of a naked foot?"[65]

Mrs Farnaby's unconventional behaviour is contrasted with that of her niece Regina when Rufus Dingwell visits them. Dingwell breaks the laws of polite conversation and is reprimanded by Regina – 'strangers are not in the habit of saying such things in England'. Mrs Farnaby apologises and explains that her niece is a 'narrow-minded young woman'.

> "You are not like the men she is accustomed to see. She doesn't understand you – you are not a commonplace gentleman. For instance," Mrs. Farnaby continued, with the matter of fact gravity of a woman innately inaccessible to a sense of humour, "you have got something strange on your hair. It seems to be melting, and it smells like soap."[66]

Significantly, it is Mrs Farnaby, whose experience allows her to take an oblique view of English society, who identifies with Dingwell and can tell him of his mistake in applying French shaving soap rather than pomatum on his hair. This essentially frivolous and comic incident serves to demonstrate some of the short-comings of the rules of propriety. Such is Regina's attention to good manners that she could not receive Rufus Dingwell in a friendly fashion or point out that his hair was in a lather. Regina is imprisoned by the rules of polite society and can only enforce them which, in this case, means not acknowledging an absurdity. Reality, in the sense of her capacity to acknowledge anything outside the rules of convention, is thus grossly obscured by her shallow adherence to manners.

Regina struggles to maintain the proprieties but she notices that Goldenheart, with whom she believes herself to be falling in love, is far from the average man. She writes to a friend that 'This curious Amelius seems to notice trifles which escape men in general, just as *we* do.'[67] Here Goldenheart's insight is seen to be on a par with that of a woman, so, to some extent, Goldenheart is feminised but within limits. Women still find him very attractive as Miss Millicent reminds him. He has a quality in his personality which is not a common masculine trait, but rather a characteristic which allows for great empathy with women; 'your manly gentleness and sweetness speaks in every tone of your voice; we poor women feel drawn towards you by an attraction which we are not able to resist'.[68] Goldenheart has the quality of 'manly gentleness' – almost a contradiction in terms – just as Mrs Farnaby combines a mothering instinct with masculine interests.

Goldenheart is in the process of being educated in these encounters. Up to this point in the novel, the reader is not sure whether his view of women is other than a vague ideal of a Christian socialist nature. But, whatever view he has of women and his own sexuality, it is put to the test when he meets Sally. After his lecture on Christian socialism, he determines to take a walk south across Waterloo Bridge and into a road containing one of the street-markets of the poor. This documentary description is reminiscent of Mayhew, replete with all the requisite characters – 'costermongers', 'lusty vagabonds', 'blind men selling staylaces', and 'a broken down soldier playing "God Save the Queen".'

> Amelius found it no easy matter to pass quickly through the people loitering and gossiping about him. There was greater freedom for a rapid walker in the road. He was on the point of stepping off the pavement, when a voice behind him – a sweet soft voice, though it spoke very faintly – said, "Are you good-natured, sir?"
>
> He turned, and found himself face to face with one of the saddest sisterhood on earth – the sisterhood of the streets.[69]

While the street-market may be described in a documentary style, there is a rhetorical shift towards sentimentalism when Collins comes to deal with the sister of the streets. Some forms of social criticism are evidently more acceptable than others. More tact is required in discussing prostitution and sexuality than describing class politics and social corruption. Collins enters controversial terrain in his interrogation of the ambivalences surrounding prostitution. It is interesting to consider just how clichéd is this attempt to describe the young prostitute, Simple Sally; her name is both patronising and sentimental.

> But for the words in which she accosted him, it would have been impossible to associate her with the lamentable life she led. The appearance of the girl was artlessly virginal and innocent; she looked as if she had passed through the contamination of the streets without being touched by it, without fearing it, or feeling it, or understanding it. Robed in pure white, with her gentle blue eyes raised to Heaven, a painter might have shown her on his canvas as a saint or an angel; and the critical world would have said, Here is the true ideal – Raphael himself might have painted this![70]

Collins juxtaposes one stereotypical representation of women with another and by showing how Sally could be contained in both stereotypes, he consequently condemns stereotypical representation of women as inadequate approximations to feminine complexity. Sally can be identified as either whore or virgin but in the sense that she is a whole human being – both whore and virgin – she transcends these inadequate categorisations. As Collins sees it, prostitutes are to be pitied because they are so often the victims of male violence and male short-sightedness. While Sally herself, is described in very sentimental terms, Collins adopts a different discourse when he is dealing with her pimp.

> Amelius turned, and saw Simple Sally with her arm in the grasp of a half-drunken ruffian; one of the swarming *wild beasts* of Low London, dirtied down from head to foot to the colour of the street mud – the living danger and disgrace of English civilization. As Amelius eyed him, he drew the girl away a step or two. "You've got a gentleman this time," he said to her; "I shall expect gold tonight, or else – !" He finished the sentence by lifting his *monstrous* fist, and shaking it in her face. Cautiously as he had lowered his tones in speaking, the words had reached the keenly

sensitive ears of Amelius. Urged by his hot temper, he sprang forward. In another moment, he would have knocked the *brute* down – but for the timely interference of the arm of the law, clad in a policeman's greatcoat. "Don't get yourself into trouble, sir," said the man good-humouredly. "Now, you Hell-fire (that's the nice name they know him by, sir, in these parts), be off with you!" *The wild beast on two legs* cowered at the voice of authority, like the wild beast on four; he was lost to sight, at the dark end of the street, in a moment.[71] (my italics)

While dealing with images of women, Collins shows the inadequacy of available stereotypes but he actually draws on this repository of stereotypes to condemn masculine violence. It is masculine violence rather than prostitution which is identified as the 'disgrace of English civilization'. Hell-fire is likened to a stalking animal and the policeman acts as a guard who protects the middle class element of society from the ravages of these wild animals, the lumpen, working class.[72] It is not just Hell-fire who is imaged in this way; before her redemption Sally is described as a wild beast in her instinctive distrust of everyone bar Goldenheart and, when she is finally captured, Mrs Sowler is described as a 'beast in a cage'.[73]

Goldenheart finds he has no option but to take care of Sally. He takes her back to his lodgings and, the next morning, is ordered to leave by his landlady. She is a woman whose moral scruples guarantee she keeps a respectable house, a house with no place for Sally. Rufus Dingwell suggests that Sally be placed in a 'Home for Friendless Women, especially adapted to receive poor girls in Sally's melancholy position'.[74] Goldenheart agrees to place Sally in this institution and then visits Regina. His love affair with Regina has been frustrated on almost all fronts, having met the combined disapproval of Mr and Mrs Farnaby and Rufus Dingwell. Regina once again refuses Goldenheart's offer of marriage and, in desperation and despair he finds himself thinking of Sally. After apparent sexual failure with one woman, Goldenheart's thoughts turn to another whom he imagines would be kinder to him.

In all probability, he would have quarrelled with any man who had accused him of actually lamenting the girl's absence, and wanting her back again. He happened to recollect her artless blue eyes, with their vague patient look, and her quaint childish questions put so openly in so sweet a voice – and that was all. Was there anything reprehensible, if you please, in an act of remembrance?[75]

There is irony in this passage when Collins writes that Goldenheart just 'happened to recollect' Sally. It is not a matter of chance and it is clear that Goldenheart's desire for this angel with her childish questions is not altogether honourable. Why else does he fear a meeting with Dingwell, the forthright American who always speaks his mind? The chances are that Dingwell will see through the conventional mask which Goldenheart is adopting, the expedient utilisation of Victorian moral rhetoric. Goldenheart now appears to the reader to be, in comparison with Dingwell, no longer an outsider or *ingenu* figure. He fears a conversation with the American because the latter 'read him like a book: the American would ask irritating questions'.[76] Rufus Dingwell has the ability to look 'below the surface and was not so easily deceived'.[77] It is for this reason that Goldenheart retreats from society – he is unsure of his motives and is afraid to be interrogated by Dingwell who, at this point, is symbolic of clear thinking. He sets up home in a quiet cottage with a new French servant Toff, a nickname given to the old man by his fellow English servants for their 'insular convenience.'[78]

Goldenheart's liaison with Regina falls into even more desperate straits when she abandons him in London and departs for Paris with her guardian, Mr Farnaby. Once again Goldenheart dreams of Sally. Again his motives are equivocal and the whole question of the masculine representation of sexuality is paramount. Sexuality and desire appear to be at the very foundations of polite society.

The slightest circumstances conspired to heighten his interest in Sally – just at the time when Regina had once more disappointed him. He was as firmly convinced, as if he had been the strictest moralist living, that it was an insult to Regina, and an insult to his own self-respect, to set the lost creature whom he had rescued in any light of comparison with the young lady who was one day to be his wife. And yet, try as he might to drive her out, Sally kept her place in his thoughts. There was, apparently, some innate depravity in him. If a looking-glass had been handed to him at that moment, he would have been ashamed to look himself in the face.[79]

The reflection in the mirror, it is suggested, would have pointed to the sexual desire – his 'innate depravity' – which Goldenheart is afraid to confront. His sense of propriety does not allow him to equate his feelings for his fiancée with the emotions which draw him towards a young prostitute. Collins is drawing attention to the Victorian double standard by distancing his reader from any full identification with Goldenheart. In fact marriage represents, for Goldenheart, a way of curbing the satyr in his loins. If he was confident in his relationship with Regina, Sally would not be such a threat to his moral standing. It is because he fears this side of himself that he determines, once again, to attempt to hasten the date of his marriage to Regina. He writes to a relative in search of a job in order to satisfy Farnaby's financial terms for allowing the wedding. Unfortunately Goldenheart's politics have reached and alienated the uncle. 'Whilst you are a Socialist, you are a stranger to me.'[80]

After Regina's speedy departure for Paris, Goldenheart's thoughts remain on questions of sex and desire. The very circumlocution in which this is described signals the problematic nature of the subject and Goldenheart is very reluctant to give space to this monster, which, it seems is slowly dominating his conscious life.

> That innate depravity which Amelius had lately discovered in his own nature, let the forbidden thoughts loose in him again as he watched the departing carriage from the door. "If poor little Sally had been in her place . . . !" He made an effort of virtuous resolution, and stopped them. "What a blackguard a man may be," he penitently reflected, "without suspecting himself!"[81]

Despite the 'virtuous resolution', it is the 'innate depravity' and the 'forbidden thoughts' which hold sway and influence Goldenheart, as becomes clear in his conversation with a servant.

> "Richard," he said, "are you engaged to be married?" Richard stared in blank surprise at the strange question – and modestly admitted that he was engaged to marry the housemaid next door. "Soon?" asked Amelius, swinging his stick. "As soon as I have saved a little more money, sir." "Damn the money!" cried Amelius – and struck his stick on the pavement, and walked away with a last look at the house as if he hated the sight of it.[82]

Though virtually unspoken, in any very direct way, the subject of this exchange is certainly given flesh. Goldenheart is keen to consummate his own relationship and also to encourage others to do the same. He is frustrated by the money–love parallel which so governs and determines his affair with Regina and is angry that money should so dictate and command the personal life.

It is Toff, the French servant, whose status as a European allows him to glance askance at the proprieties of English life, who identifies Goldenheart's problems very specifically. The young man lives in a 'suburban Paradise', but a Paradise without Eve.[83] Goldenheart needs a female companion and his poor, celibate state is contrasted with that of Toff himself who has three children and has been married three times. That evening Goldenheart falls asleep and dreams that Sally enters his library and kisses him. The dream, with its prophetic status, becomes a reality. Sally has run away from the refuge and Toff offers her shelter in the cottage. While she may be the object of sexual desire, Collins is careful not to outrage decorum and again Sally is seen in terms of a rather simple child. However, the language describing the girl's childish innocence reflects something close to pederasty in Goldenheart's response to her.

> She was clothed in the plain dress that he had bought for her; and she looked more charming in it than ever. The beauty of health claimed kindred now, in her pretty face, with the beauty of youth: the wan cheeks had begun to fill out, and the pale lips were delicately suffused with their natural rosy red. Little by little her first fears seemed to subside. She smiled and softly crossed the room, and stood at his side. After looking at him with a rapt expression of tenderness and delight, she laid her hands on the arm of the chair, and said, in the quaintly quiet way which he remembered so well, "I want to kiss you." She bent over him, and kissed him with the innocent freedom of a child.[84]

From other evidence in the text it is worth remembering that Sally is not an innocent child – she is a reformed prostitute. But the stereotypes demand that she is seen as either a child or a saint. What is being discussed here is sexual desire, but this cannot be given too explicit statement and, in the interests of the propriety and decorum, the sexual is marginalised and the attempt is made to submerge and displace it with a version of a sentimental, sanitised human love – the love which Goldenheart felt for his pets at Tadmor. So powerful is this taboo that human sexuality is trivialised by the comparison with people's love for animals.

> In his unendurable loneliness he had longed for his dog, he had longed for his fawn. There was the martyred creature from the streets, whom he had rescued from nameless horror, waiting to be his companion, servant, friend! There was the child-victim of cold and hunger, still only feeling her way to womanhood; innocent of all other aspirations, so long as she might fill the place which had once been occupied by the dog and the fawn![85]

Goldenheart had rescued Sally from a 'nameless horror', the life of a cheap prostitute, and this whole area of human sexuality must remain muted, preferably dumb. Similarly, there is no acceptable name or language in which Goldenheart can describe the sexual attraction he feels for Sally. Sexuality is usually explained away with a great deal of shame and it is to the credit of the Oneida community that it saw sex as an essential part of life which should be considered as a gift of God.

> Dividing the sexual relation into two branches, the amative and the propagative, the amative or love-relation is first in importance, as it is in the order of nature, God made woman because "he saw it was not good for man to be alone;" (Gen. 2:18) ie., for social, not primarily for propagative purposes. Eve was called Adam's "help-meet". In the whole of the specific account of the creation of woman, she is regarded as his companion, and her maternal office is not brought into view.[86]

Whether consciously or not, Collins is certainly writing in the spirit of the Oneida's community's attitude to amative sex and he appears to take a distant view of that morality which makes even Goldenheart look with such horror on his 'innate depravity'.

It is as a result of Toff's prompting and assistance that Sally becomes a permanent feature in Goldenheart's cottage. The valet prepares a room for her and after a particularly rich and relaxing dinner – when 'the effervescent gaiety of the evening was at its climax; the awful forms of duty, propriety and good manners had been long since laughed out of the room' – that the respectable reader is right to be on edge.[87] It is just at such times that the façade of polite manners and good and proper sexual behaviour is put to the test. However, the evening ends with Sally kissing Goldenheart as innocently as if she is his sister. Nevertheless, the latent and covert sexuality of the situation is only just below the surface. The sisterly kiss may be innocent but Goldenheart is frighteningly aware that 'While weeks might pass harmlessly, months might pass harmlessly – but the time must come when the innocent relations between them would be upset by peril.'[88] 'Peril' here is ambiguous. This ambiguity includes both the internal and external perspectives on sexuality. It is a reference to Goldenheart's ignorance of his own sexuality and to society's double standards. The 'peril' is from the growing sexual potential in the relationship and from the society whose hypocrisy, it is suggested, will not countenance such a liaison.

The Fallen Leaves is not a novel with two separate themes, a love plot and social critique.[89] Both these subjects are addressed in the novel but they are mutually illuminating. The social documentary extends to the love plot with its consequent concentration on the situation of women. Treatment of women as property is condemned just as much as property in the more usual sense. What I have been arguing above is that Collins uses various versions of Christian socialist thought to encompass and propose remedies for both ills. Goldenheart is more obviously and more identifiably a Christian socialist on the public front but there is a version of Christian socialism which implicitly underwrites his sexual behaviour at the end of the novel. More accurately, perhaps, there is a Christian socialist discourse available, that of Noyes' Oneida community which would save Goldenheart from the moral dilemmas he suffers at the close of the novel. But significantly Collins does not elect to invoke it. Instead he chooses to allow his hero and heroine to discover the validity of Oneida mores for themselves.

Dingwell makes a sudden return from Paris and finds Sally living in the cottage with Goldenheart. Although at first shocked to discover this ménage, he soon realises that, despite appearances, they are not cohabiting. Sally is studying the New Testament and Dingwell finds it necessary to explain the disjunction between what this book teaches and more worldly practices. The world may make a ritual genuflection to Christianity and the New Testament but

"... you see, you have got the world about you to reckon with – and the world has invented a religion of its own. There's no use looking for it in this little book of yours. *It's a religion with the pride of property at the bottom of it, and a veneer of benevolent sentiment at the top.* It will be sorry for you and very charitable towards you; in short it will do everything for you except taking you back again."[90] (my italics)

The dominance of property and the reference to the 'veneer' of sentiment is a familiar motif and, in this instance, it is just such a coupling and articulation of ideological values which render Sally's position so difficult. It is at this point that Dingwell draws the parallel between the situation of women and the rights of property. Social critique is linked with the situation of women. Here Collins, quite clearly centres his critique of Victorian mercantilism on the position of women and the limited space allowed them by the dictates of property.

The situation is made no easier by the fact that women themselves may be active agents in their own containment. This is made clear in the final pages of the novel. Goldenheart and Sally happen on a wedding when out taking a stroll. The description of this event is far from the sentimental cant which might be expected at such occasions.

> The bride was a tall buxom girl, splendidly dressed; she *performed her part in the ceremony* with the most unruffled composure. The bridegroom *exhibited* an instructive *spectacle* of aged Nature, sustained by Art. His hair, his complexion, his teeth, his breast, his shoulders and his legs, showed what the wig-maker, the valet, the dentist, the tailor, and the hosier can do for a rich old man, who wished to present a juvenile *appearance* while he is *buying a young wife. No less than three clergymen were present conducting the sale.* The demeanour of the rich congregation was worthy of the glorious bygone days of the Golden Calf. So far as could be *judged by appearances,* one old lady, in a pew close to the place at which Amelius and Sally were standing, seemed to be the only person present who was not favourably impressed by the ceremony.
>
> "I call it disgraceful," the old lady remarked to a charming young person seated next to her.
>
> But the charming young person – being the legitimate product of the present time – had no more sympathy with questions of sentiment than a Hottentot. "How can you talk so,

grandmamma!" she rejoined. "He has twenty thousand a year – and that lucky girl will be the mistress of the most splendid house in London."

"I don't care," the old lady persisted; "it's not the less a disgrace to everybody concerned in it. There is many a poor friendless creature, driven by hunger to the streets, who has a better claim to our sympathy than that shameless girl, selling herself in the house of God!"[91] (my italics)

The passage exemplifies many of the concerns of the entire novel. There is a reference to 'spectacle' and 'appearance', to the disjunction between appearance and reality in the figure of the groom and to the commerciality at the base of respectable sexuality – 'buying a young wife'. Women are seen as property and the spectacle or ceremony has all the support of convention – 'three clergymen were present' – yet the 'sale' of the young woman to the old man – 'aged Nature sustained by Art' – is legitimated, in the last instance, by the fact that he has 'twenty thousand a year'. This is all seen to be representative of modern values and the views of the 'charming young person' are contrasted with those of her grandmother who personifies the values of an older and, it is implied a better time. Here, for example, it is clear that it is not the Church itself which is being attacked but rather the present appropriation of the Church by the religious and commercial establishment which makes it the handmaiden of corruption. The Church at the time of the indignant grandmother, it is implied, would have behaved in a more scrupulous fashion. In the grandmother's opinion, even the future 'mistress of the most splendid house in London' is selling herself and her sex and is in a worse position, morally speaking, than a prostitute, 'a poor friendless creature driven by hunger to the streets'.

Goldenheart and Sally marry at the close of *The Fallen Leaves: First Series* so legitimating their sexual desire, but this is preceded by a few telling passages which can be read as Collins' attempt to describe sexual desire, give it expression and allow it to break free from the sentimental conventions of the period. Considerable value is placed on sincerity of feeling and any shame about the sexual nature of human relationships is implicitly condemned. Goldenheart is sexually attracted to Sally and Collins seems to be radically altering, at this point, the stereotype of philanthrophy, charity and good feeling which he began with. Once rescued, Sally is not a stereotype and Goldenheart cannot appreciate or understand his 'innate depravity' for some time. But he does manage to get beyond it and thus the unfolding of the plot breaks the Magdalen idea which Collins began with. Regina, on the other hand, the official 'Queen' of love is imprisoned in money and remains an incomplete human being, unable to feel passion.

Returning from their walk, where they overheard the old lady express her horror of the wedding, Sally and Goldenheart continue to discuss marriage. Sally mentions Goldenheart's proposed marriage to Regina. This is not something she could envisage for herself because she is after all a former prostitute. Yet in the sentimental rhetoric of the moment she asks

"Will you tell them to bury me in some quiet place away from London, where there are few graves? And when you leave your directions, don't say you are to be burnt. Say – when you have lived a long, long life, and enjoyed all the happiness you have deserved so well – say you are to be buried, and your grave is to be near mine. I should like to think of the same trees shading us and the same flowers growing over us."[92]

Sally describes a sentimental and transcendental solution to their problems, problems which are a result of the social conventions and restrictions which forbid a sexual relationship between them. But this is not satisfactory to either Goldenheart or the reader and that evening, back in the cottage, nothing is assuaged. For the first time ever, Sally goes to bed without giving Goldenheart her customary good-night kiss. Goldenheart ponders the situation, a state of affairs which is only to be remedied, it appears, when they recognise the sexual nature of their relationship. But because she once belonged to the 'sisterhood of the street' Goldenheart cannot marry her and maintain his social respect. The novel ends with a crushing repudiation of this empty convention; things can only be put right when Goldenheart and Sally accept the sincerity of their feelings for each other and allow themselves to be guided by this rather than what society dictates.

The time passed – and Amelius was still thinking, and still as far as ever from arriving at a conclusion, when he heard a door opened behind him. Sally crossed the room before he could rise from his chair; her cheeks were flushed, her eyes were bright, her hair fell loose over her shoulders – she dropped at his feet, and hid her face on his knees. "I'm an ungrateful wretch!" she burst out; "I never kissed you when I said good night."[93]

The scene is set for the consummation of the relationship. Sally's aroused state – the loose hair, the flushed cheeks and the dilated eyes emphasise the sexual nature of the moment.

"You shan't be angry with me!" She jumped up, and sat on his knee, and put her arms around his neck. "I was too miserable to go to sleep. I don't know what's been the matter with me today. I seem to be losing the little sense I ever had. Oh, if I could only make you understand how fond I am of you! And yet I've had bitter thoughts, as if I was a burden to you and I had done a wrong thing in coming here – and you would have told me so, only you pitied the poor wretch who had nowhere else to go." She tightened her hold around his neck, and laid her burning cheek against his face. "Oh, Amelius, my heart is sore! Kiss me, and say, 'Goodnight Sally!' "
   He was young – he was a man – for a moment he lost his self-control; he kissed her as he had never kissed her yet.[94]

Value is placed on passion and sincerity of feeling in the novel as opposed to empty manners. It is an empty manner, a hollow convention which renders it impossible for Goldenheart to have a full sexual relationship with Sally. Their love story is a critique of these proprietorial barriers and therefore has general social resonances. Collins extends the thesis novel into the private space and via an examination of the plight of women and the vagaries of personal relationships, strengthens and makes more comprehensive his criticism of Victorian society. Goldenheart and Sally have no reason to be ashamed of the sexual feelings they have for each other. As I have shown, this sense of shame is presented to the reader as a regressive convention. Here Collins may have corroboration for his own views in Christian socialist thought: the Oneida community, one of the Primitive Christian socialist societies discussed by Nordhoff, whose book was in Collins' library, had long recognised that a sense of sexual shame was the result of one of many misinterpretations of the Bible:

PROPOSITION 24 – Sexual shame was the consequence of the

fall, and is factitious and irrational. Gen. 2:25; compare 3:7. Adam and Eve, while innocent, had no shame; little children have none; other animals have none.[95]

3

Basil

It is interesting to attempt to reconstruct some notion of the aesthetic of the novel at the time of writing *Basil*. It soon becomes clear that Collins' intention is other than that espoused by the reviewers of his novel in 1852. Indeed what they prescribe, and what is disputed by Collins is the function of the novelist and the social role of literature. In October, 1853, the *Westminster Review* published a long article on the history of the novel and Collins was taken to task for his unsavoury choice of subject matter in *Basil*.

> There are some subjects on which it is not possible to dwell without offence; and Mr. Collins having first chosen one which could neither please nor elevate, has rather increased the displeasure it excites, by his resolution to spare us no revolting detail. . . . Mr. Collins . . . dwells on the details of animal appetite with a persistency which can serve no moral purpose, and may minister to evil passions even while professing condemnation of them.[1]

Collins is criticised for his choice of subject matter and this moral objection is complicated and overdetermined by a more aesthetic difficulty because *Basil* seems to combine a repertoire of effect from various genres. This problem is recognised in an unsigned review in *Bentley's Miscellany*.

> That *Basil* will be pronounced 'improbable' we do not doubt. There is a startling antagonism between the intensity of the passion, the violent spasmodic action of the piece, and its smooth, common-place environment. The scenery, the *dramatis personae*, the costumery, are all of the most familiar every-day type, belonging to an advanced stage of civilization; but there is something rude and barbarous, almost Titanic, about the incidents; they belong to a different state of society.[2]

In what follows I want to indicate the effects of these two appropriations of the novel in a reading of *Basil*.

Richard Stang's study[3] is a fine account of the critical assumptions prevalent when Collins was writing, but for our purposes, to gain some familiarity with these aesthetic norms, it is only necessary to quote from the *Westminster Review*, again speaking of Collins.

> It matters not much whether the artist hold the pencil or the pen, the same great rules apply to both. He may simply copy nature as he sees it, and then the spectator has a pleasure proportioned to the beauty of the scene copied. He may give a noble spirit-stirring scene, and he will raise high thoughts and great aspirations in those who contemplate it. He may take a higher moral ground, and move to compassion by showing undeserved suffering, or, like Hogarth, read a lesson to the idle and the dissipated. He may also paint scenes of cruelty and sensuality so gross that his picture will be turned to the wall by those who do not choose to have their imagination defiled.
>
> The novelist has a high and holy mission, for his words frequently reach ears which will hear no others, and may convey a lesson to them which the preacher would enforce in vain; . . .[4]

Collins affected to be little influenced by what the critics had to say and was content to trust the general public and to his book sales as the ultimate arbiters of his work. Yet he did take his work very seriously as is evidenced by the large number of prefaces to his novels. With particular reference to *Basil*, Dickens felt that 'the prefatory letter would have been better away, on the ground that a book (of all things) should speak for and explain itself'.[5] However, it would be wrong to assume that he equated popularity with literary merit or that he, unproblematically, offered to the public a world picture with which they could easily identify. The prefaces are proof of the seriousness with which Collins viewed literature and they also map out his differences from critical opinion. His approach to his work is never described in terms of a rigid, systematic, theoretical programme and is more easily identified by its negative features. It is a rejection of the idea of art and literature as a supplement and apologia or paean of praise to nineteenth-century morality. It is most definitely a rejection of the current theory of genre, and it advances the dialogue, interaction and dialectic of literature and society. It is a radical interpretation of Victorian mores which has little truck with dominant or established opinion. It is apparent in the novels themselves and is given some more forceful and intellectual, philosophic credence in the prefaces.

The letter of dedication in *Basil* is particularly worthy of study because it is one of the first statements of a relatively new writer. Under the rubric of the Actual Collins includes his justification for what detractors identified as his 'aesthetics of the Old Bailey' and concentration on 'The jail, the gibbet, the madhouse . . . the adultery of a wife, the jealous torture of the injured husband.'[6] Collins argues that crime is a fact in society and therefore is worthy of artistic representation. In later life Collins is to emphasise this point in a marginal note in Forster's life of Dickens. Collins was not to be convinced by a view of literature which required that it should contain nothing which could not be safely read *en famille*. So already in this letter Collins is anticipating those who were to object to the novel on moral grounds. His next comment is reserved for the critics who would complain of his reconstruction of genre.

> Directing my characters and my story, then, towards the light of Reality wherever I could find it, I have not hesitated to violate some of the conventionalities of sentimental fiction. For instance, the first love-meeting of two of the personages in this book, occurs (where the real love meeting from which it is drawn, occurred) in the very last place and under the very last circumstances which the artificer of sentimental writing would sanction. Will my lovers excite ridicule instead of interest, because I have truly represented them as seeing each other where hundreds of other lovers have first seen each other, as hundreds of people will readily admit when they read the passage to which I refer? I am sanguine enough to think not.[7]

In the interests of Reality, Collins is willing to disrupt the genre of sentimental fiction in the attempt to make his novel accord more closely to life. It is just this violation of artistic convention which is responsible for the critical disfavour which accompanies Collins. To a greater or lesser extent throughout his career, he reworks the notion of genre. For example, in this letter to Charles Ward, introducing *Basil*, there is a new articulation of novels and plays. Collins will not distinguish between them in the requisite fashion but, rather, prefers to see 'that the one is a drama narrated, as the other is a drama acted'.[8] Collins was very interested in plays throughout his career and often converted his novels into plays. On the other hand, there is evidence that *Man and Wife* started in his imagination as a play. The result of this elastic attitude to genre is that he is criticised for failing to do justice to any particular genre, either the play or the novel. For example, of *Man and Wife*, it is said that it is too stilted, written with too much regard for various entrances and exits as would be demanded by a play.[9] Yet it should be remembered that works of art, literature, novels or plays derive their specific meaningfulness for readers not by possessing any direct one-to-one correspondence with relevant aspects of the 'real world', but by slotting into particular sets of conventions which readers have learned to recognise and interpret in quite specific ways. It could be said of Collins that he refuses to recognise the individual specificity of particular genres. Different genres have different meanings and are interpreted in different ways. Genre determines how the text is read. However, in this instance, Collins utilises discourse from various genres and so does not allow the reader an easy interpretation of the text. Collins argues that by ignoring the convention of sentimental fiction he is somehow approaching nearer to life when in actual fact he is merely switching from one discourse to another and both are determined by convention, albeit different conventions. However it is the effect of this switch at pivotal points in the novel which distances the reader.

Collins gives one example of how he intends to work this. At certain key passages he will admit

> . . . as perfectly fit accessories to the scene the most ordinary street-sounds that could be heard, and the most ordinary street-events that could occur, at the time and in the place represented – believing that by adding to truth, they were adding to tragedy . . .[10]

Again what Collins is attempting to do is to add to the reality-effect of his narrative. He is disguising the conventional nature of his own writing and emphasising those qualities which suggest its adherence to the Actual.

The preface continues with a spirited defence of *Basil*. It is true that the novel is based on the Actual, yet this concentration on external reality does not limit Collins and he does not feel that it is necessary 'to adhere to everyday realities only'.[11] The reality-effects outlined above serve only as common ground to attract the reader's attention 'to begin with; but it would be only by appealing to other sources (as genuine in their way) *beyond* his own experience, that I could hope to fix his interest and excite his suspense, to occupy his deeper feelings, or stir his nobler thoughts'.[12] It becomes clear how Collins plays with genre. The conventions of realism are utilised and are forged and fused with rules from other genres to create a narrative with a new meaning. The difficulty with Collins is that he reworks his texts in such a way that it is not always easy to identify genre or convention. Hence the difficulty with prescriptive Victorian aesthetics as outlined above. But to say that he runs counter to the critics in the literary journals is not to deny him his own view of literature. Collins always had a theory of art, a set of ideas which sustains all his work. Literature, for him, has a specific function and must encompass all aspects of life including 'error and crime'. Collins has explained how he will interfere with the traditional expectations of sentimental fiction in the novel and he then concludes the dedication with a defence of his choice of subject and outline of literature's role.

To those persons who dissent from the broad principles here adhered to; who deny that it is the novelist's vocation to do more than merely amuse them; who shrink from all honest and various reference, in books, to subjects which they think of in private and talk of in public everywhere; who see covert implication where nothing is implied, and improper allusions where nothing improper is alluded to; whose innocence is in the word, and not in the thought; whose morality stops at the tongue, and never gets in to the heart – to those persons, I should consider it loss of time, and worse, to offer any further explanation of my motives, than the sufficient explanation which I have given already. I do not address myself to them in this book, and shall never think of addressing myself to them in any other.[13]

A broad concern of this work rests on the hollowness of propriety and it is possible to read Collins' aesthetic, as outlined above, as a critique of a world of polite manners where innocence is in the word and not in the thought, on the tongue but not in the heart. Collins always works from a base of thought and heart and is constantly antagonistic to word and tongue.

Collins is sufficiently modest to admit in the preface that there may be a disjunction between theory and practice, between what he intended to do in the novel and what he has actually effected. However it is my argument here that the novel cannot be read in terms of available genre, or rather, it must be allowed that literary convention serves a different purpose. Collins spotlights both the conventions of writing and also focuses on social convention and propriety. Collins demands to be read in a particular fashion and Basil establishes the rules and maps out the space which future novels explore. Obviously Collins cannot be read without reference to the rules and theory of nineteenth-century literature, but it is the peculiar and individual rearticulation and reconstruction of these conventions in Basil which marks it as a text of radical comment in mid-nineteenth-century England.

Contemporary reviews have already been cited to illustrate the reception of the novel in the 1850s. More recent criticism has little to add. In his work on Collins, Kenneth Robinson points to some of the biographical parallels between the author and the eponymous Basil.[14] Both had very strict, principled fathers and both had written or were working on historical romances. Robinson also speculates on the possibility that the novelist had recently been disappointed in love, possibly with a working-class girl. Nuer Pharr Davis argues that the plot has a basis in fact in the case of the fourth Earl of Chesterfield and his financial dealings with a certain Dr William Dodd. Chesterfield, who felt his honour was at stake allowed Dodd to be hanged for forgery.[15] However this is barren speculation and does little to elucidate the text. A detailed examination of the work is necessary to tease out these qualities in the writing which caused offence and also to show how Collins tinkered and toyed with the dominant comprehension of genre. When Basil is read in this fashion, it should also be possible to identify the topics and ideological concerns which Collins elaborates and discusses in future work.

Basil's father is the central figure in the novel and his centrality goes beyond any biographical parallel. In the description of the father, Collins reworks his interest, or in this case, gives a first statement to his interest in stereotype and gender.

> His eyes, large and gray, had something commanding in their look; they gave a certain unchanging firmness and dignity to his expression, not often met with. They betrayed his birth and breeding, his old ancestral prejudices, his chivalrous sense of honour, in every glance. It required, indeed, all the masculine energy of look about the upper part of his face, to redeem the lower part from an appearance of effeminacy, so delicately was it moulded in its fine Norman outline. His smile was remarkable for its sweetness – it was almost like a woman's smile. In speaking, too, his lips often trembled as a woman's do.[16]

This confusion of the masculine and the feminine recurs in Collins' novels. While some women are given masculine traits, there is a corresponding tendency to feminise some men, particularly those with aristocratic affectation. Frederick Fairlie in *The Woman in White* is a case in point. However this is more an undermining of a literary convention than a diatribe about the decadent ruling class. Collins is flying in the face of received opinion about stereotypes in literature. The subject is given specific attention a few years after publication of *Basil* in the essay 'A Shockingly Rude Article'.[17] The narrator of this article amplifies how gender curtails woman's position in society. 'Is it necessary, after that, to confess that I am a woman? If it is, I make the confession – to my sorrow. I would much rather be a man'.[18] So, already in *Basil*, Collins juxtaposes masculine and feminine traits and is on the way to an interrogation of gender and sex roles. The subject is returned to at a later place in *Basil* and again Basil is thinking of his father.

> I thought on his pride of caste, so unobtrusive, so rarely hinted at in words, and yet so firmly rooted in his nature, so intricately entwined with every one of his emotions, his aspirations, his simplest feelings and ideas; I thought on his almost feminine

delicacy in shrinking from the barest mention of impurities which other men could carelessly discuss, or could laugh over as good material for an after-dinner jest.[19]

Collins' attitude to sexual positioning is not at all straight-forward; it is a problem which returns in many of his works and quite often is described in conjunction with woman's place in society and the representation of women in artistic texts. It is the subject of yet another essay 'A Petition to Novel Writers'.[20] With tongue-in-cheek rhetoric, Collins here satirises the Englishman's attachment to rules, in this case, the literary conventions which determine how women are to be described in literature. Yet the essay does little more than theorise the artistic practice of *Basil* in its treatment of the narrator's sister Clara and the woman he marries, Margaret Sherwin. Basically there are two stereotypes for women, each with its incumbent ideological associations of fair and dark, good and evil, transparent and opaque. Clara is fair and has blue eyes with

> . . . a tendency to flush, not merely in moments of agitation, but even when she is walking, or talking on any subject that interests her. Without this peculiarity, her paleness would be a defect. With it, the absence of any colour in her complexion but the fugitive uncertain colour which I have described, would to some eyes debar her from any claims to beauty. And a beauty perhaps she is not – at least, in the ordinary acceptation of the term . . .
>
> The greatest charms that my sister has on the surface, come from beneath it.[21]

Collins will make use of this convention of the pale beauty, give it some credence, but, simultaneously argue that true beauty is to be found beneath the surface residing in some quality which Clara possesses over and above that of 'the most beautiful and the most brilliant women'. And, of course, Collins is already skewering convention, because, while he does place Clara in the paradigm reserved for blond beauties and stresses that she is fair, he undercuts this by having Basil explain, that despite these fair advantages she is not a beauty in the accepted sense of the word.

If it is not immediately possible to valorise Clara's appeal, Collins, through the narrator, soon throws into question the whole business of gender and sex-roles. While role and gender may be socially dictated, it is not sufficient for women to put things right by aping men. It is this very distinction between men and women which is the centre of attention and little would be achieved if the sexes merely swopped basic character, assumption and social traits.

> We live in an age when too many women appear to be ambitious of morally unsexing themselves before society, by aping the language and the manners of men – especially in reference to that miserable dandyism of demeanour, which aims at repressing all betrayal of warmth of feeling; which abstains from displaying any enthusiasm on any subject whatever; which, in short, labours *to make the fashionable impeturbability of the face the faithful reflection of the fashionable impeturbability of the mind*. Women of this exclusively modern order, like to use slang expressions in their conversation; assume a bastard-masculine abruptness in their manners, a bastard-masculine licence in their opinions; affect to ridicule those outward developments of feeling which pass under the general appellation of "sentiment". Nothing impresses, agitates, amuses, or delights them in a hearty, natural, womanly way.[22] (my italics)

Each sex has valuable properties, characteristics which it would be a loss to abandon and nothing will change if women simply act as men. In fact this could be detrimental as it would signal the end of the attributes which women possess. This passage is important, too, because the question of gender and sexuality here appears to be only a side issue and the central concern is again with the question of appearance and reality. Collins, via Basil, is only attacking women who morally unsex themselves, to the extent that this is a symptom of the greater crime of accepting surface value and taking things as they appear. Clara, like Laura Fairlie in *The Woman in White*, is transparent, a figure whose outward appearance is a true reflection of her state of mind, attitude and morality. This image of Clara is contrasted with the 'wretched trivialities and hypocrisies of modern society'.[23] Clara is sincere, appearance and reality coincide for her and she does not hide her true feelings with manners, social grace and propriety. She is a figure who completely transcends 'the hardening influence of the world' and who belongs

> . . . in solitary places far away in the country; in little rural shrines, shut up from society, among woods and fields, and lonesome boundary-hills.[24]

This equation of the countryside with essential virtue, a version of pastoralism, has a long tradition in literature and, in this case, the pastoral ideal is premised on the correspondence of appearance and reality.

Margaret Sherwin is a total contrast to Clara. In many ways, the fact that she is from a different class, a linen draper's daughter, is the least of her problems. Margaret is drawn according to the second tradition which governed and organised the portrayal of women in literature.

> She was dark. Her hair, eyes and complexion were darker than usual in English women. The form, the look altogether, of her face, coupled with what I could see of her figure, made me guess her age to be about twenty. There was the appearance of maturity already in the shape of her features; but their expression still remained girlish, unformed, unsettled. The fire in her large dark eyes, when she spoke, was latent. Their langour, when she was silent – that voluptuous langour of black eyes – was still fugitive and unsteady.[25]

Clara is fair and Margaret is the dark complement. It is interesting, too, how Basil enumerates her charms – 'latent', 'fugitive' and 'unsteady'. Whereas Clara represents a transcendental unity of appearance and reality, Margaret's appeal lies in a more liquid, mercurial quality; things are hidden, covert and unbalanced – a suggestion of other ways. The appearance of maturity is belied by a girlish expression. Appearance and reality correspond with Clara, but nothing is as it seems with Margaret. Collins reinforces and privileges the differences in the two women. Basil is back with Clara.

> Her slight figure appeared slighter than usual, in the delicate material that now clothed it. Her complexion was at its palest;

her face looked almost statue-like in its purity and repose. What a contrast to the other living picture which I had seen at sunset.[26]

Clara is white and virginal in contrast to the musky suggestiveness of Margaret. And while Clara's appeal is of a pastoral vision of bliss, removed from the world of pomp and appearance – it is exactly this urban, mannered society of pomp and circumstance, which Margaret so desperately wants to enter. Her basic reason for desiring marriage to Basil is to share the world of aristocratic signs with him. During his visits to Margaret, Basil is pleased to tell her of his family,

> . . . but whenever she questioned me directly about any of them, her inquiries invariably led away from their characters and dispositions, to their personal *appearance*, their every-day habits, their dress, their intercourse with the gay world, the things they spent their money on, and other topics of a similar nature.[27] (my italics)

Basil wants to talk of character and disposition but Margaret is more interested in the appearance of things and the world of signs.

> For instance; she always listened, and listened attentively, to what I told her of my father's character, and of the principles which regulated his life. . . . But, on all these occasions, what really interested her most, was to hear how many servants waited on him; how often he went to Court; how many lords and ladies he knew; what he said or did to his servants, when they committed mistakes; whether he was ever angry with his children for asking him for money; and whether he limited my sister to any given number of dresses in the course of the year? Again, whenever our conversation turned on Clara, if I began by describing her kindness, her gentleness and goodness, her simple winning manners – I was sure to be led insensibly into a digression about her height, figure, complexion, and style of dress.[28]

What Collins is doing here is to take a conventional representation of women in nineteenth-century popular, sentimental fiction, and rework it so it becomes associated with a new set of ideological values. The contrast between Clara and Margaret now also mediates some idea of the disjunction between appearance and reality. For Clara the two correspond in some Edenic sense whereas Margaret is a representative of the world of appearance. And this is in addition to the women as representative of two aspects of female sexuality. Clara is a sanitised Oedipal figure and Margaret is a sulky temptress and after an unsatisfactory relationship with Margaret, Basil settles down to an asexual life of domestic bliss with his sister.

> For the last five months I have lived here with Clara – here, on the little estate which was once her mother's, which is now hers. Long before my father's death we often talked, in the great country house, of future days which we might pass together, as we pass them now, in this place. Though we may often leave it for a time, we shall always look back to Lanreath Cottage as our home. The years of retirement which I spent at the Hall, after my recovery, have not awakened in me a single longing to return to the busy world.[29]

According to the stereotype the blond lady is destined for a life of matrimonial bliss and Clara, to some extent, finds this life in the secluded cottage with Basil. However Collins does twist and rework this stereotype. This is discussed in another chapter, but here it is clear that it is hardly a triumph for the family, this strange brother–sister relationship. There are Oedipal incestual undercurrents but what is important is the fact that the novel does not close on a triumphal note of praise for the nuclear family. Basil and Clara's retreat from society, generation and sex is a Pyrrhic victory. If the family cannot reproduce itself it is hardly the cornerstone of society. This pastoral bliss with Clara is far removed from the busy world which was so attractive to Margaret.

Basil's brother Ralph is the older son who is a disappointment to his father. He fails to fulfil his responsibilities and rather than be a responsible young man, proud of the family name, he elects for a dissolute life on the continent. He does eventually make amends and comes to Basil's rescue. There is little enough remarkable about this behaviour, but Ralph's function in the novel also incorporates a set of ideologies which is given favourable mention in different novels by Collins. Ralph, like Franklin Blake, is a fusion of British and European manners.

He had become a foreigner in manners and appearance. . . . He seemed to communicate to the house the change that had taken place in himself, from the reckless, racketty young Englishman to the super-exquisite foreign dandy. It was as if the Fiery, effervescent atmosphere of the Boulevards of Paris had insolently penetrated into the old English mansion, and ruffled and infected its quiet native air, to the remotest corners of the place.[30]

Collins is keen to show the familiar in a foreign perspective and Ralph's continental air is just such a device to portray English custom in an alien light. Once again, at this level, Ralph serves to remind the reader that there are alternatives to English parochialism. These ideas are demonstrated in Ralph's relationship with his father. While their father, with his pride of name and family represents aristocratic arrogance, Ralph is prepared to fly in the face of society. Their father is dogmatic about convention and the social hierarchy. He is reluctant to accept even the new aristocracy of wealth. Basil relates how his father ignores 'A merchant of enormous wealth, who had recently been raised to the peerage' in favour of an Italian Abbé 'a political refugee, dependent for the bread he ate, on the money he received for teaching languages'.[31] The foreigner is favoured because 'he was a direct descendant of one of the oldest of those famous Roman families whose names are part of the history of the Civil Wars in Italy'.[32] Ralph has a much more cavalier attitude to such social nuance and it is this social posture which allows him to come to Basil's aid when the latter offends propriety by marrying into a draper's family. Ralph is certainly no democrat and he does not condone Basil's behaviour, but his experience of life, his European as distinct from English approach, allows him to be charitable towards his younger brother. And it should be remembered that it is not just Europe, but Europe as mediated and tamed via Mrs Ralph which educates Ralph in this direction. Women are always very important but in Ralph the contrast between continental sophistication and English propriety is played out.

If the character of Basil's father is based on the Earl of Chesterfield, a symbol of aristocratic hautiness, Mr Sherwin, the linen draper is no real alternative and is not treated very sympathetically either. Where one represents the aristocracy, the other promotes the values of the merchant class. Sherwin is as aware of the advantages to him if Basil marries his daughter as Basil is conscious of his disgrace and ostricisation. Sherwin sees everything in relation to money.

> "Mrs. Sherwin, Sir," interposed her husband, "never drinks wine, and can't digest cake. A bad stomach – a very bad stomach. Have another glass yourself. Won't you, indeed? This sherry stands me in six shillings a bottle – ought to be first rate wine at that price; and so it is. Well, if you won't have any more, we will proceed to business. Ha! Ha! business *I* call it; pleasure I hope it will be to *you*."[33]

Just as he judges the quality of the wine by its price, so in referring to Basil's plans to marry Margaret, Sherwin confuses morality and parental concern with good book-keeping and business acumen. This fusion of value also afflicts Captain Wragge and is symptomatic of a system of ideas which equates civilisation with capitalism. Mannion explains that he worked his way into Sherwin's confidence by appearing to be the perfect employee, a master of sharp business technique. Sherwin never for a moment suspected that Mannion could have designs on his daughter.

> Besides the security he felt in my age, he had judged me by his own small commercial business standard, and had found me a model of integrity. A man who had saved him from being cheated, who had so enlarged and consolidated his business as to place him among the top dignitaries of the trade; who was the first to come to the desk in the morning, and the last to remain there in the evening; who had not only never demanded, but had absolutely refused to take, a single holiday – such a man as this was, morally and intellectually, a man in ten thousand; a man to be admired and trusted in every relation of life![34]

Mannion himself is a strange figure, a combination of figures drawn from literature, but again Collins reuses this stock figure to articulate an ideological repertoire which reinforces others circulating in the text. It is Mannion, for example, who emphasises how Sherwin equates morality with sound business practice. To protect Sherwin from financial hazard is the ultimate evidence for the draper of moral integrity. The final effect of all this is to give Mannion, the stock villain in the text, additional weighting. There is a warning about Mannion's position in the Sherwin family when Basil is first introduced to him. A disjunction is apparent between how Sherwin feels about his factotum and what he says about him. 'Mr. Sherwin received his clerk with the assured superiority of the master in his words; but his tones and manner flatly contradicted them.'[35] It is clear that appearance belies the reality of Mannion's situation and this point is repeated in a series of incidents and motifs throughout the work. On close examination Basil can make little of Mannion, 'it would have been impossible from his appearance to have guessed his age'.[36] He is a complete enigma who disrupts a standard reading of a person's character from their appearance. This is as true for Basil as it is for the reader of the novel. Mannion disrupts standard literary paradigms, and, just as in his description of women, Basil must learn that appearance is not reality. Just as he turns from Margaret's superficial sexual attraction, he must learn from experience not to be misled by Mannion's polite demeanour. Basil has the opinion that 'To study the appearance of a man's dwelling-room, is very often nearly equivalent to studying his own character',[37] and perhaps for this reason he gives us detailed descriptions of Mannion's apartment and Sherwin's drawing room. The contrast is great, but it is perhaps some consolation to see that Sherwin's vulgarity is reflected in his furniture. There is no shadow, shelter, secrecy, or retirement in his room. After all he is only a vulgar, shallow commercial man and the appearance does correspond with reality.

Everything was oppressively new. The brilliantly-varnished door cracked with a report like a pistol when it was opened; the paper on the walls, with its gaudy pattern of birds, trellis-work and flowers, in gold, red, and green on a white ground, looked hardly dry yet; the showy window-curtain of white and sky-blue, and the still showier carpet of red and yellow, seemed as if they had come out of the shop yesterday; the round rosewood table was in a painfully high state of polish; the morrocco-bound picture books that lay on it, looked as if they had never been moved or opened since they had been bought; not one leaf even of the music on the piano was dog-eared or worn.[38]

The brashness of the furnishings seems to depict accurately Sherwin's vulgar commerciality and cultural pretension. There is a piano, but music is not played. However, with Mannion, the situation is more complicated. He is employed as a clerk but has a

gentleman's refinement, and Basil, at first reads these signs as
definitive proof of Mannion's fine feeling.

> The personal contrast between Mr. Sherwin and his clerk was
> remarkable enough, but the contrast between the dimensions and
> furnishings of the rooms they lived in, was to the full as
> extraordinary. The apartment I now surveyed was less than half
> the size of the sitting room at North Villa. The paper of the walls
> was of a dark red; the curtains were of the same colour; the carpet
> was brown, and if it bore any pattern, that pattern was too quiet
> and unpretending to be visible by candlelight. One wall was
> entirely occupied by rows of dark mahogany shelves, completely
> filled with books, most of the cheap editions of the classical works
> of ancient and modern literature. The opposite end was thickly
> hung with engravings in maplewood frames from the works of
> modern painters, English and French. All the minor articles of
> furniture were of the plainest and neatest order – even the white
> china tea-pot and tea-cup on the table, had neither pattern nor
> colouring of any kind.[39]

Mannion's room is subdued and quietly confident in its array of
culture. Collins intends his reader to feel as comfortable here as does
Basil. However, this room is not all it seems, Sherwin's room is light
and brash, but there are shadows here and the candle-light does not
reach into all the corners. And it is this darkness which conceals
Mannion's true nature. Basil, and by implication the reader, must
learn not to accept a polite and cultured appearance as indicative of
all that is best in the world. The warnings are there, the weak
candle-light in the passage above and the flash of lightning which
illuminates Mannion's face for a split second as Basil is leaving. 'It
gave such a hideously livid hue, such a spectral look of ghastliness
and distortion to his features, that he absolutely seemed to be
glaring and grinning at me like a fiend, in the one instance of its
duration.'[40] So convinced is Basil at this stage in his narrative, of
Mannion's qualities that he distrusts the evidence of his own senses
and convinces himself that this was all an optical illusion. Yet
Mannion must remain an enigma if the text is read attentively. His
apartment may say something of the man, but Basil is at a loss when
he tries to read character from Mannion's face.

> Never had I before seen any human face which baffled all inquiry

like his. No mask could have been made expressionless enough to resemble it; and yet it looked like a mask. It told you nothing of his thoughts, when he spoke; nothing of his disposition, when he was silent. His cold grey eyes gave you no help in trying to study him. They never varied from the steady, straightforward look, which was exactly the same for Margaret as it was for me; for Mrs. Sherwin as for Mr. Sherwin – exactly the same whether he spoke or whether he listened; whether he talked of indifferent or of important things.[41]

Basil is right to wonder just who Mannion is. Mannion again foregrounds the correspondence or otherwise of appearance and reality. He exists on society's margins, socially displaced and the vacancy he occupies emphasises much of the contingent nature of society. Mannion's appropriation of respectability, if it is indeed an appropriation, is a mask which could be concealing vice or virtue.

There was the impenetrable face before you, wholly inexpressive – so inexpressive that it did not even look vacant – a mystery for your eyes and your mind to dwell on – hiding something, but whether vice or virtue you could not tell.[42]

The morality may remain a conundrum but Basil is more explicit about the social connotation of Mannion's appearance and habits. 'Before I had been in his company five minutes, his manner assured me that he must have descended to the position he now occupied.'[43] The position of the middle class is not sacred and divinely ordained, but is subject to change. While Mannion has come down in the world, Sherwin has moved up the social ladder.

Margaret Sherwin falls very much under the sway of Mannion and in her feverish meanderings towards the close of the novel echoes some of Mannion's philosophy. It could be a theorem advanced by Count Fosco.

Put roses into my coffin – scarlet roses, if you can find any, because that stands for Scarlet Woman – in the Bible, you know, Scarlet? What do I care! Its the boldest colour in the world, Robert will tell you, and all your family, how many women are as scarlet as I am – virtue wears it at home, in secret; and vice wears it abroad; in public; that's the only difference, he says.[44]

It might be expected that a death-bed scene would offer the opportunity for personal redemption and sorrow at a life ill spent. But, again, Collins does not offer the reader this satisfaction. Not only does the sinner not repent and deny her sins but the suggestion is made that her only fault was to be caught out and have her sins made public. It is implied that all women are scarlet, only that some manage to hide this with a mask of domestic virtue and purity. Collins will not allow even that degree of complacency inherent in the crime literature of the day which represented an external threat to the middle class and suggested that wrong-doing was the preserve of those people in the margins of society. Instead he indicates that crime and injustice is inherent in the middle class itself. Mannion, after all, is provoked into his way of life by Basil's father's sense of propriety which allowed this man, so bound by convention, to have Mannion's father hanged for a debt. It is propriety itself which is at fault. Mannion explains his position in a letter to Basil.

> I believed then, as I believe now, that I stood towards you both in the place of an injured man, whose right it was, in self-defence and self-assertion, to injure you. Judged by your ideas, this may read wickedly; but to me, after having lived and suffered as I have, the modern common-places current in the world are so many brazen images which society impudently worships – like the Jews of old – in the face of the living Truth.[45]

It is these 'common-places' circulating in society which provide the terrain for a radical examination of society. This project is echoed in the very structure of *Basil*. The opening sections of the novel give a vision of the way things appear to Basil and this is followed by a reinterpretation of these events, an account of what was really taking place, corresponding with Basil's education and his realisation that life is not always what it appears to be. The reference to the Jews in Mannion's letter is significant. Like the Jews in the Old Testament, Basil worships false gods and is led astray by appearance. This changes in the final section of the novel, Basil's New Testament when he discovers the Truth. After her adultery, Sherwin writes to Basil in Margaret's defence that he 'may be too ready to believe appearances'.[46] Basil decides, in response to this overture, 'to go that instant to North Villa and unmask the wretches who still thought to make their market of me as easily as ever'.[47]

Basil must transcend the world of appearance to get at the truth of things and once again Collins reminds the reader that what is at play is the market. It is money which substantiates this relationship of appearance with reality, and in the attempt to hide this fundamental cash nexus the world pretends to operate at another level.

Basil concerns itself with adultery, passion and cruel revenge. These subjects were essentially taboo in the middle class novel.[48] It was these topics to which some contemporary critics objected on the grounds that they were not fit subjects for art. This debate is now of historical interest only and does little to help produce a reading of the novel. Rather the text is better approached in terms of some notions of genre theory. There is a plastic attitude to genre and discourse in this novel – a view signalled in the dedication where Collins warns that the conventions of sentimental fiction shall not always be respected. On to what could either be a love story, a crime story or a comedy of manners, Collins introduces the ideological themes touched on above. Traditional genres are given a new function. The novel can not succeed as a love story because Basil and Margaret first see each other on a bus. Reader expectation of love stories is such that it does not allow for such an experience to occur on public transport. A similar problem occurs with the introduction of the Actual into the text. When Basil confesses to his father, the old man reacts in accordance with his sense of outrage. He collapses, and Basil dashes to his aid. The scene is set for a very sentimental/tragic/melodramatic moment.

> I ran horror-stricken to his side, and attempted to take his hand. He started instantly into an erect position, and thrust me from him furiously, without uttering a word.[49]

The scene is a cultural cliché – the collapse of the irate parent at the shocking revelation of the wayward child. There is a standard interpretation, an established vocabulary and associated ideology to describe the incident. Yet Collins does not call on this cultural repertoire. The passage continues and it is here that the reader may begin to have difficulties in placing the scene in terms of previous experience.

> At that fearful moment, in that fearful silence, the sounds out of doors penetrated with harrowing distinctness and merriment into

the room. The pleasant rustling of the trees mingled musically with the softened, monotonous rolling of carriages in the distant street, while the organ-tune, now changed to the lively measure of a song, rang out clear and cheerful above both, and poured into the room as lightly and happily as the very sunshine itself.[50]

It would be wrong to see this as a simple inversion of the pathetic fallacy. More importantly it is a switch in discourse from the language of tragic romance and melodrama to a pastoral lullaby. Such a juxtaposition may be quotidian now, but in the mid-nineteenth century, there was no available genre which could contain both registers adequately and this rendered interpretation problematic. There are many examples of this change of gear in the text. Chapter nine ends with a quotation from Shakespeare

Hope is a lover's stuff; walk hence with that,
 And manage it against despairing thoughts,

and this is followed by the horrific cityscape which opens Chapter ten.

London was rousing everywhere into morning activity, as I passed through the streets. The shutters were being removed from the windows of public houses: the drink-vampyres that suck the life of London, were opening their eyes betimes to look abroad for the new day's prey! Small tobacco and provision shops in poor neighbourhoods; dirty little eating houses, exhaling greasy-smelling steam, and displaying a leaf of yesterday's paper, stained and fly-blown, hanging in the windows – were already plying or making ready to ply their trade.[51]

The Gothic-documentary interrupts the lyricism of Shakespeare and again disrupts reader expectation. *Basil* is prone to such fusions of promiscuous detail. For example, the Actual is inserted into a description of Margaret on her death-bed.

The door closed on her; and I was left alone to watch the last moments of the woman who had ruined me!
 As I sat down near the open window, the sounds outside in the street told of the waning of the night. There was an echo of many

footsteps, a hoarse murmur of conflicting voices, now near, now afar off. The public houses were dispersing their drunken crowds – the crowds of a Saturday night; it was twelve o'clock.

Through those street-sounds of fierce ribaldry and ghastly mirth, the voice of the dying woman penetrated, speaking more slowly, more distinctly, more terribly than it had spoken yet.

"I see him," she said, staring vacantly at me, and moving her hands slowly to and fro in the air. "I see him! But he's a long way off; he can't hear our secrets, and he does not suspect you as mother does."[52]

The first and last sentence of this quotation maintain a consistent tone. But just as with the previous example where Shakespeare is followed by documentary, this passage is interrupted by the description of the drunks leaving the pub. Collins is disrupting the received genre categorisation and paradigm, thus displacing the reader and making interpretation of the text difficult. It is firstly, with this play with genre and, secondly, the concentration of subjects more appropriate for the Old Bailey which goes some way towards explaining the reception of the work.

A similar problem is brought to the fore in the concluding pages of *Basil*. Any examination of narrative must allow that it begins with equilibrium, followed by disruption and then closes with the reestablishment of an equilibrium. It is this reconstitution of the known and the familiar which guarantees the readers' satisfaction and allows for the most unlikely of coincidences towards the end of a work. Such again is reader expectation but Collins will not allow his reader this satisfaction at the close of *Basil*. He points to its inherent artificiality and has Basil argue that his autobiography cannot, in the interest of verisimilitude, have the usual closure.

One difficulty, however, still remains: – How are the pages which I am about to send you to be concluded? In the novel-reading sense of the word, my story has no real conclusion. The repose that comes to all of us after trouble – to *me* a repose in life: to others, how often a repose in the grave! – is the end which must close this autobiography: an end, calm, natural, and uneventful; yet not, perhaps, devoid of all lesson and value. Is it fit that I should set myself, for the sake of effect, to *make* a conclusion, and terminate by fiction, what has begun, and thus far, has proceeded in truth? In the interests of Art, as well as in the interest of Reality, surely not.[53]

In a post-script to the dedication, written ten years later, Wilkie Collins is still unprepared to compromise his opinions. He makes no attempt to conceal the fact that *Basil* was not universally well received but rather documents the fact that 'it was condemned off-hand by a certain class of readers as an outrage on their sense of propriety'.[54] The author is unabashed by this criticism and sees this reading of his work as representative of those who cannot distinguish between manners and justice. Collins is emphasising the difference between true and false delicacy, a nuance elaborated in future texts.

Conscious of having designed and written my story with the strictest regard to true delicacy, as distinguished from false – I allowed the prurient misinterpretation of certain perfectly innocent passages in this book to assert itself as offensively as it pleased, without troubling myself to protest against an expression of opinion which aroused in me no other feeling than a feeling of contempt.[55]

He is probably disingenuous as he did take adverse publicity and criticism very seriously as is evident from the prefaces to so many of his novels. However, at this point, it is only to be noted that Collins is totally unaffected by the charge that he disrupts society's sense of righteousness.

4

The Woman in White

The Woman in White is the story of the deception of Laura Fairlie
and it is the story of the investigation of this deception. The
narrative is presented as if written chiefly by Walter Hartright and
Marian Halcombe but includes shorter pieces from, among
others, the family lawyer and housekeeper. At one level the story
moves apace and the crime against Laura is followed by its
detection. Yet, I argue the novel deserves a closer scrutiny than
this. Collins is a very calculating writer and it will not do to
disregard and ignore his remarks.

> In the event of this book being reviewed, I venture to ask
> whether it is possible to praise the writer, or to blame him,
> without opening the proceedings by telling his story at second
> hand? As that story is written by me – with the inevitable
> suppressions which the periodical system of publication forces
> on the novelist – the telling it fills more than a thousand closely
> printed pages. No small portion of this space is occupied by
> hundreds of little 'connecting links,' of trifling value in
> themselves, but of the utmost importance in maintaining the
> smoothness, the reality, and the probability of the entire
> narrative. If the critic tells the story *with* these, can he do it in
> his allotted page, or column, as the case may be? If he tells it
> *without* these, is he doing a fellow-labourer in another form of
> Art, the justice which writers owe to one another?[1]

The story is referred to as a 'chain' which is taken up by various
characters at various times and interspaced along this chain there
are these 'little connecting links of trifling value in themselves but
of the utmost importance' in the context of the story as a whole. It
is just some of these connecting links which shall be examined
below and their cumulative effect shall be seen to have
considerable momentum and import in the development of the
tale.

Evidence of the subtlety of the work put into the construction of the text may be found in Hartright's preamble. Several views of the law are propounded in a very short space. It is said that events in the novel would have figured in a Court of Justice but that 'the law is still in certain inevitable cases, the pre-engaged servant of the long purse'.[2] Through the narrator Collins points to the class nature of the legal process; it is biased and works 'with moderate assistance only from the lubricating influences of oil of gold'.[3] Hartright explains that the law has little to do with any sense of abstract justice; it is a formality which serves the ruling groups in society, an appearance of justice only. Yet this said, this knowledge does not deter Collins from telling the story as a trial is conducted in court. The law may be biased but Collins decides to adopt some of its methods. However, the novel closes with the admission that to obtain justice the law must be surmounted. Hartright explains that his actions were vindicated because 'The Law would never have obtained me my interview with Mrs. Catherick. The Law would never have made Pesca the means of forcing a confession from the Count.'[4] It is a useful exercise to eke out the implications of Hartright's thoughts on the legal establishment. While the validity of legal formality is recognised – it is a useful exercise to arrange the novel as if it were the evidence of court-room witnesses – the arbitrary nature of legal decision is also emphasised. It is dangerous to mistake the appearance of justice for justice itself; indeed it is possible to extrapolate and say that appearance should not be taken for reality. This warning is delivered extremely early in the text and its resonance may be found even in some of the most trifling incidents in the novel. Laura Fairlie is the victim of the evil machinations of Sir Percival Glyde and Count Fosco. Laura's is an essentially trusting nature; she is unaware of contradiction and complication, life for her exists on the surface and she has little need to believe ill of anyone or anything. Things are as they appear. But in this novel where appearance is so often called into question, it is to be noted that Laura's tragedy is a result of her habit of accepting things at face value. Hartright documents this tendency in Laura.

'I hope Mr. Hartright will pay *me* no compliments,' said Miss Fairlie, as we all left the summer-house.

'May I venture to inquire why you express that hope?' I asked.

'Because I shall believe all that you say to me,' she answered, simply.

In those few words she unconsciously gave me the key to her whole character; to that generous trust in others which, in her nature, grew innocently out of the sense of her own truth. I only knew it intuitively, then, I know it by experience now.[5]

It is Laura's tragedy that she too easily accepts appearance for reality and does not recognise the danger of always accepting things at face value. This does not mean that she belongs to the corrupt world of appearance but rather represents the Edenic world where appearances and reality do coincide.

Mindful of the acknowledgment in the preface that there are many connecting links in the novel, it is a useful exercise to isolate some of these links and comment on their significance. A few pages into the narrative Professor Pesca is introduced. Hartright's first encounter with Pesca had been a matter of chance. It is known that the Italian 'once held a situation in the University of Padua; that he had left Italy for political reasons (the nature of which he uniformly declined to mention to anyone); and that he had been for many years respectably established in London as a teacher of languages.'[6] The suggestion of political intrigue is glossed over and Hartright explains that his foreign friend is a great favourite of his mother's. With his sister, however, the situation is a little more complicated.

My sister Sarah, with all the advantages of youth, was, strangely enough less pliable. She did full justice to Pesca's excellent qualities of heart; but she could not accept him implicitly, as my mother accepted him, for my sake. Her insular notions of propriety rose in perpetual revolt against Pesca's constitutional contempt for appearances; and she was always more or less undisguisedly astonished at her mother's familiarity with the eccentric little foreigner.[7]

This is an interesting passage because it sets in motion an opposition between insular propriety and what is identified as a foreign, continental disregard for appearance. Not only are Pesca's foreignness, and, by implication, politics seen as a sore on the English body politic, but this opposition is seen in terms of essence and appearance, proprietorial value challenged by the stranger, the other. This is elaborated upon in a discussion of Pesca's idiosyncratic use of the English language.

> It may be necessary to explain, here, that Pesca prided himself on being a perfect Englishman in his language, as well as in his dress, manners and amusements. Having picked up a few of our most familiar colloquial expressions, he scattered them about over his conversation whenever they happened to occur to him, turning them, in his high relish for their sound and his general ignorance of their sense, into compound words and repetitions of his own, and always running them into each other, as if they consisted of one long syllable.[8]

What has just been identified as the insular propensity for meaning and essence is contrasted with Pesca's limitless linguistic effervescence with its total disregard for meaning. With Pesca there is little limit put on language; it is relished for its sound and material existence and words are allowed to float free with little or no regard to a strict sense of meaning. The imposition of coordinates and limits on the free generation of language is not an innocent activity but is fixed by the language community to serve specific purposes. What may be identified in Pesca's language is a threat, felt in this instance by Sarah, to propriety and hence a threat to the social hierarchy. This society is recognised as being of a very fixed nature and the period one when alternatives could not be countenanced. However, Walter E. Houghton, pointing out that the corollary to dogmatic assertion is self-doubt, disagrees with the view that the smug face of Victoriana reflects freedom from doubt. Rather 'that expression, in their faces, in their style, was often put on to reassure themselves that what they believed was – of course it was – the absolute truth'.[9] *The Woman in White* should be seen in this regard. A 'truth' is asserted but then in the connecting links in the story it becomes much more problematic.

Even the form of the novel detracts from any notion of absolute truth. Narrative authority is democratised and the story is told by a number of characters, ostensibly in the interests of veracity. But, of course, not all the characters see events in the same way and the truth itself is relativised. For example, in the housekeeper's narrative, Mrs Michelson is anxious that Count Fosco should not be seen in a bad light. She fails to appreciate the extent of Fosco's evil and, as far as she is concerned, he is, essentially, a good man.

> In the first place, I wish to record my own personal conviction
> that no blame whatever, in connexion with the events which I
> have now related, attaches to Count Fosco. I am informed that
> a dreadful suspicion has been raised, and that some very
> serious constructions are placed upon his lordship's conduct.
> My persuasion of the Count's innocence remains, however,
> quite unshaken. . . . I protest, in the interests of morality,
> against blame being gratuitously and wantonly attached to the
> proceedings of the Count.[10]

Rather than an absolute truth or morality, it seems that the truth
may be different for each individual. Winifred Hughes discusses
this in her study of the sensation novel.[11] She notes that
Hartright, in performing his sacred mission, unwittingly serves
Mrs Catherick's intention. He aids her in his pursuit of Sir
Percival Glyde and with Glyde's death both Hartright and Mrs
Catherick are placated. Thus positive action can have more than
one effect. By doing his duty towards Laura, Hartright is also the
agent who serves Mrs Catherick's dubious ploy. It seems that it is
next to impossible to insist on one meaning or guarantee a single
outcome as a result of some action. Life, language and action
constantly disrupt the attempts to contain them.

The notion of propriety is invoked again and again in the novel.
It is a sense of propriety, insular propriety, which causes Sarah to
take exception to Pesca. The term recurs when Marian is
introducing herself to Hartright that first morning together in
Limmeridge House. Marian praises Laura and feels herself very
much in her half-sister's shadow. 'In short, she is an angel; and I
am – Try some of that marmalade, Mr. Hartright, and finish the
sentence, in the name of female propriety, for yourself.'[12] The
concept of propriety is apparently a system of rules which govern
behaviour, a conformity with convention in language and
conduct. But just as this appeal to decorum is made throughout
the novel, it is simultaneously undermined. Sir Percival is made
the personification for a certain time of an empty form of
propriety and the concept suffers from the association. He acts
according to its dictates and people respond to him in a reciprocal
fashion. At a difficult point in his interview with Marian, the
family solicitor, Mr Gilmore, remarks that Sir Percival is over-

attentive to the social graces. Unconsciously Gilmore recognises that Sir Percival is hollow and notes that Glyde 'resumed the subject, although he might, now, with all propriety have allowed it to drop.'[13] Glyde's empty manners have only a minimal effect on Gilmore in this discussion of the strange influence of Mrs Catherick on Sir Percival. Later Marian praises Laura for her perfect 'propriety of manner' in her encounter with her future husband.[14] Despite her various misgivings about the wedding tour, Marian must admit to herself that on the surface there is little to complain about when a man wants to take his wife on an extended honeymoon.

> Putting myself and my own feelings entirely out of the question (which it is my duty to do, and which I have done) I, for one, have no doubt of the propriety of adopting the first of these proposals. (i.e. the wedding tour)[15]

Propriety comes to be synonymous with social convention, with the status quo and with a regard for appearance. It is a sense of propriety which attempts to guarantee that the individual will act in accordance with the rules laid down by society. Propriety is a form of ideology, of cultural hegemony which both controls the individual and allows the individual to act. Marian often laments that she is not a man and at one point Collins draws attention to the fusion of gender roles and propriety. Marian is annoyed because she cannot take positive action to advance her campaign.

> If I only had the privileges of a man, I would order out Sir Percival's best horse instantly, and tear away on a night-gallop, eastward, to meet the rising sun – a long, hard, heavy, ceaseless gallop of hours and hours, like the famous highwayman's ride to York. Being, however, nothing but a woman, condemned to patience, propriety and petticoats, for life, I must respect the housekeeper's opinions, and try to compose myself in some feeble and feminine way.[16]

Marian sees propriety as a limiting factor, the convention which prevents her from acting in a positive fashion. But supplementary to this is the fact that it is this same propriety which allows her to act in the first place, however limited and curtailed this action may be. Propriety is both the product of human agency and the condition for human agency. It is not irrelevant to recall Marx at this point.

> Men make their own history but they do not make it just as they please; they do not make it under circumstances chosen by themselves but under circumstances directly encountered, given and transmitted from the past.[17]

As envisaged by Collins, propriety has a Janus-like aspect. It is positive in that it allows people to act yet negative in that it sets the limits for their behaviour, the extent to which society will countenance and allow their actions. Collins is very aware of this ambivalence about propriety just as he is aware of the complicating factors which prevent a too easy dismissal of appearance. Just as propriety both allows and controls how characters act in the novels, so appearance, at various points, can either conceal the truth or be the truth.

Count Fosco, for example, is another character who is associated with conventional decorum. Fosco appears to be all that society can demand of a gentleman who is always aware of the proprieties unlike his countryman Pesca. Fosco is even more of a gentleman than Sir Percival Glyde as Marian reports.

> The first bell for dinner separated us. Just as it had done ringing, Sir Percival and the Count returned from their walk. We heard the master of the house storming at the servants for being five minutes late; and the master's guest interposing, as usual, in the interests of propriety, patience and peace.[18]

Marian falls ill at one point, the result of her attempts to eavesdrop on Percival and the Count. Fosco finds her diary and concludes Marian's own commentary on events by completing a section of it himself. He is aware that his is not perhaps the most honourable conduct, yet he will still appeal to propriety in his own defence.

> Finally, those sentiments dictate the lines – grateful, sympathetic, paternal lines – which appear in this place. I close the book. My strict sense of propriety restores it (by the hands of my wife) to its place on the writer's table.[19]

This convention, a hallmark of the Victorian ethos and of bourgeois society in general, is not always the polite and acceptable paradigm of honest behaviour for which it is often mistaken. *The Woman in White* underscores the fact that it is often a mere convenience, an expedient mask which conceals contradiction. This becomes clear, for example, when the valetudinarian Frederick Fairlie accounts for his very selfish behaviour in terms of a sense of propriety.[20] Marian had entrusted Fanny, Laura's maid, with a note to Frederick, when Sir Percival had dismissed the young woman from his service. However, when she attempts to deliver her message, Frederick refuses to listen to the girl because 'propriety' cannot allow him to look at a member of the lower classes in distress. He asks his valet to question the girl and interpret her replies for him, but this results in great confusion and so Frederick remains unaware of Laura's sorry plight. Finally, when Fosco visits Frederick to clarify the situation and explain that Laura's wedding has not been a success, it is pointed out that only in Limmeridge may the young lady be received with 'propriety'.[21] Such are the mores of the time that scandal may only be avoided if Laura comes to stay with her uncle. However, the success of Fosco's swindle also depends on removing Laura from Blackwater Park to Limmeridge. It is a long trip and Fosco uses the excuse that he is protecting Laura in order to guarantee the success of his plans. Accordingly, he explains to Frederick Fairlie that his suggestions resolve all problems.

> Here is comfort consulted; here are the interests of propriety consulted; here is your own duty – duty of hospitality, sympathy, protection, to an unhappy lady in need of all three – smoothed and made easy, from the beginning to the end. I cordially invite you, sir, to second my efforts in the sacred interests of the Family.[22]

The importance of the family cannot be overestimated in nineteenth-century England and Collins is calling this tradition of reverence and respect into question when he allows family sentiment to shield the self-interest and comfort of a hypochondriac and the evil-doings of the villain. Propriety is in bad company and must suffer from the association. In these instances Collins demonstrates the underside of propriety by showing that it is not a quality to be relished.

Yet it appears that *The Woman in White* will not allow a total rejection of this sense of propriety. It is not a totally empty, negative concept. Eliza Mitchelson, the housekeeper at Blackwater Park, assures the reader that 'her testimony is wanted in the interests of truth' and that since she is no longer in Sir Percival's service she may mention her former mistress 'without impropriety'.[23] Propriety is Janiform, is both positive and negative. While it can be used to hide the truth, it may also be the truth. Mrs Mitchelson, however, is too severe in her views and fails to suspect Fosco of any 'impropriety' whatsoever.[24] For Mrs Mitchelson the appearance is the reality and she does not suspect any 'impropriety' when Fosco visits Marian when the latter is ill.[25] However, she is concerned about the 'propriety of our concealing the doctor's absence, as we did from Lady Glyde'.[26] In Mrs Mitchelson we see the danger of a too rigid adherence to convention. It is correct that she suspect the motives which have Fosco change Laura's maid, yet the housekeeper allows this same sense of convention to blind her when she assumes that, because of his aristocratic blood, Fosco will inevitably observe the rules.[27] At one time the instinct of propriety directs her to correct conclusions and, at other times, it makes for wrong assumption. Such is the tragedy of rigidity.

A questioning of the value of propriety is one of the connecting links evident in *The Woman in White*. In the penultimate use of the word in the novel this concept is linked with the idea of appearance and reality, a theme examined in detail below. Hartright eventually interviews Mrs Clements, the lady who looked after Anne Catherick. He is disappointed with the outcome of their meeting but his comments on their conversation are of singular importance.

> After that last reply, I waited a little, to reconsider what I had heard. If I unreservedly accepted the story so far, it was now plain that no approach, direct or indirect, to the Secret had yet been revealed to me, and that the pursuit of my object had ended in leaving me face to face with the most palpable and the most disheartening failure. But there was one point in the narrative which made me doubt the propriety of accepting it unreservedly, and which suggested the idea of something hidden below the surface.[28]

The juxtaposition of propriety and surface or appearance is hardly gratuitous. But here it is not a simple opposition between a covert reality and surface illusion. Propriety is now used in a sense which connotes a form of prudential reason and works to stop acceptance of appearance for reality.

Mention has already been made of the clash between Sarah Hartright's insular propriety and Pesca's constitutional contempt for appearance. This opposition is privileged and elaborated throughout the text culminating in Walter's interpretation of Mrs Clement's account of Anne Catherick's background, perhaps the chief secret of the novel. Between these two limit points there is much resonance and the connecting links of the novel point constantly to appearance with the suggestion that reality is elsewhere. For example, when Hartright first arrives in Limmeridge House he is struck by the contrast between Laura and her governess, Mrs Vesey.

> While Mrs. Vesey and Miss Halcombe were richly clad (each in the manner most becoming to her age), the first in silver-grey, and the second in that delicate primrose-yellow colour, which matches so well with a dark complexion and black hair, Miss Fairlie was unpretendingly and almost poorly dressed in plain white muslin. It was spotlessly pure; it was beautifully put on; but still it was the sort of dress which the wife or daughter of a poor man might have worn; and it made her, so far as externals went, look less affluent in circumstances than her own governess.[29]

Judging by appearances, Laura, the heiress, actually looks poorer than her companion and employee, Mrs Vesey.

Other incidents, trifling in themselves, emphasise this non-correspondence of appearance and reality. Hartright has conversation with Anne Catherick, the eponymous woman in white, in Limmeridge church-yard. Sir Percival Glyde is mentioned. The woman in white screams in terror and her guardian, Mrs Clements, comes to the rescue. At first she is angry with Hartright, imagining that he had injured Anne, but she relents when the situation is explained to her. She apologises to Hartright but, in her own defence says 'that appearances looked suspicious to a stranger'.[30] When it is obvious that Hartright is in love with Laura it is agreed that he should give up his post as drawing master at Limmeridge and return to London. The true reason for his departure, his love for his pupil, is to be kept from Frederick, and

Hartright needs an alibi, an excuse for breaking the terms of his contract. 'Fortunately, for the probability of this excuse, so far as appearances were concerned, the post brought me two letters from a London friend, that morning.'[31] Hartright is able to explain to Frederick that one of these letters is of such urgent import, that he must leave for London immediately. On the face of it, his excuse is plausible. Appearances are satisfied and the true reasons for his departure are successfully concealed. At this point it seems to the reader that some good may come from trusting to appearance, but then the novel suddenly changes tack.

The family lawyer is to visit Limmeridge House on the very day that Hartright decides to leave. Such is the way of the world that society has a certain pre-conceived notion of what the family lawyer looks like. A certain expectation exists and nine times out of ten this supposition is fulfilled. But Collins does not satisfy this expectation. Despite the valorisation of appearance, which has just gone before, it cannot, in the end be trusted. Gilmore is a good man and true but in 'external appearance, Mr. Gilmore was the exact opposite of the conventional idea of an old lawyer'.[32] And Gilmore himself equivocates his own attitude towards appearance. He tells Hartright that he lives 'professionally, in an atmosphere of disputation' and is not surprised that they should disagree.

'I am afraid, Mr. Gilmore. I have the misfortune to differ from you in the view I take of the case.'

'Just so, my dear sir – just so, I am an old man; and I take the practical view. You are a young man; and you take the romantic view. Let us not dispute about our views.'[33]

They are discussing Sir Percival's plans to marry Laura but what is clear is the possibility of interpreting this case in different lights. There does not appear to be one interpretation which has full purchase on the truth. Appearances can be disputed. Accordingly Gilmore is not surprised that Hartright and he should differ about the case for there is only rarely a clear correspondence between appearance and reality. Rather things exist in controversy and disputation. However, this does not stop Mr Gilmore from appealing to the body of thought which equates appearance and essence when it seems expedient. So, when he is introduced to Sir Percival Glyde for the first time, he finds him to be 'a most prepossessing man, so far as manners and appearance were concerned.'[34] The qualification is significant and, of course, Gilmore does remind us that observation is a form of conventional conjecture and that it 'is the great beauty of the Law that it can dispute any human statement, made under any circumstances, and reduced to any form'.[35] Gilmore is suggesting that language and discourse may be made to serve various interests. Rather than doggedly reflect a pre-existing actuality, discourse may be shown to create a version of reality, an expedient interpretation which serves factional interest. Accordingly, Gilmore explains that as a practising lawyer he could easily dispute and contradict Sir Percival's explanations, but, since, at this point, it is not his role ('my function was of the purely judicial kind'),[36] he must support Sir Percival's statement. Gilmore emphasises the arbitrariness of the facts in the case and further illustrates how convention dominates interpretation. There is no absolute moral right involved. Society is the final arbitrator. Marian questions Gilmore about the value to be placed on Mrs Catherick's letter, a letter which seems, on the face of it, to clear Sir Percival of all suspicion. However, Gilmore is circumspect in his reply.

'I suppose we have really and truly done all we can?' she said, turning and twisting Mrs. Catherick's letter in her hand.
'If we are friends of Sir Percival's, who know him and trust him, we have done all, and more than all, that is necessary,' I answered, a little annoyed by this return of her hesitation. 'But if we are enemies who suspect him –'[37]

It can be assumed, from what Gilmore says here, that the truth rests as much on the assumption that society will not question the matter too deeply as it does on any real validity. Marian and Gilmore are working with two conflicting definitions of the truth. Marian is interested in the peremptory truth, the eclipse of appearance by reality. Gilmore is more inclined, in this instance, to accept the pragmatic and the expeditious. Marian explains that, from Gilmore's point of view, Laura has little reason to break off her engagement to Sir Percival, yet she will support her friend to do just this. Marian is appealing and invoking her ideal truth beyond that defined by the law, so often 'the pre-engaged servant of the long purse'[38] anyway. She shall carry on regardless of legal advice.

'What excuse can she possibly have for changing her mind about a

man whom she had virtually accepted for her husband more than
two years ago?'

'In the eyes of the law and reason, Mr. Gilmore, no excuse, I
dare say. If she still hesitates, and if I still hesitate, you must
attribute our strange conduct, if you like, to caprice in both cases,
and we must bear the imputation as well as we can.'[39]

Much of the action described in the novel is centred in
Limmeridge House, the isolated family seat of the Fairlies. It is
appropriate in this house, so far removed from the social world of
refinement, manners and culture, that the correspondence of
appearance with reality should be questioned. In her journal,
Marian explains that they felt themselves to be beyond the
restrictions society normally placed on its members. 'In our wild
moorland country, and in this great lonely house, we may well claim
to be beyond the reach of the trivial conventionalities which hamper
people in other places.'[40] Here the contrast is made between nature
and culture, the laws of nature and the laws of history. It is only
when Sir Percival arrives from the world of decorum and convention
that Marian and Laura must adapt themselves to his rules. Marian
describes Laura's reaction to Percival's arrival in exactly these terms.
'Outwardly at least', Laura receives Percival's gift with 'perfect
self-possession', and the only sign Marian could 'detect of the
struggle it must cost her to preserve appearance at this trying time,
expresses itself in a sudden unwillingness, on her part, ever to be
left alone'.[41] Now that Percival is there social etiquette must be
maintained at all costs. The values of the social world have been
imported into the lonely and isolated world of Limmeridge. The
importance of manners and appearance, of decorum, is again
brought to the fore when Laura returns from her wedding tour and
when Marian discusses Sir Percival and Laura with Fosco and his
wife.[42] Mrs Catherick exemplifies this struggle to maintain
reputation at all cost, to guarantee that society thinks well of her.
Her life's ambition is answered when the local clergyman bows to
her.[43] Mrs Catherick has been ostracised by society for a long time
but she struck Mrs Mitchelson as 'a strange person in her manners,
but extremely respectable looking'.[44] And just as appearance may
conceal reality, cause and effect are not always predictable; we can
never be sure of the final outcome of our actions. This particular
problem is described by Anne Catherick. 'Why did I only do harm,
when I wanted and meant to do good?'[45]

It can be argued that the plot of the entire novel turns on this play of appearance and reality. Hartright must show that a deception has been wrought by Count Fosco and Sir Percival. He takes his evidence to Mr Kyrle, the solicitor, who clarifies the legal position for him. Things do not look good.

'The evidence of Lady Glyde's death is, on the face of it, clear and satisfactory. There is her aunt's testimony to prove that she came to Count Fosco's house, that she fell ill, and that she died. There is the testimony of the medical certificate to prove the death, and to show that it took place under natural circumstances. There is the fact of the funeral at Limmeridge, and there is the assertion of the inscription on the tomb. That is the case you want to overthrow. What evidence have you to support the declaration on your side that the person who died and was buried was not Lady Glyde?'[46]

Again the assertion is made that the law, which operates in the world of appearance, has little to do with justice. Yet it is just this latter truth which motivates Hartright. Kyrle reminds him that he can expect to find little help in the courts, because 'When an English jury has to choose between a plain fact, *on* the surface, and a long explanation *under* the surface, it always takes the fact, in preference to the explanation.'[47] Appearance is expedient and takes precedence over truth.

Hartright himself constantly has to interpret the facts in the case and is aware of the danger of misreading the evidence. He realises that Sir Percival and Mrs Catherick share a secret, but for quite some time he cannot fathom it.

Was it possible that appearances, in this case, had pointed one way, while the truth lay, all the while, unsuspected, in another direction? Could Mrs. Catherick's assertion that she was the victim of a dreadful mistake, by any possibility be true? Or, assuming it to be false, could the conclusion which associated Sir Percival with her guilt have been founded in some inconceivable error? Had Sir Percival, by any chance, courted the suspicion that was wrong, for the sake of diverting from himself some other suspicion that was right? Here, if I could find it – here was the approach to the Secret, hidden deep under the surface of the apparently-unpromising story which I had just heard.[48]

As we shall see below even language and writing cannot be trusted. It, too, serves in this deceit. Hartright has an inkling that this is the case as he stares at the registry in Old Welmingham church. 'Smoothly and fairly as appearances looked in the vestry, there was something wrong beneath them – there was something in the registry-book, for aught I knew, that I had not discovered yet.'[49]

Before examining language as a mechanism which conceals contradiction in the text and also enters into the illusion/reality dichotomy some more detailed mention must be made of Count Fosco. He is undoubtedly one of the most discussed and most vivid characters in the novel. Fosco is a pragmatist who flaunts social convention, a man willing to pit his wits against the world. He is Italian, of course, and therefore automatically exempt from English convention, but he utilises this freedom to the utmost. Remember how his fellow countryman Pesca, with his contempt for appearance, annoyed the insular propriety of Sarah Hartright. Fosco's offence is larger and he first expounds his philosophy in discussion with Laura who sees the world of appearance as a direct reflection of reality. Fosco explains that, as far as he is concerned, murder is not an absolute offence against morality, but, rather, action which may be either successful or unsuccessful. Laura, who condemns murder out of hand, rejects Fosco's categories and argues that 'truly wise men are truly good men, and have a horror of crime'.[50] Fosco immediately identifies this as sentimental nonsense, copy book morality only of value to school children. Believing in the correspondence of appearance and reality and of the efficacy of 'sentiments . . . stated at the top of copy books,' Laura challenges Fosco to give her an 'instance of a wise man who has been a great criminal'.[51] The Count patronisingly agrees with Laura on this matter, explaining that they take a different line on the case at hand. For Fosco it is not a matter of good men being totally opposed to crime, but, rather, the fact is that it is good men who are the most efficient criminals. They do not get caught because they are able to conceal their crimes. Ignoring moral absolutes as determinant of a person's character, Fosco evaluates according to function and utility. There are no absolute values, rather value is determined by success or failure. 'The fool's crime is the crime that is found out; and the wise man's crime is the crime that is *not* found out.'[52] Morality only serves to conceal the inefficiency of the state in detecting crime. While the bourgeoisie may wish to rest assured that their ideology, in this case – murder will out, crimes cause their own detection – is a true description of how things actually come about, Fosco argues that the machinery existing to detect crime is 'miserably ineffective' and moral platitudes are simply cant blinding people from ineptitude. The police and the criminal are not separated by any ideas of moral right and wrong. In the detection of crime Fosco sees a 'trial of skill between the police on one side and the individual on the other.'[53] Indeed, Fosco is at a loss how to define virtue, he has seen so many variations.

> I am a citizen of the world, and I have met, in my time, with so many different sorts of virtue, that I am puzzled, in my old age, to say which is the right sort and which is the wrong. Here, in England, there is one virtue. And there, in China, there is another virtue. And John Englishman says my virtue is the genuine virtue. And John Chinaman says my virtue is the genuine virtue. And I say Yes to one, or No to the other, and am just as much bewildered about it in the case of John with the top-boots as I am in the case of John with the pigtail.[54]

Fosco continues. In England, people are too quick to point to their neighbour's faults and too slow to identify their own. 'English society, Miss Halcombe, is as often the accomplice, as it is the enemy of crime.'[55] Fosco will not rest with cant and platitude and in a phrase pulsating with suggestion explains his approach to society.

> Ah! I am a bad man, Lady Glyde, am I not? I say what other people only think; and when all the rest of the world is in a conspiracy to accept the mask for the true face, mine is the rash hand that tears off the plump pasteboard, and shows the bare bones beneath.[56]

The images of mask and true face, pasteboard and bare bones returns us to the illusion/reality concern. Fosco seems to know intuitively that arbitrary social consensus dictates morality and truth. It is not a matter of absolute natural law but rather a cultural construction and subject to change. He equates his own machinations to gain the Fairlie legacy with legal procedure. He makes nonsense of Sir Percival's reservations about Laura's death by merely examining all the facts in the case in the manner of a lawyer.

'Your flesh? Does flesh mean conscience in English? I speak of your wife's death, as I speak of a possibility. Why not? The respectable lawyers who scribble-scrabble your deeds and your wills, look the deaths of living people in the face. Do lawyers make your flesh creep? Why should I? It is my business to-night, to clear up your position beyond the possibility of mistake – and I have now done it. Here is your position. If your wife lives, you pay those bills with her signature to the parchment. If your wife dies, you pay them with her death.'[57]

Fosco has the correct posture for all eventualities, his appearance matches his intention at any particular time. His is a fluid philosophy which is always prepared to adapt to the situation. It is a studied skill and he takes pleasure from his own artistry and technique in application. For instance when he questions Sir Percival about Anne Catherick, Sir Percival points out that Fosco even looks curious. Well aware of the uncertain connection between appearance and reality, Fosco turns this into a great compliment.

'Well, suppose it has. If it doesn't concern you, you needn't be curious about it, need you?'
'Do I look curious about it?'
'Yes, you do.'
'So! so! my face speaks the truth, then? What an immense foundation of good there must be in the nature of a man who arrives at my age, and whose face has not yet lost the habit of speaking the truth!'[58]

It is this chameleon-like ability of the Count's which allows him to charm Frederick Fairlie and Mrs Mitchelson.[59] She sees in his kindness to his pets and to the dismissed servant girl, proof of aristocratic birth.[60] Indeed such is the impression that Fosco makes on her that she concludes her narrative with a statement of belief in his innocence; such a gentleman could do no wrong, another statement of the credo which motivates Laura.

Towards the close of the novel Hartright realises that he must personally defeat Fosco if he is ever to get to the bottom of the matter. And such is Fosco's power that, in order to beat him, Hartright must adopt his strategy. Circumstances force Hartright, Marian and Laura to go into hiding and live under an 'assumed name' and an 'assumed relationship'.[61] This is the kind of life Fosco has been living for years. And in order to defeat a master of the craft,

Hartright is forced to assume a false appearance. Fosco tells Marian just what type of adversary he is.

> "Warn Mr. Hartright!" he said in his loftiest manner. "He has a man of brains to deal with, a man who snaps his big fingers at the laws and conventions of society, when he measures himself with ME."[62]

Fosco has little regard for convention. It merely supplies the wherewithal to allow him to practice his profession. Yet, of course, if it is opportune, he will be guided by convention. For example, when he mourns Sir Frederick's death, he satisfies the dictates of society, mindful always to make a good impression. 'See! I mourn his loss – inwardly in my soul; outwardly on my hat.'[63] But, in the final analysis, Count Fosco has nothing but contempt for English propriety. It has little to do with him. 'Gently, Mr. Hartright. Your moral clap-traps have an excellent effect in England – keep them for yourself and your own countrymen, if you please.'[64]

Enough has been said about Fosco for the moment. It shall become clear as this work progresses that Collins portrays very sophisticated female characters in his novels. He reacted strongly to caricatured representation of women and in his own novels seems to render problematic some very fundamental assumptions about gender. The semes which traditionally allow us to identify certain traits as either masculine or feminine exist in a state of flux in *The Woman in White*. It is sometimes difficult to identify many of the characters as essentially masculine or uniquely feminine. Marian Halcombe is the central female character in the text and it is worth examining how Collins first blends her into the narrative. Hartright describes his first meeting with Marian one breakfast time in Limmeridge House. Marian is standing by the window with her back towards him. Hartright likes what he sees. 'The instant my eyes rested on her, I was struck by the rare beauty of her form, and by the unaffected grace of her attitude.'[65] Nothing surprising so far. Marian passes as an attractive woman, at first sight, at least. As Hartright admires her, he notes that her waist was 'perfection in the eyes of a man, for it occupied its natural place, it filled out its natural circle, it was visibly and delightfully undeformed by stays'.[66] It seems that once again the reader is in the process of being introduced to a standard Victorian heroine. But this impression is not allowed to develop as Marian turns to face Hartright.

She left the window – and I said to myself, The lady is dark. She moved forward a few steps – and I said to myself (with a sense of surprise which words fail me to express), The lady is ugly!

Never was the old conventional maxim, that Nature cannot err, more flatly contradicted – never was the fair promise of a lovely figure more strangely and startingly belied by the face and head that crowned it. The lady's complexion was almost swarthy, and the dark down on her upper lip was almost a moustache. She had a large, firm, masculine mouth and jaw; prominent, piercing, resolute brown eyes; and thick, coal-black hair, growing unusually low down on her forehead. Her expression – bright, frank, and intelligent – appeared, while she was silent, to be altogether wanting in those feminine attractions of gentleness and pliability, without which the beauty of the handsomest woman alive is beauty incomplete. To see such a face as this set on shoulders that a sculptor would have longed to model – to be charmed by the modest graces of action through which the symmetrical limbs betrayed their beauty when they moved, and then to be almost repelled by the masculine form and masculine look of the features in which the perfectly-shaped figure ended – was to feel a sensation oddly akin to the helpless discomfort familiar to us all in sleep, when we recognise yet cannot reconcile the anomalies and contradictions of a dream.[67]

The shocking climax to this description of Marian Halcombe is delivered impeccably. When a woman is described so blatantly as ugly, it becomes obvious that, more generally, heroines are supposed to be beautiful. However, not only does Hartright find that Marian is ugly, she is also masculine. Her complexion was swarthy and 'the dark down on her upper lip was almost a moustache'. Marian is female, a woman, but she also combines in herself attributes generally ascribed to men and the dichotomy is called to our attention at several places in the novel. Although Hartright is in love with Laura, he is strongly drawn towards Marian and she is more his confidante than the woman he loves. It would be difficult to explain this relationship in terms of general sexual stereotyping but during the course of an intimate conversation with Marian, Hartright again comments on her masculine appearance.

I could add no more. My voice faltered, my eyes moistened, in spite of me.

She caught me by both hands – she pressed them with the strong, steady grasp of a man – her dark eyes glittered – her brown complexion flushed deep – the force and energy of her face glowed and grew beautiful with the pure inner light of her generosity and her pity.[68]

She says herself, 'My hands always were, and always will be, as awkward as a man's.'[69] Even when under great strain it seems that Marian finds it difficult to cry. And if she does cry her tears come 'almost like men's tears, with sobs that seem to tear me in pieces, and that frightens everyone about me.'[70] Marian reveals this aspect of herself in the tiniest detail. Laura recalls with glee Marian's 'horrid, heavy man's umbrella'.[71] At times Marian has the sympathies one would normally expect from a man. She bemoans the effect which Madam Fosco has on 'long-suffering male humanity'[72] – hardly a feminist feeling. Yet despite her assumed masculinity she realises that men will still patronise her, particularly Count Fosco. 'He flatters my vanity, by talking to me as seriously and sensibly as if I was a man.'[73] However, Marian will still play on the fact that she is a woman when the occasion requires it. 'My courage was only a woman's courage after all;'[74] At this point she is preparing herself to crawl along the verandah to spy on Fosco and Sir Percival. Marian is aware of her special attributes; she tells Hartright that he shall not regret that he has only a woman to help him[75] and Fosco is very aware of her special nature, 'this magnificent woman'[76] he calls her.

Can you look at Miss Halcombe, and not see that she has the foresight and the resolution of a man? With that woman for my friend, I would snap these fingers of mine at the world.[77]

Nominally, as far as appearances are concerned, Marian is a woman but such is her character, her strength and resources, that she rises beyond those qualities which society recognises as uniquely feminine. Her character is such that we must adjust our apprehensions of women. Marian is not the only character who disrupts the gender categories offered by society. Laura's childishness is often foregrounded. Houghton suggests that Victorian sexuality demanded that its women appeared as either childishly innocent or as harlots.[78] This argument is elaborated below, but, at this stage, it is proposed that when Laura is described as a child, the same categories are disturbed as in the enumeration of Marian's masculine characteristics. Society sanctioned childishness in women however and therefore it is Marian's traits which are the more abrasive. At one point Marian juxtaposes their respective qualities in a way which foregrounds their difference. She is downstairs with her 'masculine form and masculine look' whilst Laura is upstairs in her bedroom 'nursing that essentially feminine malady, a slight headache'.[79] Laura plays music with a 'delicate, womanly taste'[80] and Hartright finds when she looks at him, her eyes 'have the artless bewilderment of a child'.[81] While discussing her marriage plans with Marian, Laura twists at her hair 'with that childish restlessness in her fingers, which poor Mrs. Vesey still tries so patiently and so vainly to cure her of'.[82] Shortly before Laura is about to leave on her wedding tour, Marian refers to her as a 'poor child – for a child she is still in so many things'.[83] During the time that Walter, Marian and Laura live incognito in London, Walter writes in his journal that Laura speaks as a child and 'showed me her thoughts as a child might have shown them'.[84] Finally, this type of treatment has its effect on Laura because, just after Hartright's interview with Mrs Clements, Laura rebels against her position.

'I am so useless – I am such a burden on both of you,' she answered, with a weary, hopeless sigh. 'You work and get money, Walter; and Marian helps you. Why is there nothing I can do? You will end in liking Marian better than you like me – you will, because I am so helpless! Oh, don't, don't, don't treat me like a child!'[85]

Few of the characters in *The Woman in White* appear to be totally subsumed by the traditional markers of gender. Anne Catherick shares some of Laura's childish qualities. When she discusses the anonymous letter with Hartright, she is so startled by something he says that 'She looked up at me with the artless bewilderment of a child.'[86] Sir Percival Glyde is one of the most unlikely characters to challenge sex roles but even he has a nose 'straight and handsome and delicate enough to have done for a woman's'.[87] His feminine nose represents an ultimate lack of power. Again Frederick Fairlie's feet were effeminately small, and were clad in buff-coloured silk stockings, and little womanish bronze-leather slippers'.[88] Indeed, Frederick seems to exist in a strange limbo-land – a homosexual? – poised somewhere half way between man and woman.

Upon the whole, he had a frail, languidly-fretful, over-refined look – something singularly and unpleasantly delicate in its association with a man, and, at the same time, something which could by no possibility have looked natural and appropriate if it had been transferred to the personal appearance of a woman.[89]

Count Fosco, the ultimate villain of the piece also has character traits which are not usually emblematic of aggressive masculinity. He is fond of animals and allows his pet mice to run all over his massive bulk. He has a sweet tooth; 'A taste for sweets' he explains, 'is the innocent taste of women and children. I love to share it with them – it is another bond, dear ladies, between you and me'.[90] He lunches 'Entirely upon fruit-tart and cream'[91] before leaving Limmeridge. Marian remarks that Sir Percival is often rude about Count Fosco's 'effeminate tastes'.[92] These examples are all symptomatic of a major theme in *The Woman in White*. On the surface there are men and women with respective characteristics but the accumulating connecting links in the novel suggest that rather than describing reality the categories of masculine and feminine are insufficient to measure the entire spectrum of sexuality and gender. To credit characters with either uniquely masculine or feminine characteristics is a mere expediency which does not do full justice to a complicated subject.

The reality of sexuality and gender is concealed by a convenient division of the sexes. Collins continues this investigation in *The Woman in White* when he examines how language functions in society. The relationship of language to reality is made problematic. When Frederick Fairlie is introducing Hartright to the customs of Limmeridge House, he explains that he is a cultured man who recognises the social role of the artist. He has cast off the 'insular skin' of English 'barbarity' – propriety? – and quotes the example of Charles V who stooped to pick up Titian's brush for the artist.[93] Yet, just as he has opened up his mind to Hartright on the subject of art and society, Frederick asks the young drawing master to put away a tray of coins for him. The request suggests the master/servant relationship which Frederick had just condemned. Walter comments that 'As a practical commentary on the liberal social theory which he had just favoured me by illustrating, Mr. Fairlie's cool request rather amused me.'[94] Fairlie's actions do not correspond with what he says. He uses language to conceal the true state of affairs. He is really an old artistocrat in temperament who hides his conservative politics behind a liberal rhetoric.

Throughout *The Woman in White* there are many instances where language must be ignored if a true reading of the situation is to be obtained. Rather than describe reality, another function of language is indicated. Language may work to conceal reality and so in these situations an appeal is made to an area of experience which is free of the mediating and distorting effect of language. It is very much to be doubted that such a language-free zone exists in consciousness but it is enough that it is felt necessary to pay lip-service to it. This suggests that language in fact colours reality and that we experience reality via the rules of grammar. For example, Hartright appreciates that he misunderstands Anne Catherick's reaction to the warning letter she delivers to Laura. However, it is not sufficient that he simply note his failure. He argues, that such is the extent of his inability to comprehend that 'No words that ever were spoken could have assured me, as her look and manner now assured me, that the motive which I had assigned for her writing the letter and sending it to Miss Fairlie was plainly and distinctly the wrong one.'[95] It seems implicit here that there is an area beyond language, inaccessible to words, and apparent in Anne Catherick's face, where the ultimate truth resides. This is not the only point in the novel where the truth is seen to exist beyond the linguistic realm. This is another example of a series of connecting links which Collins wrote into the novel. When Hartright has to break his contract as drawing master at Limmeridge House, only Marian and he know his true motives. Marian signals her complicity and sympathy with Hartright in other than linguistic means, and Hartright recognises this as a sacred trust between them.

> No words could have expressed so delicately that she understood how the permission to leave my employment had been granted, and that she gave me her sympathy not as my superior but as my friend.[96]

Once something is committed to words it both expresses a view and adds weight to that view. Language can create opinion as well as reflect it. Marian is suspicious that her mail is being tampered with. She had sealed it in the normal way, but after a short time her envelope opened without sticking or tearing.

Perhaps I had fastened it insufficiently? Perhaps there might have been some defect in the adhesive gum? Or, perhaps – No! it is quite revolting enough to feel that third conjecture stirring in my mind. I would rather not see it confronting me, in plain black and white.[97]

Marian suspects that Fosco is reading her correspondence but she is unwilling to write this fear into her diary because, once it is down in black and white, it gathers momentum, writing becomes evidence, leaves a trace and has a force greater than pure speculation. To commit her thoughts to paper would somehow render them more potent as far as Marian is concerned, and gives them a greater reality. To see things in black and white also suggests a simple difference of right and wrong while the actual situation may be more complicated than this.

When Fosco arrives at Limmeridge for his interview with Frederick, the latter tries to dismiss his visitor as quickly as possible. He finds Fosco's presence so intolerable that he wonders if language is adequate to describe it.[98] During the course of this unhappy interview Fosco suggests that he has certain explanations to make which cannot be 'properly disposed of by writing only'.[99] Writing cannot be trusted to give a full explanation so Fosco supplements the written word with his presence. The inability of language always to have a purchase on the truth is again made clear when Laura discovers that Marian has been spirited away from Blackwater Park. 'No words that ever were spoken'[100] would convince her that Marian had agreed to this course of action.

Language has a dual function in this novel. Just as propriety both allows and curtails action so language both makes thought possible in the first place and also controls it. To use language correctly, is assumed to guarantee authority and also to have the monopoly on truth. Count Fosco's cook, Hester Pinhorn, voices this deferential attitude at the opening of her narrative. She knows what is 'a sin and a wickedness' but still defers to those who will write down what she says 'to put my language right'. For Hester, it is necessary, not only to have a knowledge of good and bad, but also, to be able to express this knowledge in the correct terminology.

I am sorry to say that I have never learned to read or write. I have been a hard-working woman all my life, and have kept a good character. I know that it is a sin and wickedness to say the thing which is not; and I will truly beware of doing so on this occasion. All that I know, I will tell; and I humbly beg the gentleman who takes this down to put my language right as he goes on, and to make allowances for my being no scholar.[101]

Language is a component of culture and does allow for thought in the first place, but rather than celebrate this aspect of it, the novel dwells on the corollary, the fact that language can also dictate thought. When Hartright returns from his foreign expedition, he continues to call Laura by her maiden name although he knows that she is married. The name Lady Glyde signifies her new status as Percival's wife and, as this is just the situation which Hartright cannot countenance, he continues to think of her as Laura Fairlie. Her married name, Lady Glyde, denotes for him a tragic situation and so he refuses the word. The names have different connotations, connotations which threaten to overwhelm the denotation, and determine their use. The name is more than a simple reflection of the woman, but actually influences his reaction towards her.

Hartright's family tell him of Laura's death and he visits the churchyard to see her grave. Although he is fully aware of her death, he finds it impossible to read her name on the headstone. The inscription is too powerful, too final, and is the seal on the actual fact of her death.

A second time I tried to read the inscription. I saw, at the end, the date of her death; and, above it –

Above it, there were lines on the marble, there was a name among them, which disturbed my thoughts of her. I went round to the other side of the grave, where there was nothing to read – nothing of earthly vileness to force its way between her spirit and mine.[102]

The very falseness of this inscription, the words on the marble, is proved a few moments later when Laura confronts Hartright. What then forces its way between them in the headstone is the statement, the words signifying Laura's death. Despite the appearance of Laura's name on the gravestone, written testament of her death, Laura is very much alive.

Something more of this theme is explored during Laura's time in the asylum. Sir Percival and Count Fosco have her committed and

then attempt to convince everyone that Laura is really Anne
Catherick. Not unreasonably, Laura attempts to explain this to the
authorities, but her nurse shows her Anne's name on the clothes she
is wearing and argues that this is proof of her true identity.

> This was the Asylum. Here she first heard herself called Anne
> Catherick's name; and here, as a last remarkable circumstance in
> the story of the conspiracy, her own eyes informed her that she
> had Anne Catherick's clothes on. The nurse, on the first night in
> the Asylum, had shown her the marks on each article of her
> underclothing as it was taken off, and had said, not at all irritably
> or unkindly, 'Look at your own name on your own clothes, and
> don't worry us all any more about being Lady Glyde. She's dead
> and buried; and you're alive and hearty. Do look at your clothes
> now! There it is in good marking ink; and there you will find it on
> all your own things which we have kept in the house – Anne
> Catherick, as plain as print.[103]

It may be as plain as print, down in black and white, but it is not true.
And as the novel closes this becomes an important metaphor. The
function of language, specifically writing, is foregrounded. It is the
lie offered by language, – its transparency – which Hartright must
counter if he is to win back for Laura her full status as the heiress of
the Fairlie fortunes. This task involves him in countering the lie
'written on her mother's tomb', the lie which shall be 'publicly
erased'.[104] The attempt to put things to right necessitates work to
guarantee that language again approximates to reality. Accordingly
he must turn to written records to substantiate his case and he is far
from happy with all that he reads. He suspects that there is
something wrong with the Old Welmingham registry book, despite
how 'Smoothly and fairly as appearances looked in the vestry.'[105]
Oddly enough the record at Old Welmingham is falsified, not by
erasure, but by addition. Sir Percival had made a false entry. In
actual fact his parents never married. Again the written word
conceals reality.

As events put themselves to right and the novel closes, it is not
only the inscription on the tombstone which is erased in the attempt
to make language correspond with reality. It transpires that Fosco is
a member of a secret society, a society which seeks vengeance on
him for betraying it. Eventually he is killed and his body recovered
from the Seine. He had a mark on his left arm to prove his

membership of this Brotherhood and, in avenging itself, the society not only took Fosco's life but removed its mark from his arm. The mark signified his membership of the group but, since he was a traitor to the cause, it did not reflect the true state of things. By erasing the scar, the society put things to right. All signs now reflect reality.

> When I have intimated that the foreigner with the scar was a Member of the Brotherhood . . . and when I have further added that the two cuts in the form of a T, on the left arm of the dead man, signified the Italian word 'Traditore' and showed that justice had been done by the Brotherhood on a Traitor, I have contributed all that I know towards elucidating the mystery of Count Fosco's death.[106]

The Woman in White interrogates the non-correspondence of word and meaning, appearance and reality via a series of connecting links which articulate seemingly disparate phenomena. An equilibrium is established at the end of the novel when, as a result of Hartright's efforts, some of the polarities noted above coalesce. Yet it is important to stress that it is only *some* of the polarities which coalesce. Throughout the novel Collins emphasises the arbitrary nature of this fusion of appearance with reality. It is the fact that both propriety and appearance, while serving positive ends, can also be factional which is the ultimate message of the novel. Collins stops short from a full blown indictment of propriety because, when it is often to be criticised, there are proprieties which have a positive function in society.

5

Man and Wife

Man and Wife is one of Collins' most timely books. Its discussion of the Marriage Laws was of great contemporary interest and the attack on Athleticism elaborates and goes far beyond Arnold's reservations in *Culture and Anarchy*. Collins redirects the current debate about roughs and concentrates on the 'roughs in broadcloth'.

> We have become so shamelessly familiar with violence and outrage, that we recognise them as a necessary ingredient in our social system, and class our savages as a representative part of our population, under the newly invented name of "Roughs". Public attention has been directed by hundreds of other writers to the dirty Rough in Fustian. If the present writer had confirmed himself within those limits, he would have carried all his readers with him. But he is bold enough to direct attention to the washed Rough in broadcloth – and he must stand on his defense with readers who have not noticed this variety, or who, having noticed, prefer to ignore it.[1]

Arnold sees a threat to society coming from the Hyde Park rioters.[2] Collins identifies another source of social dissolution. Polite society is as guilty of disruptive behaviour as are the working classes, and, Collins implies, even more insidious. While legislation may control the working class, middle class disruption is inherently more disruptive to society because it detracts from the middle class sense of identity and social cohesion. Social and political problems do not reside only with the lowest groups in the country but are to be found in 'the various grades of English society, in the middle and upper classes'.[3] The prime source of this bourgeois affront on society is attributed to the cult of Athleticism. *Man and Wife* fuses this crusade with an exposé of the Marriage Laws of the 1860s.

The opening paragraph of the novel describes the situation of

125

women in Victorian England. We are introduced to two school friends who are about to take their leave of each other.

> The name of one was Blanche. The name of the other was Anne.
>
> Both were the children of poor parents; both had been pupil teachers at the school; and both were destined *to earn their own bread*. Personally speaking, these were the only points of resemblance between them.
>
> Blanche was passably attractive and passably intelligent, and no more. Anne was rarely beautiful and rarely endowed. Blanche's parents were worthy people, whose first consideration was to *secure*, at any sacrifice, the future well-being of their child. Anne's parents were heartless and depraved. Their one idea, in connection with their daughter, was to *speculate* on her beauty, and to turn her abilities to *profitable account*.
>
> The girls were starting in life under widely different conditions. Blanche was going to India, to be governess in the household of a Judge, under care of the Judge's wife. Anne was to wait at home until the first opportunity offered of sending her cheaply to Milan. There, among strangers, she was to be perfected in the actress's and the singer's art; then to return to England, and *make the fortune* of her family on the lyric stage.[4] (my italics)

The two girls are described in economic terms and this language of supply and demand is interesting testimony to the pervasiveness of bourgeois ideas. Market relationships insinuate themselves into the family and women are seen as commodities to be exchanged, bought and sold, and thought of in terms of profit and loss. Hence the language of this passage – speculate, cheaply, make the fortune, profitable account, secure. This all serves to emphasise the role of women as a commodity in the great Victorian market-place. And it is a feature of society that ownership of a commodity can grant status to its owner. People are what they own and property determines their insertion in the social hierarchy.

Women are commodities and such is the insistence of this economic metaphor that it has both positive and negative connotations. There is a distinction drawn between 'security' and 'speculation'; the former describes the activity of caring parents and the latter marks a more suspect behaviour. Anne's speculative parents also wanted to put her on the stage. There is a parallel drawn between the actress and the whore. The parents were determined to prostitute, to sell their daughter on the stage. This theme is elaborated in detail throughout *No Name*.

It soons becomes clear in *Man and Wife* that if a man is fortunate enough to have the right spouse, he has gone some way towards guaranteeing his success in the world. Mr Vanborough draws attention to this aspect of marriage in the opening scenes of the novel.

"If you ever marry," he said, "don't be such a fool, Kendrew, as I have been. Don't take a wife from the stage."

"If I could get such a wife as yours," replied the other, "I would take her from the stage tomorrow. A beautiful woman, a clever woman, a woman of unblemished character, and a woman who truly loves you. Man alive! what do you want more?"

"I want a great deal more. I want a woman highly connected and highly bred – a woman who can receive the best society in England, and open her husband's way to a position in the world."[5]

Vanborough wants a woman who will contribute to his social standing. He is ambitious to have a Parliamentary career and become a Peer. The only obstacle to this he can identify is his 'estimable wife'. She is not the woman who can help him 'make my place in society?' – who can smooth my way through social obstacles and political obstacles, to the House of Lords?'[6] Apparently a woman is something you acquire to help you make your way in life. However, the implication is that this is a very superficial approach to the business of love and marriage. Vanborough enlists the aid of a lawyer, Mr Delamayn to help him in his divorce and this gentleman is described in such a way that it becomes clear that the two men only deal in appearance and social ephemera and are prepared to ignore the finer, moral issues of life, questions which lie beneath surface reality.

Externally speaking, the rising solicitor, who was going to try his luck at the Bar, looked like a man who was going to succeed. His hard, hairless face, his watchful grey eyes, his thin resolute lips, said plainly, in so many words, "I mean to get on in the world; and, if you are in my way, I mean to get on at your expense." Mr. Delamayn was habitually polite to everybody – but he had never been known to say one unnecessary word to his dearest friend. A man of rare ability; a man of unblemished honour (as the code of the world goes); but not a man to be taken familiarly by the hand.[7]

Both Vanborough and Delamayn may operate in strict accordance with the code of the world and observe the manners and laws of society but their behaviour is contrasted most ill-favourably with another, as yet unspoken code which presents them in a much more unfavourable light. It is insufficient merely to be answerable to the dictates of society. Eventually Vanborough gets his divorce and marries a woman he assumes will further his career and although he has acted all above board it is clear that, despite the lack of social censure, his behaviour is not applauded.

In three months from the memorable day when his solicitor had informed him that he was a free man. Mr. Vanborough possessed a wife he desired, to grace the head of his table and to push his fortunes in the world – the Legislature of Great Britain being the humble servant of his treachery, and the respectable accomplice of his crime.[8]

As for the first Mrs Vanborough,

It is due to Mr. Vanborough to admit that he broke her heart, with the strictest attention to propriety.[9]

Again it is worth paying attention to the language used at this instance in the novel. Normally respectable institutions and conventions become associated with nefarious purpose and wrong doing. Bourgeois institutions are unmasked; they lose their respectable appearance and in this instance marriage is shown to be a social convenience which may be used, with the full approbation of the law, to advance a man's career. And all this is possible with the most rigid adherence to propriety. Propriety, like the legislature of Great Britain is the humble servant of treachery and the respectable accomplice of crime. Despite the appearance of things, despite adhering to the law, it is still possible to be guilty of great injustice. Delamayn can sympathise with the treatment meted out to Mrs Vanborough. It may be very shoddy, but he can also justify it to himself. 'Yes in his own impenetrable way the rising lawyer owned it was hard on her. But the law justified it. There was no doubt in this case. The law justified it.'[10]

In the eyes of the law Vanborough really does no wrong to the woman. The narrative guarantees that we should find no fault with the man on legal grounds. So far as social convention, propriety and the legal system are concerned, it appears that no wrong has been done. Yet the entire novel questions this legal apparatus and those rules of polite behaviour which allow for the situation described. Women become synonymous with property and it is hardly surprising that the law should support the property owners. Collins is determined to describe this property system in its true light and advertise the plight of women. It is worth recalling that Marx accounts for the legal system in a similar fashion. Étienne Balibar explains it succinctly.

(Legal forms) are necessary and yet 'irrational', *expressing and codifying* the 'economic' reality which each mode of production defines in its own way, and yet simultaneously *masking* it.[11]

In similar terms to Balibar's gloss on Marx, Collins investigates the juxtaposition of property and the apparatus of the law. The appearance/reality dichotomy is common to both writers and *Man and Wife* investigates some of the problems inherent in these ambivalences and duplicities. The parallels may be extended even further. Marx shows how capitalist law appropriated the local laws of custom and made them serve in its interest. Custom and tradition in the novel are shown to be agents preventing change, a change in the law for the benefit of all. 'The Story' opens with a strange description recounting the struggle between some owls and several workmen in the summerhouse of a country seat in Perthshire. An allegorical reading is invited and the passage deals with the relationship of custom to law and the difficulty of challenging present social arrangements. The owls feel the mansion, Windygates, is theirs because they had settled there. The house had once been the centre of a law suit and the grounds had become desolate when the owls had invaded the summerhouse. 'For years the owls had lived undisturbed on the property which they had acquired by the oldest of all existing rights – the right of taking.'[12] Collins draws a parallel with humanity.

> So for years the Owls slept their happy sleep by day, and found their comfortable meal when darkness fell. They had come, with the creepers, into the possession of the summerhouse. Consequently the creepers were a part of the constitution of the summerhouse. And consequently the Owls were the guardians of the constitution. There are some human owls who reason as they did, and who are in this respect – as also in respect of snatching smaller birds of their roosts – wonderfully like them.[13]

The owls are identified with the ruling bloc in society, the guardians of the English constitution, whose power comes from their property. And this property, too, was initially stolen but custom, tradition and the law legitimated the theft.[14] Little sympathy is shown for the owls; they represent tradition and fear of change, but, eventually, they are defeated. 'The summerhouse was cleared of the rank growth that had choked it up, while the rotten woodwork was renewed – while all the murky place was purified with air and light.'[15] It is implied that it is just a tradition, convention and constitution which dictates the present condition of the country and, in particular, the Marriage Laws.

However, Collins is aware, unfortunately, that these Marriage Laws are not as easy to change as it is to shift the owls. It is quite a simple matter to indicate social abuse and point to faults in society, but it is a different matter to effect change. This becomes clear, later in the novel, in Hester Dethridge's manuscript.

> Indeed, through all my trouble, I must say I have found one thing hold good. In my experience, I have found that people are oftener quick than not to feel a human compassion for others in distress. Also, that they mostly see plain enough what's hard and cruel and unfair on them in the governing of the country which they help to keep going. But once ask to get on from sitting down and grumbling about it to rising up and setting it right; and what do you find them? As helpless as a flock of sheep – that's what you find them.[16]

Collins was prompted to write *Man and Wife* by the publication of The Report of the Royal Commission to examine the workings of the Marriage Laws and since the first appearance of the book an Act of Parliament had been passed to protect, to some degree, the property of married women. The novel itself may have contributed something to this change of mood.

The theorem is advanced that the Marriage Laws do little more than give the appearance of respectability to a situation which is very unfair to women. As the novel gets under way the entire world of appearance is held up for examination. Blanche Lundie has all the accoutrements of a fashionable young woman of 1868.

> Age, at the present time, eighteen. Position, excellent. Money, certain. Temper, quick. Disposition, variable. In a word, a child of the modern time – with the merit of the age we live in, and the failings of the age we live in – and a substance of sincerity and truth and feeling underlying it all.[17]

Lady Lundie, Blanche's step-mother had a 'cruel aquiline nose, an obstinate straight chin, magnificent dark hair and eyes' and 'a lazy grace of movement which was attractive at first sight, but inexpressibly monotonous and wearisome on a longer acquaintance'.[18] The nose and chin hint at Lady Lundie's personality and while she may have the apparent attributes of an attractive woman, her charm is really superficial. Collins did not have much time for fashionable beauties and his description of Lady Lundie contrasts interestingly with his treatment of her governess Anne Silvester.

> "She has not a single good feature in her face." There was nothing individually remarkable about Miss Silvester, seen in a state of repose. She was of the average height. She was as well made as most women. In hair and complexion, she was neither light nor dark, but provokingly neutral, just between the two. Worse even than this, there were positive defects in her face, which it was impossible to deny. A nervous contraction at one corner of her mouth drew up the lips out of the symmetrically right line, when they moved. A nervous uncertainty in the eye on the same side narrowly escaped presenting the deformity of a "cast". And yet with these indisputable drawbacks, here was one of those women – the formidable few – who had the hearts of men and the peace of families at their mercy.[19]

Blanche and her step-mother comply with the fashions of the time, but, with Anne, her sex appeal cannot be expressed so well in polite statement, so, as with her relationship to Lady Lundie, 'there was something smouldering under the surface here'.[20]

Anne emerges in contrast to Lady Lundie and Blanche. Geoffrey Delamayn, 'a magnificent human animal' is compared to Sir Patrick Lundie who is 'socially dreaded for a hatred of modern institutions'. Sir Patrick takes the view that 'It's the cant of the day . . . to take these physically-wholesome men for granted as being morally-wholesome men into the bargain.'[21] Sir Patrick represents the values of a better time and explains to Arnold Brinkworth, Blanche's suitor why he dislikes Geoffrey.

> Your friend is the model young Briton of the present time. I don't like the model young Briton. I don't see the sense of crowing over him as a superb national production, because he is big and strong, and drinks beer with impunity, and takes a cold shower-bath all the year round. There is far too much glorification in England, just now, of the mere physical qualities which an Englishman shares with the savage and the brute.[22]

Collins traces the degeneration of the British university from a centre of scholarship to a glorified gymnasium in a sharp exchange between Sir Patrick and Geoffrey. Sir Patrick had just quoted Dryden.

> Lady Lundie looked unaffectedly shocked. Mr. Delamayn went a step further. He interfered on the spot – with the air of a man who feels himself imperatively called upon to perform a public duty.
>
> "Dryden never said that," he remarked, "I'll answer for it."
>
> Sir Patrick wheeled round with the help of his ivory cane, and looked Mr. Delamayn hard in the face.
>
> "Do you know Dryden, Sir, better than I do?" he asked.
>
> The Honourable Geoffrey answered, modestly, "I should say I did, I have rowed three races with him, and we trained together."
>
> Sir Patrick looked round him with a sour smile of triumph. "Then let me tell you, Sir," he said, "that you trained with a man who died nearly two hundred years ago."

Mr. Delamayn appealed in genuine bewilderment, to the company generally:

"What does this old gentleman mean?" he asked, "I am speaking of Tom Dryden, of Corpus. Everybody in the university knows *him*."

"I am speaking," echoed Sir Patrick, "of John Dryden the Poet. Apparently, everybody in the University does *not* know Him!"[23]

Geoffrey is ridiculed as a product of the modern university which concentrates on the physical development of its students. Geoffrey is a fine looking man but it soon becomes obvious that his appeal is all on the surface. Morally and intellectually he is hollow. Unfortunately Anne Silvester had fallen in love with him, and now pregnant by him, wants to marry. It is only now when it is too late that she sees Geoffrey for what he is 'below the surface' but it is impossible to blame her for her infatuation.

She had seen him, the hero of the river-race, the first and foremost man in a trial of strength and skill which had roused the enthusiasm of all England. She had seen him the central object of the interest of a nation; the idol of the popular worship and the popular applause. *His* were the arms whose muscle was celebrated in the newspapers. *He* was the first among the heroes hailed by ten thousand roaring throats as the pride and flower of England. Is it reasonable – is it just – to expect her to ask herself, in cold blood, what (morally and intellectually) is all this worth? – and that, when the man who is the object of the apotheosis, notices her, is presented to her, finds her to his taste, and singles her out from the rest? No. While humanity is humanity, the woman is not utterly without excuse.[24]

Anne's appeal for Geoffrey to marry her meets with little success and as he makes his excuses the true nature of marriage, as it strikes Collins, is unfolded before the reader. Geoffrey is not the eldest son and is dependent on his father's good grace for every penny. 'You're a lady, and all that, I know. But you're only a governess. It's your interest as well as mine to wait till my father has provided for me. Here it is in a nutshell: if I marry you now, I'm a ruined man.'[25] It has become a matter of attempting to square finance and property with honour and propriety. Anne's immediate response to Geoffrey is that if he does not marry her she is a 'ruined woman'. 'Moral ruin to the woman, meant money ruin to the man' because 'One more outrage on his father's rigid sense of propriety, and he [Geoffrey] would be left out of the will as well as kept out of the house.'[26] Anne decides that a private marriage is the answer to their problem and Geoffrey agrees as this might avoid any awkward scandal reaching his father.

So the first potential man and wife are introduced in the novel, a text with three couples vying to be the eponymous pair. Blanche has a suitor in Arnold Brinkworth and the stereotypical language in which they are described allows the supposition that Arnold and Blanche may prove to be the happy couple in contrast to Anne's tragic situation. Arnold is encouraged to make love to Blanche 'within limits'. Decorum is never forgotten. Everything is perfectly acceptable. Their passion is strong but is circumscribed by propriety and manners. Accordingly Arnold asks Sir Patrick, Blanche's guardian, for permission to marry and it is in this interview that a less pleasant aspect of marriage is revealed. It becomes evident that even Arnold's feeling for Blanche must be substantiated by more than love and affection. Sir Patrick feels it his duty to explain this to the young man. Arnold asks if Sir Patrick would advise him to marry. The old lawyer draws a comparison with the purchase of moist sugar. Understandably Arnold is confused so Sir Patrick elaborates.

"You go to the tea-shop, and get your moist sugar. You take it on the understanding that it *is* moist sugar. But it isn't anything of the sort. It's a compound of adulterations made up to look like sugar. You shut your eyes to that awkward fact, and swallow your adulterated mess in various articles of food; and you and your sugar get on together in that way as well as you can. Do you follow me so far?"

Yes, Arnold (quite in the dark) followed, so far.

"Very good," pursued Sir Patrick. "You go to the marriage-shop, and get a wife. You take her on the understanding – let us say – that she has lovely yellow hair, that she has an exquisite complexion, that her figure is the perfection of plumpness, and that she is just tall enough to carry the plumpness off. You bring her home and you discover that it is the old story of the sugar over again. Your wife is an adulterated article. Her lovely yellow hair is – dye. Her exquisite skin is – pearl powder. Her plumpness is – padding. And three inches of her height are – in the bootmaker's heels. Shut your eyes, and swallow your adulterated wife as you swallow your adulterated sugar – and, I tell you again, you are one of the few men who can try the marriage experiment with a fair chance of success."[27]

Again the equation is made between women and commodities.

And there is also a 'Trade Description Act' aspect of the comparison. Collins is making the structural analogy in the old idea of cosmetic deceit with the commodity. Where, for example, Dickens will give us Mrs Skewton in *Dombey and Son*, whose whole existence is a cosmetic fraud, Collins reworks the individual example to show the entire structure of rules which makes this possible.

Despite the romantic world-view of Arnold and Blanche they still must satisfy the dictates of property and make their relationship legal in the eyes of the law. This is brought home to Arnold when Sir Patrick decides that events force him to bring forward the date of the marriage. Arnold immediately agrees to this and Sir Patrick explains that it now all depends on the lawyers. Once again Arnold is baffled.

"What have the lawyers got to do with it?"
"My good fellow, this is not a marriage in a novel! This is the most unromantic affair of the sort that ever happened. Here are a young gentleman and a young lady, both rich people; both well matched in birth and character; one of age and the other marrying with the full consent and approval of her guardian. What is the consequence of this purely prosaic state of things? Lawyers and settlements of course!"[28]

There is nothing particularly new in the description of marriage as a matter of defending and enlarging property but Collins' concentration on the role of the law in this business is an interesting departure. The law makes proper and gives propriety to this defence of the rights of property. The law glosses what is really happening and gives everything the appearance of the utmost respectability. The law is a false appearance. It is not an impartial apparatus but serves its own interest and is often an apologia for property and finance. Any notion of abstract justice is eradicated. Sir Patrick, himself a retired lawyer, explains this aspect of his profession to Arnold. 'The law will argue anything with anybody who will pay the law for the use of its brains and its time.'[29]

Anne has left Windygates for a neighbouring inn at Craig Fernie where Geoffrey has agreed to meet and marry her according to Scottish law. Unfortunately for her a telegram from London has Geoffrey leave immediately for London as his father is dangerously ill. Geoffrey convinces Arnold that he should visit Anne and explain the situation. Arnold is in Geoffrey's debt, he had saved his life, and so cannot refuse. Arnold arrives at the inn and in order to protect Anne's position asks for her as his wife. Geoffrey does not tell him that according to Scottish law this is sufficient to make him Anne's husband. Intent to save Anne's reputation Arnold is only too willing to play the role of Anne's husband and give the appearance of man and wife to all at the hotel. He is so successful, that the head-waiter Bishopriggs, taking appearance for reality is convinced that he is dealing with a case of elopement. He is even more convinced of his reading of the action when Sir Patrick arrives and Arnold rushes to hide himself.

Sir Patrick's arrival allows Collins to comment on the fashion of the moment which he identifies as 'striking a pose'.[30] This translates easily into an obsession with appearance at the expense of genuine feeling.

> Sir Patrick affected nothing of the sort. One of the besetting sins of *his* time was the habitual concealment of our better selves – upon the whole, a far less dangerous national error than the habitual advertisement of our better selves, which has become the practice, publicly and privately, of society in this age.[31]

To illustrate the corruptions of the 1860s Collins has Sir Patrick play a figure from the past, a version of Pastoral again, whose manner contrasts sharply with the hollow virtues of the present day. And again this transformation is imaged in terms of appearance. Contemporary values privilege posture at the expense of honesty.

The next important scene involves Geoffrey and his father's dying efforts to reinstate his second son. Here the connection between marriage and social and financial success is again emphasised; it is now made clear to the reader that Geoffrey may only regain his good standing with his father if he now makes a good marriage.

Geoffrey's brother Julius attempts to argue the athlete's case but Lord Holchester is convinced that his younger son has only the appearance of a civilised man.

"My brother is not a savage, Sir."

"His stomach is generally full, and his skin is covered with linen and cloth, instead of red ochre and oil. So far, certainly, your brother is civilised. In all other respects your brother is a savage. . . . Give him his books to read for his degree, and, strong as he is, he will be taken ill at the sight of them. You wish me to see your brother. Nothing will induce me to see him, until his way of life (as you call it) is altered altogether. I have but one hope of it ever being altered now. It is barely possible that the influence of a sensible woman – possessed of such advantages of birth and fortune as may compel respect, even from a savage – might produce its effect on Geoffrey."[32]

Anne, a poor governess, would not answer these requirements although, in the same interview, Lord Holchester advises Julius to be generous to a woman called Anne Silvester. He remembers the legal injustices wrought against her mother. Geoffrey is soon to be faced with a moral choice. Either he can stand by Anne, the honourable thing, or he may attempt to win his way back into the family by making a good marriage. The question is if Geoffrey's athletic education is the correct preparation for such a decision. Lady Holchester had already picked a suitable woman for Geoffrey. Julius explains to his brother.

"Birth, beauty, and money are all offered to you. Take them – and you recover your position as Lord Holchester's son. Refuse them – and you go to ruin your own way." . . . "The lady in question was formally Miss Newenden – a descendant of one of the oldest families in England. She is now Mrs. Glenarm – the young widow (and the childless widow) of the great iron-master of that name. Birth and fortune – she unites both. Her income is a clear ten thousand a year."[33]

There seems little doubt that Geoffrey will abandon Anne completely. 'A disinterested anxiety for the welfare of another person was one of those refinements of feeling which a muscular education had not fitted him to understand.'[34] On his return to

Windygates Geoffrey hears Arnold explain that he is not at all happy with the turn of events. Geoffrey is not at all troubled with such a conscience and identifies Arnold's inner perturbation by referring to his outward appearance.

> "The fact is – I'm out of sorts, this morning. My mind misgives me – I don't know why."
>
> "Mind?" repeated Geoffrey, in high contempt. "Its flesh – that's what's the matter with *you*. You're nigh on a stone over your right weight. Mind be hanged! A man in healthy training don't know that he has got a mind. Take a turn with the dumb-bells, and a run up hill with a great-coat on. Sweat if off, Arnold! Sweat it off!"[35]

Geoffrey's character continues to be presented in a poor light. He is the 'personified antithesis of poetry' and Blanche is unafraid to talk to Arnold in Geoffrey's presence because rather than another person in the library with them she explains 'There's only an animal in the room. We needn't mind him.'[36] But it is of crucial importance to the plot that Geoffrey should indeed be in the library with Blanche and Arnold. Blanche is suddenly reminded of Anne and a conversation ensues, overheard by Geoffrey, where they discuss the laws governing Irregular Marriages in Scotland. It is very difficult for a man to pretend to marry in Scotland without really doing it. Arnold does not appear to comprehend just what this means to him since he had introduced himself at Craig Fernie as Anne's husband. Geoffrey, despite the muscular education, is not so slow this time.

> "He asked for her by the name of his wife at the door. He said, at dinner, before the landlady and the waiter, 'I take these rooms for my wife.' He made *her* say he was her husband at the same time. After that he stopped all night. What do the lawyers call this in Scotland? – (Query: a marriage?)"[37]

Again the point worth drawing out is that what appears to be a marriage is more likely to be accepted as a genuine legal marriage in Scotland than anywhere else in Britain at this time. Those who appear to act as if they are married are declared married in Scottish law. Geoffrey is only too prepared to take advantage of this moot point but he does decide to confirm the position with Sir Patrick, who is after all a retired lawyer.

Geoffrey finds the old man arguing with some athletes in the garden. Sir Patrick is once again arguing against Athleticism and claims that this concentration on the body will result in moral turpitude.

"Will the skill in rowing, the swiftness in running, the admirable capacity and endurance in other physical exercises, which he has attained, by a strenuous cultivation in this kind that has excluded any similarly strenuous cultivation in other kinds – will these physical attainments help him to win a purely moral victory over his own selfishness and his own cruelty?"[38]

A healthy appearance is no guarantee of a healthy mind. However, with Geoffrey the case is even more complicated. In his case it is suggested by a surgeon visiting Windygates that his health is not to be relied on and that his fine muscles may detract from the fact that he is really a sick man.

"The training authorities at his college, or elsewhere, take him in hand (naturally enough again) on the strength of outward appearances. And whether they have been right or wrong in choosing him is more than they can say, until the experiment has been tried, and the mischief has been, in many cases, irretrievably done. How many of them are aware of the important psychological truth, that the muscular power of a man is no fair guarantee of his vital power?"[39]

Geoffrey's appearance may be false on two counts. It is just possible that his lack of intellectual discipline, as he admits himself, lays him open to crime; and the doctor is of the opinion that the healthy body may conceal internal physiological problems.

The point is made in the next chapter. 'The man who first declared that "seeing" was "believing" laid his finger (whether he knew it himself or not) on one of the fundamental follies of humanity.'[40] This prefaces a conversation between Geoffrey and Sir Patrick which is described as a 'conference between the two men, so trifling in appearance, so terrible in its destined influence, not over Anne's future only, but over the future of Arnold and Blanche'.[41] Geoffrey wants to satisfy himself about the law of Scotland on marriage. He believes that Arnold has, in effect, married Anne as a result of his misplaced gallantry at Craig Fernie. Sir Patrick explains just how confused the Marriage Laws are, and unaware that he is deliberating about Arnold and Anne, concludes that he doubts the couple Geoffrey mentions are married, although evidence could be advanced in favour 'of possibly establishing a marriage – nothing more'.[42] Geoffrey, of course is blind to such subtlety and feels his way is clear to marry the iron-master's widow as Anne is now married to Arnold. Anne soon hears of Geoffrey's intentions when she meets him in the Windygates library while on a secret visit to see Blanche. She faints and he abandons her just before Blanche re-appears. Again, fooled by the evidence of her eyes, Blanche imagines that Anne has fainted from fatigue and so misses the opportunity of discovering that Geoffrey is the man who has wronged her friend. In Collins' terms Blanche had mistaken the cause of Anne's loss of consciousness and was too quick to accept appearance for reality.

> If she had been less ready in thus tracing the effect to the cause, she might have gone to the window to see if anything had happened, out of doors, to frighten Anne – might have seen Geoffrey before he had time to turn the corner of the house – and, making that one discovery, might have altered the whole course of events, not in her coming life only, but in the coming lives of others. So do we shape our own destinies, blindfold. So do we hold our poor little tenure of happiness at the capricious mercy of Chance. It is surely a blessed delusion which persuades us that we are the greatest product of the great scheme of creation, and sets us doubting whether other planets are inhabited, because other planets are not surrounded by an atmosphere which *we* can breath![43]

Cause and effect is juxtaposed with appearance and reality and the tendency to confuse one for the other is attributed to the laws of Chance. When the law, propriety and, by implication, culture is not actively campaigning for the interests of property, they are acting in accord with a blind destiny based on fortuitous phenomena.

Anne recovers from her faint, leaves Windygates, and later in the evening, the neighbourhood, all without informing anyone. She writes to Blanche to say that they must never see each other again. In an attempt to placate his ward, Sir Patrick decides to bring forward the date of Blanche's wedding to Arnold. It is important that Blanche should try to forget Anne. But again the reader is never allowed to forget that while things had reached an equilibrium on the surface still 'Signs of perturbation under the surface, suggestive of some hidden influence at work, were not wanting, as the time passed on.'[44] Anne had meanwhile got herself to Glasgow, consulted lawyers about her marital status and had then taken ill and had a miscarriage. Anne's beauty is much admired by the lawyers she consults. 'Mr Crum was the older lawyer of the two and the harder lawyer of the two; but he, too, felt the influence which the charm that there was in this woman exercised, more or less, over every man who came in contact with her.'[45]

This theme of female attractiveness is elaborated in the scenes at Swanhaven Lodge, Julius' country house. To the delight of his family Geoffrey is courting Mrs Glenarm, the iron-master's widow. Geoffrey is attracted to her because of his family obligations although she is not without superficial appeal. And it is this aspect which is emphasised. Mrs Glenarm 'looked what she was, a person possessed of plenty of superfluous money, but not additionally blest with plenty of additional intelligence to correspond.'

Reduced to the plain expression of what it is really worth, the average English idea of beauty in women may be summed up in three words – youth, health, plumpness. The more spiritual charm of intelligence and vivacity, the subtler attraction of delicacy of line and fitness of detail, are little looked for and seldom appreciated by the mass of men in this island. It is impossible otherwise to account for the extraordinary blindness of perception which (to give one instance only) makes nine Englishmen out of ten who visit France come back declaring that they have not seen a single pretty Frenchwoman, in or out of Paris, in the whole country. Our popular type of beauty proclaims itself, in its fullest material development, at every shop in which an illustrated periodical is sold. The same fleshy-faced girl, with the same inane smile, and with no other expression whatever, appears under every form of illustration, week after week, and month after month, all year round. Those who wish to know what Mrs. Glenarm was like, have only to go out and shop at any bookseller's or news-vendor's shop, and there they will see her in the first illustration, with a young woman in it, which they discover in the window.[46]

Mrs Glenarm's appeal, a stereotype enforced by the popular press, lies on the surface. It is physical rather than intellectual or spiritual and seems to be focused on such accessories as her brooch 'a single diamond of resplendent water and great size' and 'The fan in her hand [which] was a master-piece of the finest Indian workmanship.'[47] Of course Geoffrey can compete with her and as she watches him train for an important race, Geoffrey's physical presence, and sexual attractiveness is stressed.

> Dressed in a close-fitting costume, light and elastic, adapting itself to every movement, and made to answer every purpose required by the exercise in which he was about to engage, Geoffrey's physical advantages showed themselves in their best and bravest aspect. His head sat proud and easy on his firm, white throat, bared to the air. The rising of his mighty chest, as he drew in deep draughts of the fragrant summer breeze; the play of his lithe and supple loins; the easy elastic stride of his straight and shapely legs, presented a triumph of physical manhood in its highest type. Mrs. Glenarm's eyes devoured him in silent admiration.[48]

To some extent Geoffrey and Mrs Glenarm seem to deserve each other and Collins is not afraid to signal the attraction which the young widow sees in the athletically-trained masculine frame – the 'lithe and supple loins'. Yet this same body, apparently in perfect condition, is ultimately inadequate even to athletic test. Perry, Geoffrey's trainer, soon spots that Geoffrey is suffering from an internal complaint and secretly backs the northern champion, the man Geoffrey is running against.

The next event of import in the novel is Arnold's wedding and the whole description of this seems to point to the inadequacy of the institution to contain and be equivalent to the true importance of the action. Marriage is a mystery, its success or failure a mystery, and the outward show of the marriage ceremony is an inadequate indication of the reality of the situation. Collins has fun listing Arnold and particularly Blanche's 'outrages on propriety' and then describes the service.

Village nymphs strewed flowers on the path to the church door (and sent in the bill the same day). Village swains rang the joy bells (and got drunk on their money the same evening).[49]

The first phrase in each sentence, the Pastoral appearance, is immediately undermined by what follows in parenthesis, an indication of a more quotidian and cost-conscious world. The passage continues to concentrate on the ritual nature of the wedding and its inadequacy to account for the depth of human emotion.

There was the proper and awful pause while the bridegroom was kept waiting at the church. There was the proper and pitiless staring of all the female spectators when the bride was led to the altar. There was the clergyman's preliminary look at the licence – which meant official caution. And there was the clerk's preliminary look at the bridegroom – which meant official fees. All the women appeared to be in their natural element; and all the men appeared to be out of it. Then the service began – rightly considered, the most terrible, surely, of all mortal ceremonies – the service which binds two human beings, who know next to nothing of each other's natures, to risk the tremendous experiment of living together till death parts them – the service which says, in effect if not in words, Take your leap in the dark: we sanctify, but we don't insure it![50]

The religious and legal ceremony represents an attempt to give meaning to an aspect of life which is in reality, a leap in the dark. Marriage and its contingent ceremonies are condemned because, as with Geoffrey and his intended, Mrs Glenarm, it is a legal and religious seal on the demands of property or, as with Blanche and Arnold, at best, an attempt to deny Chance.

Arnold is only a few days into his honeymoon in Baden when a letter from Anne notifies him of the horror of his situation. The Glasgow solicitors have told her that there are grounds which could be argued to prove that she is his wife and that the service with Blanche is now null and void. Arnold and Blanche return immediately to join Sir Patrick at Ham Farm. Working in Arnold and Blanche's best interests Anne meanwhile visits Swanhaven Lodge to attempt to see Mrs Glenarm, explain the situation to her and perhaps prevent the marriage to Geoffrey. Collins describes the interview between the two women in terms which are by now familiar to the reader. Mrs Glenarm, the fashionable young woman, dressed in accordance with magazine illustration, is credited with having a nature 'as shallow as it appeared to be on the surface', whereas Anne, a much more interesting and appealing creature is presented in more mysterious terms.

> The dawning surprise in Mrs. Glenarm's face became intensified into an expression of distrust. Her hearty manner vanished under a veil of conventional civility, drawn over it suddenly. She looked at Anne. "Never at the best of times a beauty," she thought. "Wretchedly out of health now. Dressed like a servant, and looking like a lady. What *does* it mean?"[51]

Mrs Glenarm can use 'conventional civility' to her advantage; it can become a mask to conceal her real emotions whereas, by her very appearance, Anne seems to disrupt these very categories. She may be dressed like a servant, but she looks like a lady. It is shortly after this interview that Mrs Glenarm informs Lady Lundie that Arnold is married to Anne as a result of their behaviour at Craig Fernie. Again Collins takes this opportunity to undermine the notion of civility and manners. Lady Lundie's reaction to the news of the Craig Fernie adventure is recorded.

> A smile – the dangerous smile of an inveterately vindictive woman thoroughly roused – showed itself with a furtive suddenness on her face. Mrs. Glenarm was a little startled. Lady Lundie below the surface – as distinguished from Lady Lundie *on* the surface – was not a pleasant object to contemplate.
> "Pray try to compose yourself," said Mrs. Glenarm. "Dear Lady Lundie, you frighten me!"
> The bland surface of her ladyship appeared smoothly once more; drawn back, as it were, over the hidden inner self, which it had left for the moment exposed to view.[52]

Of course such a bland surface is often a social necessity. Lady Lundie's doctor has 'the necessary bald head and the indispensable white cravat'. And he is armed with all the other professional signs which allow him to practice medicine, explaining symptoms as the patients want to hear.

He felt her ladyship's pulse, and put a few gentle questions. He turned his back solemnly, as only a great doctor can, on his own positive internal conviction that his patient had nothing whatever the matter with her. He said with every appearance of believing himself, "Nerves, Lady Lundie. Repose in bed is essentially necessary. I will write a prescription."[53]

Lady Lundie determines to go immediately to Ham Farm and rescue Blanche from Sir Patrick and Arnold who she decides are conspiring against Blanche and herself. Her mission is successful and Sir Patrick, to clear the air, proposes a meeting of all the parties involved. But almost as a delaying device to increase the reader's appetite for a resolution of this problem, the novel turns to a further exploration of Athleticism. Mr Speedwell, the doctor who had first noticed Geoffrey's precarious health had now confirmed his diagnosis when he examined the young man for a second time at his retreat in Fulham. If Geoffrey runs he does so at the risk of his life.

A very cold eye is cast on the entire proceedings concerning this race. The event is explained as if to an anonymous foreigner.

The colour of the North is pink. The colour of the South is yellow. North produces fourteen pink men, and South produces thirteen yellow men. The meeting of pink and yellow is a solemnity. The solemnity takes its rise in an indomitable national passion for hardening the arms and legs, by throwing hammers and cricket-balls with the first, and running and jumping with the second. The object in view is to do this in public rivalry. The ends arrived at are (physically) an excessive development of the muscles, purchased at the expense of an excessive strain on the heart and the lungs – (morally) glory; confirmed at the moment by the public applause. Any person who presumes to see any physical evil in these exercises to the men who practice them, or any moral obstruction in the exhibition itself to those civilizing influences in which the true greatness of all nations depends, is a person without a biceps, who is simply incomprehensible. Muscular England develops itself and takes no notice of him.[54]

Again it is emphasised that an athletic training is a charade which conceals internal physical damage and is a substitute for moral and intellectual development. Further, it has political and social implications: 'Preserve us from enjoying anything but jokes and scandal! Preserve us from respecting anything but rank and money!'[55] The jokes and scandal may conceal the reality of the position of rank and money.

Mr Speedwell's diagnosis is confirmed. Geoffrey collapses towards the end of the race.

> There the conquered athlete lay: outwardly an inert mass of strength, formidable to look at, even in its fall; inwardly a weaker creature, in all that constitutes vital force, than the fly that buzzed on the window-pane.[56]

He survives but the truth is that he is a very weak man despite his overtly healthy constitution. Two days later, at the meeting Sir Patrick has arranged, it will be seen whether his outward strength is a true reflection of moral certitude.

By this stage Athleticism has been fiercely attacked and Collins is able to turn his attention to the position of women as rendered and dictated by the Marriage Laws. It is not an utter change of tack however because the same critique is applied to the laws governing marriage as to the cult of Athleticism. We have just left Geoffrey, a desolate man despite appearances and to guarantee that the following scene is framed within a similar paradigm, the play of appearance and reality, there is a description of Mrs Glenarm's relative, Captain Newenden.

> He was painted and padded, wigged and dressed, to represent the abstract idea of a male human being of five and twenty in robust health. There might have been a little stiffness in the region of the waist, and a slight want of firmness in the eyelid and the chin. Otherwise there was the fiction of five and twenty, founded in the appearance on the fact of five and thirty – with the truth invisible behind it, counting seventy years.[57]

The captain's appearance is a fiction; his dress conceals the fact that he is an old man. In a few moments, when the contending parties enter the room, the Marriage Laws and in particular their treatment of women, shall be exposed as a fiction in relation to their supposed correspondence with an abstract ideal of justice.

This becomes clear in Sir Patrick's appeal to Blanche. He wants her to forget the formality of the law, look to her heart and see the justice of the case he is arguing.

"You believe what Arnold Brinkworth has said; you believe what Miss Silvester has said. You know that not even the thought of marriage was in the mind of either of them, at the inn. You know – whatever else may happen in the future – that there is not the most remote possibility of either of them consenting to acknowledge that they have ever been, or ever can be, Man and Wife. Is that enough for you? Are you willing, before this enquiry proceeds any farther, to take your husband's hand; to return to your husband's protection; and to leave the rest to me – satisfied with my assurance that, on the facts as they happened, not even the Scotch Law can prove the monstrous assertion of the marriage at Craig Fernie to be true?"[58]

Sir Patrick appeals to a realm of abstract truth as distinct from the mere legal technicalities and Blanche, to a certain extent, agrees with him. She is willing to admit that Arnold has not 'Knowingly done me any wrong' but she cannot return to him until she is certain that she is his wife. Mr Moy, Blanche's solicitor, in explaining the wisdom of her decision, focuses on the real point at issue in the proceedings. Mr Moy sticks to the letter of the law. Both he and another Scottish lawyer dispute Sir Patrick's interpretation of the events at Craig Fernie. For their part, they insist on the validity of the peculiarities of the Scottish marriage laws. Mr Moy's reason for this scrupulous attention to the legalities of the question is of paramount importance.

Who is to say that circumstances may not happen in the future which may force Mr. Brinkworth or Miss Silvester – one or the other – to assert the very marriage which they repudiate now? Who is to say that interested relatives (*property being concerned here*) may not, in the lapse of years, discover motives of their own for questioning the asserted marriage in Kent?[59] (my italics)

Ultimately the law is concerned with protecting property and it is the rights of property which conflict here with the personal sentiments of the litigants. Sir Patrick is aware that he is contradicting professional etiquette and apologises to his colleagues, explaining that his

". . . position is one of unexampled responsibility and indescribable distress. May I appeal to that statement to stand as my excuse, if I plead for a last extension of indulgence toward the last irregularity of which I shall be guilty, in connection with these proceedings?"[60]

Sir Patrick is attempting to protect Anne from being legally bound to 'return' to Geoffrey. He knows that to prove the point that Blanche and Arnold are man and wife, Anne must claim the errant Geoffrey as her husband. It is Sir Patrick who, once again, points to the idiocy of the situation. Scottish law decrees that a deserted woman may be forced back on the villain who betrays her. This is exactly what happens to Anne. A dreadful picture of Anne's married life is envisaged, but, after all, the law is on Geoffrey's side.

> "The law tells her to go with her husband," he said. "The law forbids you to part Man and Wife."
> True. Absolutely, undeniably true. The law sanctioned the sacrifice of her as unanswerably as it had sanctioned the sacrifice of her mother before her. In the name of Morality, let him take her! In the interests of Virtue, let her get out of it if she can![61]

The contrast between virtue and morality is interesting. If not synonymous, they are certainly not antonyms as they seem to be made here. But such is the force of the law, that, in the interests of property, contradiction is overdetermined and all this is

> Done, in the name of Morality. Done, in the interests of Virtue. Done, in an age of progress, and under the most perfect government on the face of the earth.[62]

By this stage the message is clear. No one could offer protection to Anne. 'Law and Society armed her husband with his conjugal rights. Law and Society had but one answer to give, if she appealed to them – you are his wife.'[63] Such is the strength of Geoffrey's position that he may even appeal to 'the proprieties of life'[64] to defend his treatment of Anne. After the scene in Portland Place he holds Anne a virtual prisoner in a very isolated cottage in Fulham, a cottage owned by Hester Dethridge, Lady Lundie's former housekeeper. Anne's situation is likened to a living death, a familiar metaphor to describe the situation of women in the nineteenth century.[65]

To a woman, escape from the place was simply impossible. Setting out of the question the height of the walls, they were armed at the top with a thick setting of jagged broken glass. A small back-door in the end wall (intended probably for the gardener's use) was bolted and locked – the key having been taken out. There was not a house near. The lands of the local growers of vegetable surrounded the garden on all sides. In the nineteenth century, and in the immediate neighbourhood of a great metropolis, Anne was as absolutely isolated from all contact with the humanity around her as if she lay in her grave.[66]

And not only does Geoffrey appeal to the proprieties of life when visitors call to see his wife, but all of a sudden he takes to reading. However, his choice of reading matter – *The Newgate Trials* – is lamented by his brother Julius.

"You won't cultivate your mind," he said, "with such a book as that. Vile actions, recorded in vile English, make vile reading, Geoffrey, in every sense of the word."[67]

Geoffrey is also reading this volume selectively. He had marked for his private study only cases involving murder. It becomes clear that Geoffrey is planning to murder Anne. And at this point the critique of Athleticism reaches a crescendo.

Will his skill in rowing (as Sir Patrick once put it), his swiftness in running, his admirable capacity and endurance in other physical exercises, help him to win a purely moral victory over his own selfishness and his own cruelty. No! The moral and mental neglect of himself, which the material tone of public feeling about him has tacitly encouraged, has left him at the mercy of the worst instincts in his nature – of all that is most vile and all that is most dangerous in the composition of the natural man.[68]

At this point *Man and Wife* may be compared with *Mary Barton* in that the murder plot appears to subvert social critique. However, this murder plot is actually integrated with the social critique in *Man and Wife* and the same metaphors are at work in this closing section of the novel. Anne must learn to be wary of appearances and Hester's journal emphasises the role of the Marriage Laws in the subjection of women. It is when Geoffrey is attempting to find a way of disposing of Anne that he discovers the secret manuscript of his landlady, Hester Dethridge. Even at Windygates, while Lady Lundie's housekeeper, this mute woman had reacted very strangely towards Geoffrey. The manuscript explains why. Collins is generally credited for his insightful treatment of servants and with Hester Dethridge he combines this with a further investigation of woman's plight in marriage. Hester is not actually a member of the working class; her father was often away 'travelling for business',[69] and she had a 'little fortune' left to her by her aunt. Her manuscript explains how she determines to marry for very pragmatic reasons. Marriage is not a grand romance for her, but, rather, provides the means by which she can escape her invalided and tyrannical mother. At chapel she has met a young man, Joel Dethridge; however as she admits he was 'only a journeyman, his worldly station was below mine'.[70] Her family object to the wedding because of Dethridge's class and because of a series of bad character reports. Despite this Hester marries and discovers her mistake. She gives two-thirds of her fortune to her new husband and furnishes their home with the remainder. It is then that she discovers that Joel is an alcoholic and he soon drinks his way through the fortune and then sells the furniture to finance the habit. It is at this point that Hester's narrative again illuminates how the law treats married women. Hester decides to take her case to the police and her experience is worth attention. Her reasoning is without fault.

> My money had not only bought the furniture – it had kept the house going as well; paying the taxes which the Queen and the Parliament asked for among other things. I now went to the magistrate to see what the Queen and the Parliament, in return for the taxes, would do for *me*.[71]

The police are sympathetic but Hester does not have a marriage settlement and the furniture is not in her name. The law is on the side of the powerful and the wealthy, 'poor people in this condition of life don't even know what a marriage settlement means. And, if they did, how many of them could afford to pay the lawyer's charges?'[72] The law can do nothing for her. A policeman explains,

"My good creature," says he, "you are a married woman. The law doesn't allow a married woman to call anything her own – unless she has previously (with a lawyer's help) made a bargain to that effect with her husband before marrying him. You have made no bargain. Your husband has a right to sell your furniture if he likes. I am sorry for you; I can't hinder him."[73]

Hester's sad story continues. It is the account of her attempts to protect herself from her vindictive husband. But just as much as he is to blame, it is also suggested that society is not protecting all its members. As Hester demands of the policemen,

"Please answer me this, Sirs," I says. "I've been told by wiser heads than mine that we all pay our taxes to keep the Queen and the Parliament going; and that the Queen and the Parliament make laws to protect us in return. I have paid my taxes. Why, if you please, is there no law to protect me in return?"[74]

Hester finds work, but again her husband turns up and creates a disturbance. She does her job and again goes to the police for help. This time she hears that it may be possible for her to be granted a legal separation which would keep her husband away. Unfortunately she would have to pay for the litigation. 'After allowing my husband to rob me openly of the only property I possessed – namely my furniture – the law turned round on me when I called upon it and held out its hand to be paid.'[75] And despite all her attempts to rid herself of her husband, Hester is forced to conclude that 'there is no limit in England, to what a bad husband may do – as long as he sticks to his wife.'[76]

Eventually Hester murders her husband, by burrowing through a 'lath-and-plaster' wall, smothering him and then making the wall perfect again. Her crime goes undetected but she is haunted by a strange phantom which goads her to murder again. The manuscript stops and Geoffrey realises he has Hester in his power. He determines to repeat the 'lath-and-plaster' wall trick and so murder Anne. However, the plot fails, and, significantly, it fails because Anne does not trust appearance. On the surface she has no cause to worry '– what proof could she produce to satisfy the mind of a stranger? The proofs were all in her husband's favour'.[77] However, in this novel where a critique of appearance is united with a devastating study of the Marriage Laws and both are forcibly undermined, it is a distrust of appearance which helps save Anne's life. She is rightly suspicious of the innocent-seeming Geoffrey.

> She looked all round the room; examining the fire place, the window and its shutters, the interior of the wardrobe, the hidden space under the bed. Nothing was anywhere to be discovered which could justify the most timid person living in feeling suspicion or alarm. Appearances, fair as they were, failed to convince her. The presentiment of some hidden treachery, steadily getting nearer and nearer to her face in the dark, had rooted itself firmly in her mind.[78]

This does appear to be a very conventionalised conclusion but it is saved from cliché by the fact that the metaphor of appearance and reality, so dominant in the text, is again foregrounded. The murder plot fails because, despite all the appearance of domestic security, Anne refuses to rest easy with apparent external comfort. In his attempt to kill his wife Geoffrey has a heart attack and is the victim of Hester's savage revenge.

An epilogue describes the happy outcome for most of the main characters. Collins works on the premise that an athletic education produces people with warped morals, apparently healthy but with an inner weakness. This is articulated with a reading of the Marriage Laws which show how they attempt to give a reasonable façade to a set of regulations which viciously exploit women. *Man and Wife* demonstrates Collins' interest in topical events – in this case the lobbying to change the Marriage Laws – and, further, shows how this overtly political mission can be seen as part of a whole series of other issues which informs his novels.

6

No Name

Names are very important in *No Name*. The title itself gives a clue to the content of the novel and few pages are turned before Collins introduces the theme.

> Magdalen! It was a strange name to have given her? Strange indeed; and yet, chosen under no extraordinary circumstances. The name had been borne by one of Mr. Vanstone's sisters, who had died in early youth; and, in affectionate remembrance of her, he had called his second daughter by it – just as he had called his eldest daughter Norah, for his wife's sake. Magdalen! Surely, the grand old Bible name – suggestive of a sad sombre dignity; recalling in its first association, mournful ideas of penitence and seclusion – had been here, as events had turned out, inappropriately bestowed? Surely, this self-contradictory girl had perversely accomplished one contradiction more, by developing into a character which was out of all harmony with her own Christian name![1]

We are reminded that names should have a degree of appropriateness, that proper names, ideally, should give us some indication of the character or thing they nominate. And so our attention returns to the title, *No Name* with its implications about illegitimacy. What else can the absence of a name signify? And in the passage above, describing Magdalen 'born with all the senses – except the sense of order', it is bemoaned that she should seem to frustrate the expectation of her Biblical name.

A condition of no-name suggests chaos and anarchy, a complete lack of social ordering and control. The process of naming is itself a system of understanding and control. In this novel, this situation of no-name comes about because of the death of the father and this can be interpreted in terms of the death of order, civilisation and culture and the rise of indeterminacy. This indeterminacy is marked by Magdalen's quest for identity on the death of her father. Yet the irony of the situation is that *No Name*

153

opens with a description of domestic bliss, and apparently well-ordered family life. The author describes a spring morning in the Vanstone household in Coombe-Raven, Somerset. However, it is a safe assumption to make, that if a novel opens with a scene of content, comfort and social equilibrium, that condition will soon change. *No Name* is no exception and this first scene of peaceful family life is soon to collapse. This is the first example of the difference which separates appearance from reality in the novel. More than 'the steady ticking of the clock, and the lumpish snoring' of the family dog disturbs the peace and quiet of the Vanstone family.[2]

There are quite a number of indications in the first few chapters of the novel that the apparent equilibrium in Coombe-Raven is not too well sustained. The novel is positive about Mr Vanstone but it should be noticed that he is nothing at all like a sober Victorian burgher and *pater familias*.

Tall, stout, and upright – with bright blue eyes, and healthy florid complexion – his brown plush shooting-jacket carelessly buttoned awry; his vixenish little Scotch terrier barking unrebuked at his heels; one hand thrust into his waistcoat pocket, and the other smacking the bannisters cheerfully as he came down stairs humming a tune – Mr. Vanstone showed his character on the surface of him freely to all men. An easy, hearty, handsome, good-humoured gentleman, who walked on the sunny side of the way of life, and who asked nothing better than to meet all his fellow-passengers in this world on the sunny side, too. Estimating him by years, he had turned fifty. Judging him by lightness of heart, strength of constitution, and capacity for enjoyment, he was no older than most men who have only turned thirty.[3]

Vanstone may show his character 'on the surface of him' but it is also worth bearing in mind that there is a discrepancy between his chronological age and his temperament, which is that of a thirty-year-old man. Miss Garth, the governess, seems to personify an opposite character trait. Although only forty she dresses and has all the appearance of an old woman. Miss Garth actually looks older than she really is.

No observant eyes could have surveyed Miss Garth without

seeing at once that she was a north countrywoman. Her hard-featured face; her masculine readiness and decision of movement; her obstinate honesty of look and manner, all proclaimed her border birth and border training. Though little more than forty years of age, her hair was quite gray; and she wore over it the plain cap of an old woman. Neither hair nor head-dress was out of harmony with her face – it looked older than her years.[4]

It is also worth recording that Miss Garth is credited with a 'masculine readiness'; she is a woman but has some of the characteristics of a man. Some of this she shares with Magdalen, one of her old pupils. There are suggestions in the description of Vanstone's younger daughter which again indicate a possible turbulence in the family. Magdalen is certainly no stereotype.

The eyes, which should have been dark, were incomprehensibly and discordantly light; they were of that nearly colorless gray which, though little attractive in itself, possesses the rare compensating merit of interpreting the finest gradations of thought, the gentlest changes of feeling, the deepest trouble of passion, with a subtle transparency of expression which no darker eyes can rival. Thus quaintly self-contradictory in the upper part of her face, she was hardly less at variance with established ideas of harmony in the lower. Her lips had the true feminine delicacy of form, her cheeks the lovely roundness and smoothness of youth – but the mouth was too large and too firm, the chin too square and massive for her sex and age. . . . The whole countenance – so remarkable in its strongly opposed characteristics – was rendered additionally striking by its extraordinary mobility. The large, electric, light-gray eyes were hardly ever in repose; all varieties of expression followed each other over the plastic, ever changing face, with a giddy rapidity which left sober analysis far behind in the race. Her figure – taller than her sister's, taller than the average of a woman's height; instinct with such a reductive, serpentine suppleness, so lightly and playfully graceful, that its movements suggested, not unnaturally, the movements of a young cat – her figure was so perfectly developed already that no one who saw her could have supposed that she was only eighteen.[5]

Magdalen's appearance belies her age and she is taller than average for a woman. Her chin and mouth also detract from her ideal femininity and her 'plastic, ever changing face' is matched in her 'serpentine suppleness' of movement. Her eyes too are rarely at rest and it does seem difficult to account for this 'self-contradictory' girl. Her name itself, of course, suggests both penitence and transgression so that when she becomes an actress later in the novel the theatrical metaphor equates the actress with the whore. Magdalen's plastic features, which are foregrounded here indicate much of what is to come as they suggest acting ability.

Despite the apparent order of life in Coombe-Raven, 'Magdalen was born with all the senses – except a sense of order' and this is apparent in her 'flighty disregard of all punctuality'.[6] Things are not at all as settled as they, at first, appear. As Mr Vanstone remarks to Miss Garth, 'the sexes are turned topsy-turvy with a vengeance; and the men will have nothing left for it but to stop at home and darn the stockings'.[7] Miss Garth wonders to herself what is going on and her explanation is indicative of things to come. 'What does it mean? Change? I suppose I'm getting old. I don't like change.'[8] Miss Garth is no longer sure she can appreciate what is happening. Things no longer correspond, so that 'If a stranger had entered the house that day, he might have imagined that an unexpected disaster had happened in it, instead of an unexpected necessity for a journey to London.'[9] Magdalen may have had a 'subtle, transparency of expression' but it soon becomes obvious that little is transparent in No Name. This is compounded for us when Miss Garth, accompanied by Norah and Magdalen, encounter Captain Wragge for the first time. Again Wragge is a figure of contradiction. Collins first draws attention to his surface appearance. 'What did he look like, on the face of him? He looked like a clergyman in difficulties.' The contradictions continue, characterised 'by eyes of two different colors – one bilious green, one bilious brown, both sharply intelligent' and are fully exemplified in the difference between seeing him from the front or from behind.

The front view of him was the view in which he looked oldest; meeting him face to face, he might have been estimated at fifty or more. Walking behind him, his back and shoulders were almost young enough to have passed for five and thirty.[10]

The novel consists of an entire series of motifs, which on the one hand suggest the difficulty of apprehension and, yet, on the other suggest that there is no difficulty, and, with a little patience, all enigmas may be resolved. For example, in the preface, Collins writes that 'these pages [have] been constructed on a plan which differs from the plan followed in my last novel, and in some other of my works published at an earlier date. The only Secret contained in this book is revealed midway in the first volume'.[11] And this is confirmed by a direct statement in the novel itself.

> Nothing in this world is hidden for ever. The gold which has lain for centuries unsuspected in the ground, reveals itself one day on the surface. Sand turns traitor, and betrays the footstep that has passed over it; water gives back to the tell-tale surface the body that has been drowned. Fire itself leaves the confession, in ashes, of the substance consumed in it. Hate breaks its prison-secrecy in the thoughts, through the door-way of the eyes; and Love finds the Judas who betrays it by a kiss. Look where we will, the inevitable law of revelation is one of the laws of nature: the lasting preservation of a secret is a miracle which the world has never yet seen.[12]

The secret which Collins refers to in the preface is soon revealed and is a secret involving names. Through an unfortunate early marriage Andrew Vanstone leaves his daughters unprovided for in his will. Not only do Norah and Magdalen lose all their wealth, but they also lose their names. This becomes clear in a letter from Miss Garth to Mr Pendril, the family solicitor.

> The last time you were so good as to come to this house, do you remember how Magdalen embarrassed and distressed us by questioning you about her right to bear her father's name? Do you remember her persisting in her inquiries, until she had forced you to acknowledge that, legally speaking, she and her sister had No Name?[13]

I will now proceed with an investigation into the significance of names in this novel and will advance the thesis that behind this problem of nomination lurks the appearance/reality debate.

Because Andrew Vanstone's will predated his marriage to the

girl's mother, they were automatically disinherited and rendered nameless on a legal technicality. In fact the legal system took away their identities and left them 'Nobody's children' with no name. It is a fact of the nineteenth-century world that the legal system is empowered to do just this. The law is authorised to take from people their identity as subjects. The entire organisation of society, supported by the legal system, is determined by this category of the fixed subject. And it is a specifically masculine force which comes from the Father. With the death of the Father, in this case Noel Vanstone, his daughters lose their sense of themselves as subjects and individuals. Things become indeterminate and the coordinates of appearance and reality are confused. This confusion is usually avoided when people have a sense of themselves as subjects.

In a famous essay the French Marxist philosopher, Louis Althusser identifies the subject as 'constitutive of all ideology'[14] and it is part of the function of ideology in society to ensure that the relations of production are guaranteed: 'it is by an apprenticeship in a variety of know-how wrapped up in a massive inculcation of the ideology of the ruling class that the *relations of the production* in a capitalist social formation, i.e. the relations of exploited to exploiters, are largely produced'.[15] The category of the subject is essential for this smooth running of society and this categorisation ensures that people know their place in society. Thus the state guarantees the continuation of the relations of production and hence its own survival as a viable organisation.

No Name undermines this entire social-ideological fabrication. When Magdalen Vanstone discovers that, in the eyes of the law, she has no name, that she is a character, an individual but not a legal subject, her role in society becomes problematic. There are normally a fixed number of roles for the individual in society and the direction in which an individual may act as a subject is decided by a selection of social norms. Previous to her father's death, Magdalen, as legal subject, was a young heiress, an eligible young woman who should have been searching for a husband among the rich young men of the neighbourhood. That this is the role that is expected of her is made clear by the upset she causes when she declares her intention of marrying the unfortunate Frank Clare, the son of a good family, but without a penny to his name. The marriage is agreed to but Frank must first make his fortune.

Magdalen's name, resonant with Biblical significance, suggests possibilities of sin and redemption. She begins with a name over-determined by these cultural connotations only to have the law deprive her of any name at all. But, rather than accept her fate and take refuge with her old governess, Miss Garth, Magdalen decides to regain the family wealth by whatever means come to hand. She refuses the status quo, the laws of legitimacy which grant her the meagre sum of £100 and cast her into the world an unprotected woman. This is Magdalen's first offence against society. Evidently, she does not appreciate that for the smooth running of the community, the law must have its ways. She is convinced that it is possible to fly in the face of the law and recoup all that she considers to be rightly hers, rightfully in a sense which undermines the law of the land and makes it appear a nonsense. It is at this point that the relativity of society's value system is made apparent. First, and foremost the law protects property and it is little concerned with the individual justice of a particular case. It is Captain Wragge who points out to Magdalen that, because what she is attempting is so unconventional, despite the justice of her case, only a rogue can help her. An honest man would be on the side of the law.

> "For the sake of argument, let us say I am a Rogue. What is Mr. Huxtable?"
>
> "A respectable man, or I should not have seen him in the house where we first met."
>
> "Very good. Now observe! You talked of writing to Mr. Huxtable a minute ago. What do you think a respectable man is likely to do with a young lady who openly acknowledges that she has run away from her home and her friends to go on the stage? My dear girl, on your own showing, its not a respectable man you want in your present predicament. It's a Rogue – like me."[16]

Once Magdalen has taken the decision to dispute the distribution of her father's estate, she must enter a world very different from that of her childhood in the country-house at Coombe-Raven. Necessarily her life changes completely, and more to the point, she changes her name. It is this change of name which marks her transformation. Wragge records this in his journal.

> The trifling responsibility of finding a name for our talented Magdalen to perform under has been cast on my shoulders. She feels no interest whatever in this part of the subject. "Give me any name you like," she said; "I have as much right to one as another. Make it yourself." I have readily consented to gratify her wishes.[17]

Deprived of her father's name, Magdalen loses all interest in what she should be called. She feels she has no right to any particular name as all names are but social practice and, if she cannot have her original name, she is prepared to leave the matter with Wragge. Once removed, as a legal subject, from the dominant social establishment, Magdalen no longer has official identity as Magdalen Vanstone and her new role as an actress requires that she have a new name. One of the primary metaphors in the novel for the ironic relation between appearance and reality is again the theatrical and this 'acting a part' rehearses the Althusserian notion of subjectivity.

In Coombe-Raven, Magdalen's ability as a mimic was something to be discouraged, but this dramatic ability now allows her to switch roles quickly and it is significant that each role has its accompanying name. When she goes in disguise to visit Noel Vanstone she introduces herself as Miss Garth. Even more telling is the conversation between Admiral Bartram and Magdalen. She has managed to smuggle herself into the admiral's house as his new parlour-maid and, true to form, she has again changed her name. This time, she is to be called Louisa, the name of her own former maid. She introduces herself to the admiral as Louisa but he will not hear of it.

> "Ay! ay! ay! here's the new parlour-maid, to be sure!" he began, looking sharply, but not at all unkindly, at Magdalen. "What's your name, my good girl? Louisa is it? I shall call you Lucy, if you don't mind."[18]

Here the process of naming is given an apt demonstration. Let us ignore, for a moment, the fact that Magdalen is not using her 'real' name in the first place. The admiral is meeting a **new** servant called Louisa and in the social contract they establish between them, the servant must lose some of her identity as an individual and a free subject. Some of her autonomy must be sacrificed, and she must be willing to place the admiral's interests before her own. This is marked by the change of name. Louisa identifies the woman as a free individual. Lucy is her new identity as a servant. The admiral, as employer, is allowed to change her identity at will. The servant is passive and is not allowed to act as a free agent.

Normally people have one name and one identity which, for all practical purposes, is fixed and finds its level in the organisation of the social world. In fact, for society to function as a viable whole it is essential that people recognise their identity and fulfil their proper roles. As Althusser explains, the entire thrust of ideology is to ensure that this happens. *No Name* makes us aware of the importance of naming and its functioning in society. When Magdalen is declared illegitimate and has no name, she not only moves out of but also, beyond social codification, and reality, for her, becomes a very arbitrary structure. Names normally fix character and while the novel demonstrates just how arbitrary this may be, Collins also utilises names in their more traditional function. At the end of the day when all Magdalen's plans have come to nothing and she is about to be shifted to the poor house she is saved from this tragic fate by a Captain Kirke, a name suggesting the staunchness of the Protestant faith. Kirke has fallen in love with Magdalen sometime before in Aldborough. Significantly, too, the man who comes to her rescue is also the master of a vessel called 'Deliverance'. The importance of names is recognised by the characters themselves. When Old Mazey finds Magdalen snooping among the Admiral's private papers he immediately refers to her as 'young Jezebel'.[19] Magdalen/Louisa/Lucy now functions in another role. Even in the most traditional way, Collins provides insight into the functioning of names in the novel. Frank Clare, the young neighbour, is generally well thought of by most of the Vanstone family. Nora is the exception and this is explained by Collins.

The example thus set by the master of the house was followed at once by the family – with the solitary exception of Norah, whose incurable formality and reserve expressed themselves, not too graciously, in her distant manner towards the visitor. The rest (led by Magdalen who had been Frank's favourite playfellow in past times glided back into their old easy habits with him, without an effort. He was "Frank" with all of them but Norah, who persisted in addressing him as "Mr. Clare."[20]

In *No Name* these difficulties are investigated in terms of appearance and reality. Andrew Vanstone's family, to all intents and purposes, personifies bourgeois respectability, but, this only serves to conceal the fact that Vanstone's marriage is not legal. The couple may be in love, considerate towards their children, pillars of the local community, but the fact is, that in legal terms they are not married. And the law must be satisfied otherwise it will have its revenge. Life must be organised around the dictates of the law rather than the dictates of the heart and the emotions. The law determines how we should lead our lives and a challenge to the law is an attack on society itself. Despite the fact that Vanstone wanted his children to inherit his wealth, the law punishes him and his family for ignoring it for so long. This apparently happy family count for nothing when confronted with the reality of the legal world. Papers, documents and government decrees, ultimately the state, rule the individual and little attention is paid to the justice of an isolated case. Miss Garth archly raises this very point just before Mr Pendril, the lawyer, arrives at Coombe-Raven. Magdalen had objected to the governess's interference in her courtship.

"Mr. Pendril is coming tomorrow; and Mr. Vanstone seems remarkably anxious about it. Law, and its attendant troubles already! Governesses who look in at summer-house doors are not the only obstacles to the course of true-love. Parchment is sometimes an obstacle. I hope you may find Parchment as pliable as I am – I wish you well through it."[21]

Magdalen's struggle to regain the inheritance which she feels belongs to Norah and herself is a confrontation with parchment. The legal world is not interested in the actual existence of things but only in these things as they are represented on paper. Andrew Vanstone was a happily married man – only the law would deny it. But the law has the last word. Magdalen's marriage to Noel is expedient and loveless but it is a relationship which is fully endorsed by the law. This is the vital difference. The law which refused to countenance her parent's relationship will support her own unhappy liaison through thick and thin. Magdalen draws attention to this anomaly in a letter to Miss Garth. The legal world which refused her protection when she was an innocent victim of circumstance will now offer her its protection. And yet, to gain this legal sponsorship, Magdalen had, at first, to flout the law. However, she was particularly careful not to overstep 'the general sense of propriety', the appearance of things, which glosses the contradictions in society. It was this sense of propriety which her parents had ignored.

> My position has altered. I am no longer the poor outcast girl, the vagabond public performer, whom you once hunted after. I have done what I told you I would do – I have made the general sense of propriety my accomplice this time. Do you know who I am? I am a respectable married woman, accountable for my actions to nobody under heaven but my husband. I have got a place in the world, and a name in the world at last. Even the law, which is the friend of all you respectable people, has recognised my existence, and has become *my* friend too! The Archbishop of Canterbury gave me his license to be married, and the vicar of Aldborough performed the service. If I found your spies following me in the street, and I chose to claim protection from them, the law would acknowledge my claim. You forget what wonders my wickedness has done for me. It has made Nobody's Child Somebody's Wife.[22]

In the light of what has been said at the beginning of this chapter it is interesting that Magdalen should equate a place in the world with a name in the world and that she should parallel the Church and law in this manner. Both institutions are concerned with propriety and the corresponding preservation of the laws of property, and it is via the operation of such systems that the individual finds a sense of identity. Magdalen's father had a perfect marriage in all but the fact that it required official validation. Her own marriage is a farce but it is legally recognised. This gives her an identity; she is now a person, whereas before she had to exist in a world where there was no legal subject called Magdalen Vanstone. If appearance is all, it is the case that all value is arbitrary and relative. The best of motives can have the worst of consequences; the end can justify the means, as above when Magdalen must lie and cheat to win legal recognition and a place in society.

This world-view is best represented by Captain Wragge,

Magdalen's suspect mentor and guardian in the course of her various deceptions. Wragge is a self-confessed rogue and moral agriculturalist, 'a man who cultivates the field of human sympathy'.[23] On one level he is a swindler, but he can justify his behaviour in a way which makes a nonsense of Christian charity. He is master of rhetoric and can use language in such a fashion that there is a gulf between his meaning and a more general appreciation of language. Parodying Christianity, as he later parodies Utilitarianism, he forces the community to do its duty by being charitable to him.

> "Now, observe," he began. "Here am I, a needy object. Very good. Without complicating the question by asking how I come to be in that condition, I will merely inquire whether it is, or is not, the duty of a Christian community to help the needy. If you say No, you simply shock me; and there is an end of it. If you say Yes, then I beg to ask, Why am I to blame for making a Christian community do its duty? You may say, Is a careful man who has saved money bound to spend it again on a careless stranger who has saved none? Why of course he is! And on what ground, pray? Good heavens! On the ground that he *got* the money, to be sure. All the world over, the man who has not got the thing, obtains it, on one pretence or another, of the man who has – and, in nine cases out of ten, the pretence is a false one. What! your pockets are full, and my pockets are empty; and you refuse to help me? Sordid wretch! do you think I will allow you to violate the sacred obligations of charity in my person? I won't allow you – I say distinctly, I don't allow you. Those are my principles as a moral agriculturalist.[24]

Wragge's appeal for justification of his actions is unnervingly plausible. He can call on the best values of society to justify his actions, actions which, nevertheless, amount to swindling. Despite appearance the reality is that he remains a rogue. Yet this is unsettling because he is also a representative of the entrepreneurial side of capitalism, the progressive force of the nineteenth century. He is the up and coming nineteenth-century man. His defence of his actions is the vindication of the nineteenth-century business man. This is disturbing, however, because Collins lets us see that, whatever the appearance, Wragge is still a rogue at heart. But he can still argue his case and give himself the appearance of a legitimate business man. Defending himself to Magdalen, he explains that she should not 'think me mercenary – I merely understand the age I live in'.[25] Collins uses Wragge to point to some of the contradictions which are at the centre of the industrialisation and commercialisation of society. It is significant that when Wragge makes his fortune with his notorious Pill, he takes full advantage of the power of advertising. There is undoubtedly a covert criticism of this new industry in the exposition. The advertising industry emphasises appearance and its claims for its products has often little purchase on the actual effectivity of the goods. Wragge's exaggerated claims for his wonder-drug seems a case in point. He describes his publicity campaign to Magdalen.

> "It's no laughing matter to the public, my dear," he said. "They can't get rid of me and my Pill; they must take us. There is not a single form of appeal in the whole range of human advertisement which I am not making to the unfortunate public at this moment. Hire the last new novel, there I am, inside the boards of the book. Send for the last new Song – the instant you open the leaves, I drop out of it. Take a cab – I fly in at the window in red. Buy a box of tooth-powder at the chemist's – I wrap it up for you in blue. Show yourself at the theatre – I flutter down on you in yellow. The mere titles of my advertisements are quite irresistible. Let me quote a few from last week's issue. Proverbial Title: 'A Pill in time saves Nine.' Familiar Title: 'Excuse me, how is your stomach?' Patriotic Title: 'What are the three characteristics of a true-born Englishman? His Hearth, his Home, and His Pill.' Title in the form of a nursery dialogue: 'Mamma, I am not well.' 'What is the matter my pet?' 'I want a little Pill.' Title in the form of a Historical Anecdote: 'New Discovery in the Mine of English History. When the Princes were smothered in the Tower, their faithful attendant collected all their possessions left behind them. Among the touching trifles dear to the poor boys, he found a tiny Box. It contained the Pill of the Period. It is necessary to say how inferior that Pill was to its successor, which prince and peasant alike may now obtain?' – Et caetera, et caetera."[26]

What was once only available to princes is now sold to the general public. Wragge's production of the Pill seems to encapsulate all of the advantages of industrial and democratic progress. He opens up a shop with an exposed front, submitting his employees to public gaze. It is a good description of alienated labour in an industrialising society.

> The place in which my Pill is made is an advertisement in itself. I have got one of the largest shops in London. Behind one counter (visible to the public through the lucid medium of plate-glass) are four-and-twenty young men, in white aprons, making the Pill. Behind another counter are four-and-twenty young men, in white cravats, making the boxes. At the bottom of the shop are three elderly accountants, posting the vast financial transactions accruing from the Pill in three enormous ledgers. Over the door are my name, portrait, and autograph expanded to colossal proportions, and surrounded in flowing letters, by the motto of the establishment, 'Down with the Doctors!'[27]

It is true that the workers are visible to the world through the 'lucid medium of plate-glass' but Wragge's name is superimposed above all this and despite the real contribution of the workforce in the manufactory of the Pill, the real credit seems to go to the individual entrepreneur himself. Despite the fact that the workers are fully visible, they are still dominated by Wragge.

Nobody should doubt Wragge's ability always to have the correct appearance. A true personification of the spirit of commerce, he has a note-book which he consults to insure that he will not fall foul of the law. It is his habit to register his exploits in a ledger and so avoid the possible repetition of his deals in the same town. This magic book-keeping extends to his identity and it is here that some of the strands outlined above begin to converge. Appearance and reality correspond with the identity and name which Wragge assumes. It is in this area that he is of such use to Magdalen when she wishes to change her identity in her attempt to marry Noel Vanstone. Wragge refers to these different identities as 'different skins' in his journal.

> "Our new name has been chosen with a wary eye to your suggestion. My books – I hope you have not forgotten my Books? – contain, under the heading of *Skins To Jump Into*, a list of individuals retired from this mortal scene, with whose names, families, and circumstances I am well acquainted. Into some of those Skins I have been compelled to Jump, in the exercise of my profession, at former periods of my career. Others are still in the condition of new dresses, and remain to be tried on. The Skin

which will exactly fit us originally clothed the bodies of a family named Bygrave. I am in Mr. Bygrave's skin at the moment – and it fits without a wrinkle. If you will oblige me by slipping into Miss Bygrave (Christian name, Susan); and if you will afterward push Mrs. Wragge – anyhow; head foremost if you like – into Mrs. Bygrave (Christian name, Julia), the transformation will be complete."[28]

Wragge, with his constant ability to adopt the correct position in society, is the ultimate accolade to Victorian commerce. Capitalism, as personified by Wragge, is a matter of false representation even to the point of impersonating the dead. Jumping into other people's skins is a metaphor for jumping into the grave. At the end of the novel, he presents himself to Magdalen as 'a grand Financial Fact. Here I am, with my clothes positively paid for; with a balance at my banker's; with my servant in livery, and my gig at the door; solvent, flourishing, popular – and all on a Pill'.[29]

Yet, despite this apparent success, Wragge is a rogue, a parody of the values he appears to endorse. Collins draws this burlesque figure so successfully that he appears to be the genuine article. The novelist has to resort to quite awkward means to remind the reader that, while Wragge is a 'grand Financial Fact' and may utilise current, commerical mannerisms, it is a mere mechanical production and differs totally from any genuine application of such methods.

He opened one of the books. Magdalen was no judge of the admirable correctness with which the accounts inside were all kept; but she could estimate the neatness of the handwriting, the regularity in the rows of figures, the mathematical exactness of the ruled lines in red and black ink, the cleanly absence of blots, stains or erasures. Although Captain Wragge's inborn sense of order was in him – as it is in others – a sense too inveterately mechanical to exercise any elevating moral influence over his actions, it had produced its legitimate effect on his habits, and had reduced his rogueries as strictly to method and system as if they had been the commercial transactions of an honest man.[30]

It is here that there is the suggestion of an indictment of Utilitarianism. Wragge's operations have all the appearance of respectable business practice but it is an appropriation of these actions beyond the standard moral coordinates. His book-keeping reaches its apogee when he records his financial dealings with Magdalen. This is during the time she works as an actress and Wragge is her manager. His sense of appearance becomes very convoluted indeed. Magdalen's false representation of herself as an actress on the stage is echoed in Wragge's manipulation of the accounts. Wragge is cheating her and not only does he record the apparent profits from the performance as he reports them to Magdalen, but he also notes the actual profits and the actual divisions of the dividends –

Financial Statement	Third Week in January
Place Visited Newark	Performances Two
Net Receipts, In black and white £25	Net Receipts Actually Realised £32.10s.
Apparent Division of Profits Miss V .... £12.10 Self £12.10	Actual Division of Profits Miss V .... £12.10 Self £20.00

Private Surplus of the Week
Or Say
Self-presented Testimonial
£7.10s.

Audited, H. Wragge	Passed correct, H. Wragge [31]

All this is in his own chronicle, presumably for his eyes only. This mechanical reproduction of the commercial ethic is followed up even more because Wragge signs this peculiar account passing it as correct. This may well be an example of the complexities of the Protestant conscience, but for my purposes, bearing in mind that Protestantism marches in step with mercantilism, it is sufficient to underline the weight which Wragge places on appearance.[32] As it transpires in the course of the novel, Magdalen knew all along that she was being swindled, so Wragge was keeping up appearance for himself alone.

At another point in his journal he recounts how he feels he has met his match in a Derby music seller. He needs financial aid at this point, and, though unwilling to have a third party in his dealings, he finds consolation in the fact that he may swindle the music dealer. But:

> The music seller extorts my unwilling respect. He is one of the very few human beings I have met in the course of my life who is not to be cheated. He has taken a masterly advantage of our helplessness; and has imposed terms on us, for performances at Derby and Nottingham, with such a business-like disregard of all interests but his own, that – fond as I am of putting things down in black and white – I really can not prevail upon myself to record the bargain.[33]

Here the point is reached, where it seems that the reality of the situation is such that, not even Wragge can accommodate the facts in a suitable masking form. This is the nadir of Wragge's career in the novel. But he is still not beaten, and, as events develop, he is once again master of the situation. For example, when he opens the campaign to convince Mrs Lecount that Magdalen would be an eligible wife for Noel Vanstone, he appears to take the young man into his confidence. He explains to Noel that he is playing a role, attempting to ensure that events are represented correctly, and he describes his part in the drama as a matter of taking off his 'honest English coat' and dressing in a 'Jesuit gown'.[34] This Jesuit gown must be seen in a very broad light because Wragge adopts a range of strategy in the process of ingratiating himself with Mrs Lecount. He explains one of his plans to Magdalen. Mrs Lecount's weakness

> . . . if she has such a thing at all, is a taste for science, implanted by her deceased husband, the professor. I think I see a chance here of working my way into her good graces, and casting a little needful dust into those handsome black eyes of hers. Acting on this idea when I purchased a lady's tea at Ipswich, I also bought on my own account that far-famed pocket-manual of knowledge, 'Joyce's Scientific Dialogues.' Possessing, as I do, a quick memory and boundless confidence in myself, I propose privately inflating

my new skin with as much ready-made science as it will hold, and presenting Mr. Bygrave to Mrs. Lecount's notice in the character of the most highly informed man she has met with since the professor's death.[35]

Wragge is a difficult man to fix yet his eventual success suggests that his chameleon character is one which is best able to interpret his times. His unfathomable nature is made clear in a description of his clothes. Even his jacket colludes with the sense of disguise and counterfeit, it hides 'the dark secret of its master's linen from the eyes of a prying world'.[36] It is appropriate that his business should be to conceal the truth from people and disguise reality. He throws dust in Mrs Lecount's eyes with an affected knowledge of science just as he will win others to his side with the advertising campaign for the Pill.

Life as it is represented in *No Name* is counter and difficult and it is suggested that it is very foolish to draw conclusions from a superficial reading of events. This is made clear early in the novel when Miss Garth is seeking to console herself during the time Magdalen is taking part in the amateur dramatics.

> No well-regulated mind ever draws its inference in a hurry; Miss Garth's mind was well regulated; therefore, logically speaking, Miss Garth ought to have been superior to the weakness of rushing at conclusions. She has committed that error, nevertheless, under present circumstances. In plainer terms, the consoling reflection which had just occurred to her, assumed that the play had by this time survived all its disasters, and entered on its long-deferred career of success. The play had done nothing of the sort. Misfortune and the Marrable family had not parted company yet.[37]

It is only 'practised eyes'[38] which can sometimes go beyond the immediate appearance and find the truth. There are many motifs in the novel which emphasise the care which must be exercised in the reading of events. Noel Vanstone lectures a servant on this very subject. 'Don't you know the value of words? The most dreadful consequences sometimes happen from not knowing the value of words.'[39] It is worth keeping this caveat in mind when reading the novel. Even in one of the most 'straightforward' documentary sections, the passage may be read in a fashion which suggests it is more in key with the mood of the novel than may at first appear. Collins is drawing attention to the wretched living standards of the London poor. He focuses on Lambeth.

> The net-work of dismal streets stretching over the surrounding neighborhood contains a population for the most part of the poorer order. In the thoroughfares where shops abound, the sordid struggle with poverty shows itself unreservedly on the filthy pavement; gathers its forces through the week; and, strengthening to a tumult on Saturday night, sees the Sunday morning dawn in murky gas-light. Miserable women, whose faces never smile, haunt the butchers' shops in such London localities as these, with relics of the men's wages saved from the public house clutched fast in their hands, with eyes that devour the meat they dare not buy, with eager fingers that touch it covetously, as the fingers of their richer sisters touch a precious stone. In this district, as in other districts remote from the wealthy quarters of the metropolis, the hideous London vagabond – with the filth of the street outdirtied in his clothes – lounges, lowering and brutal, at the street corner and the gin-shop door; the public disgrace of his country, the unheeded warning of social troubles that are yet to come. Here, the loud self-assertion of Modern Progress – which has reformed so much in manners, and altered so little in men – meets the flat contradiction that scatters its pretensions to the winds. Here, while the national prosperity feasts, like another Belshazzar, on the spectacle of its own magnificence, is the Writing on the Wall, which warns the monarch, Money, that his glory is weighed in the balance, and his power found wanting.[40]

Obviously, there is overt social concern expressed in this passage. And the poor are not the only 'disgrace' to the nation. There are cruel words about the laws of legitimacy as Mr Pendril makes clear to Miss Garth.

"A cruel law, Mr. Pendril – a cruel law in a Christian country."

"Cruel as it is, Miss Garth, it stands excused by a shocking peculiarity in this case. I am far from defending the law of England as it affects illegitimate offspring. On the contrary, I think it a disgrace to the nation. It visits the sins of the parents on the children; it encourages vice by depriving fathers and mothers of the strongest of all motives for making the atonement of marriage; and it claims to produce these two abominable results in the names of morality and religion.[41]

Morality and religion are façades which allow for this 'disgrace to the nation' and this argument has much in common with the thoughts expressed about the poor in Lambeth. Here the excuse is 'Modern Progress', 'national prosperity' and 'Money' and the poor are to be ignored or considered as unavoidable consequences of these greater goods and social advance. But Collins is actually arguing that in Lambeth is to be found the reality of Victorian progress. Prosperity is an illusion and a mere appearance. It is in these poorer parts of London that the true results of progress are to be found. Riches and wealth, significantly imaged as a 'spectacle', are a mask which conceals the reality of the situation. Rather than allow the Victorian burgher to rest easy, Collins warns that the situation in Lambeth proves that all is far from well. Behind the complacency allowed by wealth and splendour, it is implied, the rule of capital is challenged. 'Modern progress' has only managed to change appearance, outwardly a minority may have become more polite, but society is still riddled with contradiction. The 'Writing on the Wall', the signs for the future, is that the 'flat contradiction' of 'Modern Progress' will guarantee its downfall.

Little can be taken at face value; appearance is not to be trusted. Above, there is a discussion of the pliability of the law, of parchment. It was concluded that the legal system allowed for little oscillation, that it was rigid and held to its dictates ignoring the subtleties of justice. The law provided a respectable appearance and this appearance paid scant regard to the actuality of any particular case. However, at one point in the novel, even the infallibility of legal documentation is called into question. Mr Loscombe, Magdalen's solicitor, has been instructed to examine her husband's will. Subsequently he reports to Magdalen.

"Simple as they may seem to you, these are very remarkable words. In the first place, no practical lawyer would have used them in drawing your husband's will. In the second place, they are utterly useless to serve any plain straightforward purpose. The legacy is left unconditionally to the admiral; and in the same breath he is told that he may do what he likes with it! The phrase points clearly to one of two conclusions. It has either dropped from the writer's pen in pure ignorance, or it has been carefully set where it appears to serve the purpose of a snare. I am firmly persuaded that the latter explanation is the right one. The words are expressly intended to mislead some person – yourself in all probability – and the cunning which has put them to that use is a cunning which (as constantly happens when uninstructed persons meddle with law) has overreached itself. My thirty years' experience reads those words in a sense exactly opposite to the sense which they are intended to convey."[42]

This is a rather paradoxical situation. Words are used in such a way in a legal document to convey the opposite of what they apparently say. The will in question is, in fact, a disguise and its true meaning may only be discovered when the codicil is unearthed. Just as the wealth of society is itself a mere 'spectacle' concealing a painful truth, the law, functioning for the preservation of the interests of property is a system of disguise.

This element of disguise in the law is suddenly made apparent on the death of the father, Michael Vanstone, which renders the situation and position of his daughters problematic. Where before the patriarchal system had given meaning to life, supplied the daughters with a name and a position which allowed them to negotiate their lives, the position on Vanstone's death is one of indeterminancy and confusion. Appearance and reality become confused and this confusion is given even greater prominence through the figure of Captain Wragge. But, as is usual with Collins, the major themes permeate incidental episodes in the novel and the most minor and casual occurrences contribute to the development of the major premises.

Appearance is undermined in the world of No Name. This is sometimes worked via an attack on sexual and gender stereotyping. Stereotypes give us an all too easy appropriation of reality so Miss Garth contradicts expectation and Magdalen is 'not made for the ordinary jog-trot of a woman's life'.[43] Francis Clare lacks the positive attributes of his ancestors and 'his gentle wandering brown eyes would have looked to better advantage on a woman's face – they wanted spirit and firmness to fit them for the face of a man',[44] and while Frank is handsome, it is stressed that it is 'In his own effeminate way'.[45] Noel Vanstone has a complexion which is 'as delicate as a young girl's'.[46] But not all the characters in the novel are duped by appearance. Mr Clare, Frank's father, casts a cold eye on society. He has a 'contempt for all social prejudices'[47] and 'has outlived all human prejudices'.[48] He explains his philosophy to Mr Vanstone.

"In your presence and out of it," continued Mr. Clare, "I have always maintained that the one important phenomenon presented by modern society is – the enormous prosperity of Fools. Show me an individual Fool, and I will show you an aggregate Society which gives that highly-favored personage nine chances out of ten – and grudges the tenth to the wisest man in existence. Look where you will, in every high place there sits an Ass, settled beyond the reach of all the greatest intellects in this world to pull him down. Over our whole social system, complacent Imbecility rules supreme – and hoots, owl-like, in answer to every form of protest. See how well we all do in the dark! One of these days that audacious assertion will be practically contradicted, and the whole rotten system of modern society will come down with a crash."[49]

The statistics here are interesting and are repeated later in the novel where they are linked to the concept of propriety. Miss Garth is explaining to Magdalen that Norah has lost her job as a governess. Norah's employers asked her to leave when they discovered that Magdalen was an actress and so beyond the social pale. Again the actress is seen as akin to the whore. Norah may be well out of this particular position:

But the harm does not stop here. For all you and I know to the contrary, the harm may go on. What has happened in this situation may happen in another. Your way of life, however pure your conduct may be – and I will do you the justice to believe it pure – is a suspicious way of life to all respectable people. I have lived long enough in this world to know that the sense of Propriety, in nine Englishwomen out of ten, makes no allowance and feels no pity.[50]

This sense of propriety and good appearance is a large contributing factor to what Mr Clare identifies as the dominance of 'complacent Imbecility' in society. Appearance is taken for reality and this error is further compounded because the relationship between the two is credited to the workings of Providence while in actual fact any correspondence has more to do with the blind machinations of chance. This shall all be elucidated and emphasised by focusing on several incidents in the novel.

Appearance is certainly not to be trusted. Mrs Lecount is immediately suspicious of Magdalen when she first visits Noel Vanstone. Mrs Lecount is not fooled by Magdalen's disguise and refers to the visit as 'the performance of a clever masquerade'.[51] Similarly the housekeeper has reservations about Wragge and Magdalen when they present themselves in Aldborough wearing the skins of the Bygrave family. It is during this Aldborough interlude that Wragge emphasises the need to 'keep up domestic appearances'[52] and explains Mrs Wragge's seclusion in terms of an illness which is not apparent to the eye. 'There is some remote nervous mischief which doesn't express itself externally. You would think my wife the picture of health if you looked at her, and yet, so delusive are appearances, I am obliged to forbid her all excitement.'[53] Mrs Lecount is far from satisfied by these explanations and queries them in terms of surface meaning and deep truth, of appearance attempting to conceal reality.

> An incomprehensible resemblance to some unremembered voice in the niece; an unintelligible malady which kept the aunt secluded from public view; and extraordinary range of scientific cultivation in the uncle, associated with a coarseness and audacity of manner which by no means suggested the idea of a man engaged in studious pursuits – were the members of this small family of three, what they seemed on the surface of them?[54]

Appearance may be completely deceptive. Wragge and Mrs Lecount maintain a truce when they go on picnic together with Noel and Magdalen and the true state of relations between them bears no resemblance to the way they behave.

> Mrs. Lecount accepted the proposal. She was perfectly well aware that her escort had lost himself on purpose, but that discovery exercised no disturbing influence on the smooth amiability of her manner. Her day of reckoning with the captain had not come yet – she merely added the new item to her list, and availed herself of the campstool. Captain Wragge stretched himself in a romantic attitude at her feet, and the two determined enemies (grouped like two lovers in a picture) fell into as easy and pleasant a

conversation as if they had been friends of twenty years standing.[55]

However it seems, at times, that to flaunt this sense of propriety, the socially acceptable formulas is to fly in the face of God and risk the wrath of Providence. The female members of the congregation at Magdalen's wedding 'murmured among themselves at the inexcusable disregard of appearances implied in the bride's dress'.[56] This refusal to behave according to pattern is spelled out for us in a conversation between Magdalen's maid and a servant in the hotel.

"Did you ever hear of anything like this!" said the house-servant, entering on the subject immediately.
"Like what?"
"Like this marriage, to be sure. You're London bred, they tell me. Did you ever hear of a young lady being married without a single new thing to her back? No wedding veil, and no wedding breakfast, and no wedding favors for the servants. It's flying in the face of Providence – that's what I say. I'm only a poor servant, I know. But it's wicked, downright wicked – and I don't care who hears me!"[57]

The implication here is that appearance corresponds to reality which is God-given and to ignore it is to encroach on the divine order of the universe. However, there is also another line of argument in *No Name* which would suggest that Providence has little to do with the divine ordering of the world. Rather the correspondence of appearance with reality is more a matter of chance. Magdalen raises the issue when she decides to resolve her struggles 'by setting her life or death on the hazard of a chance'.

On what chance?
The sea showed it to her. Dimly distinguishable through the mist, she saw a little fleet of coasting-vessels slowly drifting toward the house, all following the same direction with the favoring set of the tide. In half an hour – perhaps in less – the fleet would have passed her window. The hands of her watch pointed to four o'clock. She seated herself close at the side of the window, with her back toward the quarter from which the vessels were drifting down on her – with the poison placed on the window sill, and the watch on her lap. For one half-hour to come **she**

determined to wait there and count the vessels as they went by. If in that time an even number passed her, the sign given should be a sign to live. If the uneven number prevailed, the end should be Death.

With that final resolution, she rested her head against the window, and waited for the ships to pass.

The first came, high, dark, and near in the mist, gliding silently over the silent sea. An interval – and the second followed, with the third close after it. Another interval, longer and longer drawn out – and nothing passed. She looked at her watch. Twelve minutes, and three ships. Three. The fourth came, slower than the rest, larger than the rest, farther off in the mist than the rest. The interval followed; a long interval once more. Then the next vessel passed, darkest and nearest of all. Five. The next uneven number – Five.

She looked at her watch again. Nineteen minutes, and five ships. Twenty minutes. Twenty-one, two, three – and no sixth vessel. Twenty-four, and the sixth came by. Twenty-five, twenty-six, twenty-seven, twenty-eight, and the next uneven number – the fatal Seven – glided into view. Two minutes to the end of the half-hour. And seven ships.

Twenty-nine, and nothing followed in the wake of the seventh ship. The minute-hand of the watch moved on half-way to thirty, and still the white heaving sea was a misty blank. Without moving her head from the window, she took the poison in one hand, and raised the watch in the other. As the quick seconds counted each other out, her eyes, as quick as they looked from the watch to the sea, from the sea to the watch – looked for the last time at the sea – and saw the EIGHTH ship.

She never moved, she never spoke. The death of thought, the death of feeling, seemed to have come to her already. She put back the poison mechanically on the ledge of the window, and watched, as in a dream, the ship gliding smoothly on its silent way – gliding till it melted dimly into shadow – gliding till it was lost in the mist.

The strain on her mind relaxed when the Messenger of Life had passed from her sight.

"Providence?" she whispered faintly to herself. "Or chance?"[58]

Captain Kirke answers this question for her when he finds **Magdalen** close to death in a hovel in Camden Town. Kirke has her nursed back to health and, when he realises just who she is, wonders; ' "What brought me here?" he said to himself in a whisper. "The mercy of chance? No. The mercy of God." '[59] This final accolade to Christianity may be interpreted as the ultimate acknowledgement of the correspondence of appearance with reality and the divine order of the world but it is rather flat and unconvincing when considered alongside the passage which describes how Magdalen rejects suicide. It is these nuanced resonances between Providence and chance, appearance and reality that are interrogated in *No Name*. And while Kirke does answer Magdalen's question, his all too succinct and complacent reply is a poor counter-statement to the very forceful passage where chance is given such room to operate. Kirke is allowed to focus on the mercy of God, but in the text, this belief in divine Providence is counter-balanced by this insistence on the role of chance.

7

Women in Collins

Gail Cunningham's profile of the representation of women in Victorian fiction is cogent and fair.[1] She is particularly perceptive in her observation on Dickens. At first sight it appears that

> Dickens is making out the argument found in many of the New Woman novels – that marriage is too often a sordid financial bargain, that women are forced to deck themselves out to attract the highest bidder and to go through the socially approved motions which are in essence shameful and degrading.[2]

Yet Cunningham argues that this view of marriage is actually denied in the plot. The sale of Edith to Mr Dombey, for example, 'is designed primarily as an illustration of the novel's main theme, the subordination of human affection to financial ambitions, and in the end, selflessness and generosity triumph sufficiently strongly to make the mercenaries appear as aberrations, rather than typical representatives of human conduct'.[3] Dickens may well be typical of this projection in Victorian fiction but it is not a monopoly opinion. Collins is very aware of the stereotype in art and literature and while it can only be argued in part that he anticipates the feminist consciousness of the New Woman novelists, his treatment of women in his work makes it necessary to differentiate him from any notion of a uniform mainstream. Collins' treatment of women is also complicated by the fact that his intervention may be seen as either a purely formal reaction against specifically artistic stereotyping – (literature needs more colourful female characters) – or, his dispute, with what he sees as the traditional treatment of women, may have ideological and political connotations and mark the gestation of an early feminist consciousness. Collins revamps the stereotype because it will intensify literature, give it more colour and brio and also make it approximate more tightly to life.

Collins wrote two articles for *Household Words* on this subject and they provide a good point of entry into this territory. Some care must be exercised in reading these essays as they are first person narratives, one 'Communicated by a Romantic Old Gentleman' and the other by a 'Charming Woman'.[4] This is an ironic choice of narrators given the subject matter, and, while it may allow Collins' own opinion to float free and difficult to specify, it still foregrounds the entire debate. 'A Petition to the Novel Writers' opens with a spirited and amusing defence of novels and novel reading. 'Dull people . . . people of all degrees of rank and education [who] never want to be amused . . . are the people who privately as well as publicly, govern the nation.'[5] The romantic old gentleman defends the institution of literature against these people, yet he would also like to see a little variety in the literature of the future.

Let me say something, first, about our favourite two sisters – the tall, dark one, who is serious and unfortunate: the short light one, who is coquettish and happy.

Being an Englishman, I have, of course, an ardent attachment to anything like an established rule, simply because it is established, I know that it is a rule that, when two sisters are presented in a novel, one must be tall and dark, and the other short and light. I know that five feet eight of female flesh and blood, when accompanied by an olive complexion, black eyes, and raven hair, is synonymous with strong passions and an unfortunate destiny. I know that five feet nothing, golden ringlets, soft blue eyes, and a lily brow, cannot possibly be associated by any well-constituted novelist, with anything but ringing laughter, arch innocence, and final matrimonial happiness. I have studied these great first principles of the art of fiction too long not to reverence them as established laws; but I venture respectfully to suggest that the time has arrived when it is no longer necessary to insist on them in novel after novel. I am afraid there is something naturally revolutionary in the heart of man. Although I know it to be against all precedent, I want to revolutionize our favourite two sisters. Would any bold innovator run all risks, and make them both alike in complexion and in stature? Or would any desperate man (I dare not suggest such a course to the ladies) effect an entire alteration, by making the two sisters change characters? I tremble when I see to what lengths the spirit of innovation is leading me. Would the public accept the tall, dark-haired sister, if she exhibited a jolly disposition and a tendency to be flippant in her talk? Would readers be fatally startled out of their sense of propriety if the short charmer with the golden hair appeared before them as a serious, strong-minded, fierce-spoken, miserable, guilty woman? It might be a dangerous experiment to make this change; but it would be worth trying – the rather (if I may be allowed to mention anything so utterly irrelevant to the subject under discussion as real life) because I think there is some warrant in nature for attempting the proposed innovation.[6]

As the argument is presented, the case is made that women are represented in a stereotypical fashion in literature, and actual experience of the world is then addressed to point to the fact that these literary conventions have no basis in reality. Implicitly, it is suggested that rather than reflect the world, the literary paradigms may be articulating our attitudes to the world. So, rather than describing the world in a transparent manner, literature is actually helping to create an impression of this reality and bolstering an attitude to the world which has little to do with individual experience. However, it is important to handle this problem with a certain nuance and sophistication. The question of the relationship of life to literature is vexed and fissured. 'Petition' may be objecting to the established representation of women in fiction in purely formal terms, – women should be described differently simply to add to the variety of literature, rather than as a result of more political, ideological objection. The irony of the essay, the fact that the narrator is this romantic, old gentleman complicates the issue. He is such a benign figure that it is difficult to accept that he would take political issue with the sexual status quo. Yet, there is an undercurrent of ideological distaste when the narrator evokes his own experience of the women in his family to signal the implausible description of women in novels.

Judging by my own small experience, I should say that strong minds and passionate natures reside principally in the breasts of little, light women, especially if they have angelic blue eyes and a quantity of fair ringlets. The most facetiously skittish woman, for her age, with whom I am acquainted, is my own wife, who is three inches taller than I am.[7]

So while objection is made to established images of women because literature as a form should be more varied, there is also the point that it is also untrue to life in its continual resort to outmoded paradigms in its representation of women. However, while there may be cause for a certain amount of optimism here, it must be admitted that the argument has both conservative and progressive connotations. There is also a rhetorical double-take going on in that the speaker is a romantic old gentleman whose consciousness and point of view are being distanced and satirised. But, at this point it can be said that the argument in the essay is progressive to the extent that it points to the inadequacies of the treatment of women in contemporary novels. Yet it is also conservative and reactionary in that it will only allow change in representation within certain paradigms. These paradigms are essentially masculine; women are still regarded as objects and their subservient position is emphasised.

In the article, the old gentleman takes issue with the 'established Heroine' but he is also far from happy with 'her modern successor – a bouncing, ill-conditioned, impudent young woman, . . . I venture to call this wretched and futile substitute for our dear, tender, gentle, loving old Heroine, the Man-Hater'.[8] This most recent figure is then delimited with regard to her personal attributes, all of which appear to challenge accepted behaviour and masculine complacency. Particular exception is taken to the Man-Hater because of her negative approach to marriage. The narrator is especially appalled when he considers what future this implies for his son.

> In a short time, this boy will be marriageable, and he will go into the world, to bill and coo, and offer his hand and heart, as his father did before him. My unhappy offspring, what a prospect awaits you! One forbidding phalanx of Man-Haters, bristling with woman's dignity, and armed to the teeth with maidenly consciousness, occupies the wide matrimonial field, look where you will.[9]

In search of a wife, he advises his son to ignore these women and

Go rather to the slave-market at Constantinople – buy a Circassian wife, who has heard nothing and read nothing of man-haters – bring her home (with no better dowry than pots of the famous Cream from her native land to propitiate your mother and sisters) – and trust to your father to welcome an Asiatic daughter-in-law, who will not despise him for the unavoidable misfortune of being a Man![10]

The prejudices become absurd here. Because these contemporary women, these man-haters, are refusing to be treated as commodites on the marriage-market, the narrator encourages his son to go and purchase a wife in the Constantinople slave-market. This, of course, reminds the reader of the current masculine attitude to marriage. Just why Collins has elected a 'romantic old gentleman' as narrator suddenly makes sense. The prejudice aimed at women is so great that it overdetermines racial difference. What at first appears to be a liberal, progressive manifesto transpires to be a call for the defence of an essential femininity in women.

As represented in books of the period this new heroine finds

. . . it is her mission from first to last to behave as badly as possible to every man with whom she comes into contact. She enters on the scene with a preconceived prejudice against my sex, for which I, as a man abominate her.[11]

She displays a 'maidenly consciousness' which the old gentleman finds is, for him, synonymous with 'bad manners. And I am the more confirmed in this idea, because, on all minor occasions, the Man-Hater is presistently rude and disobliging to the last'.[12] Is it too much to suggest that these women are so consistently rude because they see the world of manners and cultural behaviour as a masculine charade?

However, the old gentleman fumes on and calls for the total removal of man-haters from the novel.

The new-fashioned heroine is a libel on her sex. As a husband and father, I solemnly deny that she is in any single respect a natural woman.[13]

It is difficult to contextualise this argument, but in the fury of his declamation, the narrator attacks these new heroines on the grounds that they were not natural women. John Stuart Mill's *The Subjection of Women (1869)*, arguing for the equality of the sexes, pointed to the pressures which are put on women and the indoctrination which guarantees the perpetuation of the sex-roles.

All women are brought up from the very earliest years in the belief that their ideal of character is the very opposite to that of men; not self-will, and government by self-control, but submission, and yielding to the control of others. *All the moralities tell them that it is the duty of women, and all the current sentimentalities that it is their nature, to live for others*; to make complete abnegation of themselves, and to have no life but in their affections.[14] (my italics)

It is clear that the sentiment and morality which, Mill is arguing, contributes to the lowly situation of women is to be found in the views of Collins' romantic old gentleman. However, I feel it must be said that by giving this opinion to a 'romantic old gentleman' Collins satirises this entire argument. Thirteen years before Mill, Collins is showing how literature functions as a 'current sentimentality' which contributes to the inferior status allowed to women in society.

Interestingly, too, the man-hater is attacked because she is not a 'natural woman'. The defence of natural femininity has long been a factor in the case of all those opposed to the feminist cause. More sophisticated thinking has always pondered the distinction between 'natural' and 'cultural'. It can be argued that it is the function of ideology to present the cultural order as somehow natural, and the results of history come somehow to be equated with the notion of a fixed and permanent, general human order. Again Mill in *Subjection of Women* argues against the idea that there can be such a thing as the naturally feminine.

Women have always hitherto been kept, as far as regards spontaneous development, in so unnatural a state, that their nature cannot but have been greatly distorted and disguised; and no one can safely pronounce that if women's nature was left to choose its direction as freely as men's, and if no artificial bent were attempted to be given to it except that required by the conditions of human society, and given to both sexes alike, there would be any material difference, or perhaps any difference at all, in the character and capacities which would unfold themselves.[15]

Mill is denying the notion that there is such a thing as a 'natural woman'. Rather culture and society determine the position women occupy and literature is one of the factors which contributes to this subjection. The idea of a natural femininity is one of the elements which fixes women's position in society.

'A Petition to the Novel Writers', therefore cuts both ways. It illustrates the stereotypical nature of the representation of women in novels and demands change on the grounds that these figures have little to do with life. Yet, it also cautions and attempts to limit these changes within established masculine coordinates which see women as objects. However, because the article is narrated by a 'romantic old gentleman' it is possible to see through the limits of these very same paradigms and by drawing attention to the fact that they could belong to such a narrator, the paradigms themselves are seen as having a factional interest. They are not natural and god-given but rather reinforce the dominant order.

Of course, the fact that man-haters were now a recognised type in literature indicates that a movement was afoot which challenged literary protocol. 1868 saw the publication of Mrs Lynn Linton's article 'Girl of the Period' in the *Saturday Review*.[16] This flanking action in defence of a natural femininity argued in terms of cultural fall. It identified a time in the past when young ladies were naturally feminine, content to serve men and happy to be the angels of the hearth. This type of woman is contrasted with a kind, akin to Collins' man-haters, who have renounced all notion of the natural woman. Mrs Linton was to continue this attack elsewhere.

Possessed by a restless discontent with their appointed work, and fired with a mad desire to dabble in all things unseemly, which they call ambition; blasphemous to the sweetest virtues of their sex, which until now have been accounted both their own pride and the safeguard of society; holding it no honour to be reticent, unselfish, patient, obedient and swaggering to the front, ready to try conclusions in aggression, in selfishness, in insolent disregard of duty, in cynical abasement of modesty, with the hardest and the least estimable of the men they emulate; *these women of the doubtful gender* have managed to drop all their own special graces while unable to gather up any of the more valuable of men.[17]

Discussing this quotation, John Goode points to the equation which balances the naturally feminine with sexual attractiveness. In other words, women are still the objects of male desire and the man-hater denies this objectivity in an attempt to win her own subjectivity. It is this desire to have masculine power, to be the subject of discourse rather than the object, which is often rehearsed by Collins' female characters.

Collins returns to this subject of sexual stereotyping and the representation of women in literature in another article written for *Household Words* in 1858, entitled 'A Shockingly Rude Article'. Here the stereotypical representation of women is made explicit and once it has been recognised as a stereotype has little or no effect on the reader whatever. The narrator is discussing novels by men.

Look where I may, I find, for instance, that the large proportion of the bad characters in their otherwise very charming stories, are always men. As if women were not a great deal worse! Then, again, most of the amusing fools in their books are, strangely and unaccountably, of their own sex, in spite of its being perfectly apparent that the vast majority of that sort of character is to be found in ours. On the other hand, while they make out their own half of humanity (as I have distinctly proved) a great deal too bad, they go to the contrary extreme the other way, and make out our half a great deal too good.[18]

This may be a good thing as, if literature is seen to be so rife with stereotypes, it may be ideologically neutered and so no longer contribute to that collection of moralities, identified by Mill, which adds to the subjection of women. However, the negative connotation is that literature has little or no effect whatsoever in society and becomes a distinct series of works with no bearing on life. Collins had too much regard for his work to accept that it could only exist in a vacuum, sealed off from society.

By the time he had written these articles for *Houshold Words* he was already the author of three novels. Already in *Basil* he had

put into practice some of the points enumerated in the essays for
Dickens' magazine. Collins always had a serious and intense
commitment to literature and its effect and functioning in society.
'A Petition to the Novel-Writers' has much to say both about and
to the 'dull people' who, unfortunately rule the country and yet
refuse to read works of fiction. *A Rogue's Life* and *Armadale*
continue this discussion about the effects of literature and in *The
Evil Genius (1886)*, Collins is still arguing that good literature
should have a challenging effect on its audience. Mrs Lindley
disturbs her mother sleeping in the sitting room, a book slipping
out of her hand.

"Oh Mamma, I am so sorry! I was just too late to catch it."
    "It doesn't matter, my dear. I dare say I should go to sleep
again, if I went on with my novel."
    "Is it really as dull as that?"
    "Dull?" Mrs. Prestey repeated. "You are evidently not aware
of what the new school of novel writing is doing. The new
school provides the public with soothing fiction."
    "Are you speaking seriously, Mamma?"
    "Seriously, Catherine – and gratefully. The new writers are
so good to old women. No story to excite our poor nerves; no
improper characters to cheat us out of our sympathies; no
dramatic situations to frighten us; exquisite management of
details (as the reviews say), and a masterly anatomy of human
motives which – I know what I mean, my dear, but I can't
explain it."
    "I think I understand, Mamma. A masterly anatomy of
human motives which is itself a motive of human sleep. No; I
won't borrow your novel just now. I don't want to go to
sleep."[19]

Collins is obviously unhappy with literature as placebo and
anodyne. It has another task, and while this is overt in the later
work, overt and detrimental if we are to accept established
reading, it is argued here that even the early novels reject easy
classification within established frameworks.

I shall now discuss representations of women in a range of
Collins' novels. He is not a feminist by any means, and in *The Evil
Genius* appears to defend that *bête-noire* of the feminists, the
double standard, but what I want to suggest is that in his

representation of sexuality and gender he is consistently more sophisticated than any easy appropriation might suggest. In his description of gender, Collins is presenting an articulation of sex roles which point to their cultural determination and shows how notions of gender are constructed in society. These notions, for Collins, are the results of the reworking of various ideologies and moralities rather than reflective of essential difference. Marian Halcombe in *The Woman in White* is a fusion of masculine intellect and female physique. The lawyer, Mr Sarrazin in *The Evil Genius* exclaims to his client 'What a lawyer you will make when the rights of women invade my profession.'[20]

But to begin with *Basil*. Collins reworks, both confirming and nuancing the rule, described above, that when two sisters, two women appear in a novel, one is fair and the other is dark. The two women in this case are Basil's sister Clara and Margaret Sherwin who is so powerfully attractive to him. There is a considerable play on darkness and light in the novel and it may be read as a record of Basil's education and experience which allows him to recognise the goodness of light and put to rest his fascination with the dark. In established terms this means that he recognises the wholesomeness of the 'golden ringlets', the heroine whom the hero should marry according to literary protocol. It further insists that he break away from the impropriety of the sexual attraction offered by the dark lady, Margaret Sherwin. Collins complicates this paradigm by making the fair lady the hero's sister and also introduces a class theme by making Margaret Sherwin a linen draper's daughter. Before his involvement with Margaret, Basil speaks of 'the morning sunshine of life',[21] and in this bright, cloudless world, Clara, with her pale complexion is very appropriate. Such is her incandescent beauty that she 'eclipsed'[22] other women, and, with the advantage of hindsight, Basil images her as kindling a 'pure light' compared to the 'darkness of crime and grief' which now surrounds him. Clara's attraction is not sexual; she would not turn many heads at the opera, and few men would look after her in the street. Yet it is just such a quiet and modest appeal, not apparent on the surface, which Basil must learn to value. The normal site for sex in a novel is in the relationship between husband and wife and the family is held in high esteem. Sex is licensed between husband and wife and they bring up their children in the family unit. In *Basil* there is a strange shift in emphasis with regard to the family and sex and it appears to run counter to the original idea. Basil does retire into a quiet family life at the close of the novel but he sets up home with Clara so the possibility of sex and the generation of children is frustrated. This rather strange, sexless ménage is further complicated by the fact that, throughout the novel, Clara is a mother-substitute for Basil and so the Oedipus myth is also given a bizarre resonance. Before Basil confronts his father with his secret, Clara reminds him of her maternal regard. 'All that our mother would have done for you, if she had been still among us, *I* will do. Remember that, and keep heart and hope to the very last.'[23]

So while Clara is the fair sister (and mother), Margaret represents the other side of the equation which, tradition insists, demands an 'olive complexion, black eyes and raven hair'. Basil is attracted by Margaret's obvious beauty, yet it is an appeal which is all on the surface, all appearance and it is part of the project of the novel to educate Basil into a recognition of the fact that appearance and reality are not always synonymous. Margaret is 'tall for a woman' and

> She was dark. Her hair, eyes, and complexion were darker than usual in English women. The form, the look altogether, of her face, coupled with what I could see of her figure, made me guess her age to be about twenty. . . . The fire in her large dark eyes when she spoke was latent. . . . The smile about her full lips (to other eyes they might have looked *too* full) struggled to be eloquent, yet dared not. Among women, there always seems something left incomplete – a moral creation to be superinduced on the physical – which love alone can develop, and which maternity perfects still further when developed.[24]

Margaret's appeal is obviously sexual and as Basil studies her he wonders how she would look when pregnant. Concentrating on her lips, Basil decides that maternity would somehow complete her. He wants to make eloquent and productive those other lips and have her bear children.[25] However the novel suggests that Basil is infatuated with appearance here and this becomes clear as the novel progresses. When he eventually discovers that Mannion and Margaret are cheating on him, he finds himself in a situation which allows him to reinterpret these appearances, these surface details and finally recognises Margaret in a true *light*. As Basil recovers in his father's house he parallels his dawning consciousness of how he had been cheated and deceived with a blind person's recovery of sight.

> In the moment of their restoration, the blind have had one glimpse of light, flashing on them in an overpowering gleam of brightness, which the thickest, closest veiling cannot extinguish. . . . It was so with my mental vision. After the utter oblivion and darkness of a deep swoon, consciousness flashed like light on my mind, when I found myself in my father's presence, and in my own home. . . .
> Now instead of placing implicit trust in others, as I had done; instead of failing to discover a significance and a warning in each circumstance as it arose, I was suspicious from the first – suspicious of Margaret, of her father, of her mother, of Mannion, of the very servants in the house.[26]

From an initial opposition of darkness and light epitomised by the two young women in the novel, the paradigm is extrapolated to contain a whole series of ideological values ranging from good and evil, reality and appearance, to sensuality and asceticism or asexuality. Basil must labour his way through darkness to find the light, the truth. The original representation of the two women and its requisite association becomes analogous to the central drama of the novel.

Just after his first encounter with Margaret, Basil has a dream whose imagery condenses and reworks much of the detail discussed above. He is in a position when he must decide between two women, one translucently pure in beauty, and the other, dark and sensual. Indeed the dream seems to give imaginative fulfilment of his desires to have sex with Margaret. The dream is worth quoting at length because in the dichotomies and oppositions it reveals may be found the foundation for an entire repertoire of ideological connotation. I shall interrupt the quotation at various points to indicate how the imagery concentrates and condenses various themes. Around the cluster of fair and dark, good and evil, reality and appearance, Collins reworks the traditional representation of women and connects this with broader social concerns.

> I stood on a wide plain. On one side, it was bounded by thick

woods, whose dark secret depths looked unfathomable to the eye: on the other, by hills, ever rising higher and higher yet, until they were lost in bright, beautifully white clouds, gleaming in refulgent sunshine. On the side above the woods, the sky was dark and vaporous.

A contrast is created between black and white, dark and light together with the qualification that there are mysteries and secrets in the darkness. It is difficult to establish a sense of reality there whereas in the sunlight everything is apparent to the eye.

As I still stood on the plain and looked around, I saw a woman coming toward me from the wood. Her stature was tall; her black hair flowed about her unconfined; her robe was of the dun hue of the vapour and mist which hung above the trees, and fell to her feet in dark thick folds . . .
   I looked to the other side, toward the hill; and there was another woman descending from their bright summits; and her robe was white, and pure, and glistening. Her face was illuminated with a light, like the light of the harvest-moon.

At this point the two women are differentiated in terms of black and white with the connotations of good and evil inevitably suggesting themselves to the reader. Collins is utilising the traditional representation of women which sees them in terms of good and evil.

Meanwhile, the woman from the dark wood still approached; never pausing on her path like the woman from the fair hills. And now I could see her face plainly. Her eyes were lustrous and fascinating, as the eyes of the serpent – large, dark and soft, as the eyes of the wild doe. Her lips were parted with a languid smile; and she drew back the long hair, which lay over her cheeks, her neck, her bosom, while I was gazing on her.

The sexual attractiveness of the dark, mysterious woman begins to be foregrounded. Sexual power has long been associated with serpents and Basil's sexual curiosity is obvious from the long and lingering attention he gives to lips, cheeks, neck and bosom. This is the beginning of sexual arousal. But then conscience stirs him and he turns his attention to the white, virginal woman.

Then, I felt as if a light were shining on me from the other side. I turned to look, and there was the woman from the hills beckoning me away to ascend with her towards the bright clouds above. Her arm, as she held it forth, shone fair, even against the fair hills; and from her outstretched hand came long thin rays of trembling light, which penetrated to where I stood, cooling and calming wherever they touched me. But the woman from the woods still came nearer and nearer, until I could feel her hot breath on my face.

The fair lady from the hills is cool conscience coming to his aid in the battle with his hot passion. Conscience and purity are cool and light whereas passion is hot and dark.

This dream-scape preempts the themes of the novel and just as Basil is overawed by Margaret so it is the dark lady who is victorious in his dream. His desire for Margaret is overtly sexual in nature. He had tried to imagine how she would improve when pregnant, when he first saw her. The dream satisfies this wish and as he disappears with the dark woman into the trees, the suggestion is that they slide into sexual embrace. The secret recess is the concealed vagina.

For now the woman from the wood clasped me more closely than before, pressing her warm lips on mine; and it was as if her long hair fell round us both, spreading over my eyes like a veil, to hide from them the fair hill-tops, and the woman who was walking onward to the bright clouds above.

I was drawn along in the arms of the dark woman, with my blood burning and my breath failing me, until we entered the secret recesses that lay amid the unfathomable depths of trees. There, she encircled me in the folds of her dusky robe, and laid her cheek close to mine, and murmured a mysterious music in my ear, amid the midnight silence and darkness of all around us.[27]

Basil is blinded in the dream by his sexual passion and this is the case on a conscious level in the rest of the novel. The story is that which involves his rejection of a sexual passion which blinds him to the truth of things and the fact that Mannion and Margaret use him as a pawn in their greater plans.

Basil must also rethink his attitude to Mrs Sherwin, the other main female character in the novel. At first, Mrs Sherwin appears to him as little more than a cypher, but a cypher which suggests misery and unhappiness.

> Poor Mrs. Sherwin. . . . Her pale, sickly, moist-looking skin; her large, mild, watery, light-blue eyes; the restless timidity of her expression; the mixture of useless hesitation and involuntary rapidity in every one of her actions – all furnished the same significant betrayal of a life of incessant fear and restraint; of a disposition full of modest generosities and meek sympathies, which had been crushed down past rousing to self-assertion, past ever seeing the light.[28]

Mrs Sherwin lives in the shadows – and again the metaphor is significant – she is totally dominated by her husband, and while Basil does sympathise with her sorry state, it is an unstudied sympathy and he is glad that it is Mrs Sherwin who chaperones him and Margaret.

> She always kept far enough away to be out of hearing when we whispered to each other. We rarely detected her even in looking at us. She had a way of sitting for hours together in the same part of the room, without ever changing her position, without occupation of any kind, without uttering a word, or breathing a sigh.[29]

Basil must learn to distinguish between Mrs Sherwin's appearance as it initially strikes him and the reality of the situation. With the greater insight afforded him towards the end of the novel he realises that he had misinterpreted Mrs Sherwin.

> I saw immediately, that she suspected Mannion, and dared not openly confess her suspicions; I saw, that in the stillness, and abandonment, and self-concentration of her neglected life, she had been watching more vigilantly than others had watched; I detected in every one of her despised gestures, and looks, and halting words, the same concealed warning ever lying beneath the surface.[30]

When the novel opens it seems that Mrs Sherwin is a minor character with little importance in the plot and of little interest to the reader. She is the victim of her husband's ambition and her daughter's arrogance. Yet this poor long-suffering creature is in possession of the secret of her daughter's duplicity. What at first appears as a figure of suffering, and, unfortunately, little interest, transpires, as the novel develops, to hold the 'secret' of the plot. Women are often given this degree of importance in Collins' novels. Female sexuality is often to the fore in some form or other. Often it represents a threat to men and masculine values. Perhaps Margaret's ultimate rejection of Basil is connected with the fact that he did not fulfil her expectations of what constituted a real man. 'A nice wife I've been to him, and a nice husband he has been to me – a husband who waits a year! Ha! ha! he calls himself a man, doesn't he? A husband who waits a year!'[31]

Armadale is not ostensibly about the rights and wrongs of women; it is written at the time of the dominance of sensationalism and much of its effect is a revaluation of the importance of dreams. However much of the contemporary reaction to this novel was focused around the character of Miss Lydia Gwilt, and if the novel is approached from this direction, a reading concentrating on Miss Gwilt and associated representations of sexuality and gender, it can be seen that Collins is again giving considerable regard to the position of women. The warning letter to Midwinter is much concerned with the relationship of Fate to Providence, but, interestingly, it also warns him to avoid 'the maid whose wicked hand smoothed the way to marriage'.[32] This maid is the twelve-year-old Lydia Gwilt and her knowledge of the existence of two Armadales is of great importance in the unfolding of the plot. And Lydia Gwilt is even more important than this. While it is often argued that no novelist of this period, who wished to arouse sympathy for a fallen woman would risk portraying her as remotely sensual,[33] Collins endows Gwilt with an overpowering sensuality. She uses her sexual power to get the better of men and this behaviour is little criticised in the novel. Indeed she has all the advantages and enjoys all the pleasures associated with cultivated and elegant ladies. She is fond of Beethoven and can speak several languages. She is also very aware of herself as a sexual creature, and creature is perhaps an operative term because, on several occasions, she is identified and compared to a 'cat', 'tigress' and 'boa-constrictor'.[34] Lydia is fully cognisant of this power. In a remarkable scene of self-awareness, which stresses her obvious sexual favours, **she** studies herself in a mirror.

The house-clock struck the hour and roused her. She sighed, and walking back to the glass, wearily loosened the fastenings of her dress; wearily removed the studs from the chemisette beneath it, and put them on the chimney-piece. She looked indolently at the reflected beauties of her neck and bosom, as she unplaited her hair and threw it back in one great mass over her shoulders. "Fancy," she thought, "if he saw me now!" She turned back to the table, and sighed again as she extinguished one of the candles and took the other in her hand.[35]

Lydia uses her sexuality for her own ends. She is no longer simply the object of the male gaze but is an active sexual subject. It is this active sexuality which disrupts the sexual status quo and also contributed to the contemporary critical disapprobation in which she was held. The *Spectator* notes that *Armadale*

. . . Gives us for its heroine a woman fouler than the refuse of the streets, who has lived to the ripe age of thirty-five, and through the horrors of forgery, murder, theft, bigamy, gaol, and attempted suicide, without any trace being left on her beauty.[36]

The reference to the fact that Miss Gwilt is still beautiful confirms Cunningham's point as generally true. The contemporary reader did expect that such a woman could no longer be attractive, yet the review also emphasises the case that Collins is placing Miss Gwilt in a different league. The review may be seen as a typical reaction to a fallen woman and what appears to be most contentious about her portrayal is the description of her beauty, sexual desirability and sensitivity. A certain poignancy is added to this treatment of Miss Gwilt if it is remembered that it is the clergyman, Mr Brock, who first 'observed that she (Miss Gwilt) was a remarkably elegant and graceful woman', so much so, in fact, that he 'looked after her as she bowed and left him'.[37] Because Miss Gwilt's appearance is of such importance, Collins is subtle enough to hint at it rather than offering full description so that, when he does attempt to enumerate her attractions, the reader already has a strong expectation of what they might be. Some of these indications will be examined below, but it is important to place the first sustained description in context.

Midwinter has just returned to Thorpe Ambrose and meets Miss Gwilt. She has just come back from a *rendezvous* with Bashwood, all the time shadowed by Armadale's spy. She left Bashwood, who is hopelessly in love with her 'as a cat goes on her way when she has exhausted the enjoyment of frightening a mouse'.[38] She then risks a physical confrontation with the spy and, after knocking his hat off, considers further violence. Significantly, she is 'taller and (quite possibly) the stronger of the two'.[39] Another man is then spotted in the distance.

Some women would have noticed the approach of a stranger at that hour and in that lonely place with a certain anxiety. Miss Gwilt was too confident in her own powers of persuasion not to count on the man's assistance before hand, whoever he might be, *because* he was a man. She looked back at the spy with redoubled confidence in herself, and measured him contemptuously from head to foot for the second time.

"I wonder whether I'm strong enough to throw you after your hat?" she said. "I'll take a turn and consider it." She sauntered on a few steps towards the figure advancing along the road. The spy followed her close. "Try it," he said brutally. "You're a fine woman – you're welcome to put your arms round me if you like."[40]

What is stressed in passages and scenes of this kind is Miss Gwilt's power over men. They become strongly attracted to her and are helpless victims of her beauty and sexuality. She is confident of her power and is prepared to use it to her own advantage. It is this active feminine power which is such a challenge to established gender roles. However, she is not an archetypal *femme fatale*. Midwinter falls victim to her as she serves him tea. He believes he has just 'rescued' her from the incident with the spy.

"Women are not all coquettes," she said, as she took off her bonnet and mantilla, and laid them carefully on a chair. "I won't go into my room, and look in my glass, and make myself smart – you shall take me just as I am." Her hands moved about among the tea-things with a smooth, noiseless activity. Her magnificent hair flashed crimson in the candle-light, as she turned her head hither and thither, searching with an easy grace, for the things she wanted in the tray. Exercise had heightened the brilliancy of her complexion and had quickened the rapid alternations of expression in her eyes – the delicious langour that stole over them when she was listening or thinking, the bright intelligence that flashed from them as softly as she spoke. In the lightest word she said, in the least thing she did, there was something that gently solicited the heart of the man who sat with her. Perfectly modest in her manner, possessed to perfection of the graceful restraints and refinements of a lady, she had all the allurements that feast the eye, all the Siren-invitations that reduce the sense – a subtle suggestiveness in her silence, and a sexual sorcery in her smile.[41]

Miss Gwilt is also simultaneously 'the pink of propriety',[42] possessing all the attributes of a lady, but she puts these qualities to other uses than those officially sanctioned by society. There is a 'suggestiveness' in her silence and sexual sorcery in her smile but she is not a *femme fatale*. Rather, she subverts propriety from within. Mrs Oldershaw, the old procuress and cosmetician reminds Lydia that

"A woman . . . with your appearance, your manners, your abilities, and your education, can make almost any excursions into society that she pleases, if she only has money in her pocket and a respectable reference to appeal to in cases of emergency.[43]

However, Collins can react to stereotypes with stereotypes. Miss Milroy, for example, is painted in terms other than those associated with the romantic heroine.

She was pretty; she was not pretty – she charmed, she disappointed, she charmed again. Tried by recognized line and rule, she was too short, and too well-developed for her age. And yet few men's eyes would have wished her figure other than it was . . . these attractions passed, the little attendant blemishes and imperfections of this self-contradictory girl began again. Her nose was too short, her mouth was too large, her face was too round, and too rosy.[44]

A stereotypical notion of female attractiveness is rejected, a positive factor, but Collins does not push for a too radical alternative. Rather, he sets his rejection of the existing rubric for determining female beauty within a paradigm which is still dominated by men. Despite her obvious shortcomings few men would ignore Miss Milroy. This is not the case with Miss Gwilt. While Miss Milroy is still the object of male attention and still satisfies male desire, Lydia Gwilt is a free subject who is in control of her sexuality and can use it as a power source and work with it to gain her own ends. Miss Milroy is still the object of male attention, a creature to be courted and flattered whereas Lydia Gwilt courts and flatters men, takes the sexual initiative and appropriates to herself masculine gender characteristics. In a recent article discussing the trace of phrenology and its effects on the representation of women in nineteenth-century fiction, Jeanne Fahnestock points to the significance of Marian Halcombe's strong chin and Valeria Macallan's aquiline nose.[45] It is of interest to note that Miss Gwilt also has an aquiline nose,[46] whereas, unfortunately Miss Milroy's nose is too short. If the significance of the nose is foregrounded and if the nose is a signifier for the phallus, it may be seen that Lydia Gwilt has phallic power which allows her to operate as a man. Miss Milroy is without the power of the phallus and so remains the object of phallic power. However, Miss Milroy is not completely defenceless and does have a battery of feminine wiles which she can call on in her dealings with Armadale. Concealed behind a tree, Lydia Gwilt watches her in action with the young Armadale and is much impressed by her manoeuvres. Indeed they provide the opportunity for Miss Gwilt to remark that manners are themselves a charade which scheming young women can, at times, manipulate to their own ends.

> For downright brazen impudence, which a grown woman would
> be ashamed of, give me the young girl whose "modesty" is so
> pertinaciously insisted on by the nauseous domestic
> sentimentalists of the present day.[47]

Miss Gwilt can manipulate her almost classic carriage and appearance to her own ends. Miss Milroy has limited powers of persuasion and is only interested in manipulating men towards marriage, a traditional female pursuit in literature. And Miss Gwilt is very impressed by Miss Milroy's ability to flirt when she considers Miss Milroy's shortcomings – bad legs and no waist.[48]

That Lydia Gwilt controls the phallus becomes clear in her relationship with Midwinter and Bashwood. This covert appropriation of masculine power is supplemented at times in the text when Miss Gwilt is admired for her masculine intellect and powers of reasoning. Pedgift Senior, Armadale's lawyer, grudgingly admits that her plot to win his client is virtually foolproof. He admires her letter to the young Armadale and in its praise exclaims 'What a lawyer she would have made . . . if she had only been a man!'[49] Yet, despite the fact that this public sphere is closed to Miss Gwilt, she is able to operate as a man in her various manipulations of Midwinter and Bashwood.

Midwinter is an easy target. It is brought to the reader's attention quite early in the novel that he has a 'sensitive feminine organization'[50] and Miss Gwilt is able to manage this aspect of his character to her own advantage. The phallic woman is able to sway the feminine man to her own desires. Lydia Gwilt is, at first, amused by her evident power over Bashwood, 'this feeble old creature'.[51] When they first meet it is Bashwood who blushes like a young girl, 'he turned all manner of colours, and stood trembling and staring'.[52] Bashwood behaves like a young girl before her first lover and Lydia Gwilt is made apprehensive by such behaviour. 'I felt quite startled for the moment, – for of all the ways in which men have looked at me, no man ever looked at me in that way before'.[53] Miss Gwilt is, of course, accustomed to being looked at by men, but with Bashwood, she realises that she can control this look and turn it to her own advantage. She is unable to describe her power over Bashwood other than by reference to animals. The language of human desire is inadequate in its repertoire of other metaphor.

> Did you ever see the boa-constrictor fed at the Zoological Gardens? They put a live rabbit into his cage, and there is a moment when the two creatures look at each other. I declare Mr. Bashwood reminded me of the rabbit![54]

It is no coincidence that such imagery is used to identify Miss Gwilt at other points in the text. The elder Pedgift refers to her as a 'tigress' and as she sports with Bashwood, the text refers to their exchange and meeting as the behaviour of a 'cat (who has) exhausted the enjoyment of frightening a mouse'.[55] There is a tradition which identifies women with animals. In Genesis, for example, the Devil, Eve and the snake are juxtaposed, but here the juxtaposition is given a particular tone which privileges Miss Gwilt's peculiar power in her relationship with men. Miss Gwilt is herself aware of the contribution of language to the depiction of such problems. It is appropriate, and worth bearing in mind, at this point that she appears to be aware of the fact that language is not arbitrary but does have ideological implications and reverberations. In a strange aside in her diary, she remarks how men refer to ships and boats as 'she' and she continues to illuminate some further connotations of this seemingly innocent use of language.

> "The yacht. As a relief from hearing about Miss Milroy, I declare the yacht in the harbour is quite an interesting subject to me! She (the men call a vessel 'She;' and I suppose if the women took an interest in such things, *they* would call a vessel 'He'); she is a beautiful model; and her 'top-sides' (whatever they may be) are especially distinguished by being built of mahogany. But, with these merits, she has the defect, on the other hand, of being old – which is a sad drawback – and the crew and the sailing-master have been 'paid off,' and sent home to England – which is additionally distressing. Still, if a new crew and a new sailing-master can be picked up here, such a beautiful creature (with all her drawbacks) is not to be despised. It might answer to hire her for a cruise and see how she behaves. (If she is of *my* mind, her behaviour will rather astonish her new master!)[56]

Miss Gwilt picks up that men refer to boats as 'she' and then in a free-ranging extrapolation decodes the further ramifications of this and shows that boats, like women, can have the misfortune of being old, and can have especially attractive topsides. Great enjoyment may be had from seeing how they perform and behave. In what amounts to a trial marriage, men decide whether or not to buy a particular vessel, but only after they have given her a run to see how she behaves. And Lydia would like boats to surprise their masters. She likes neither women nor boats to be servile.

After this conversation with Armadale, Lydia Gwilt has a 'tigerish' tingling all over, but decides to control her evident anger and irritation because 'We all know that a lady has no passions'.[57] This is not the only time that Gwilt sublimates her feelings. She is a passionate woman but the social conventions so control her behaviour that she is forced to find refuge in drugs. 'Drops you are a darling! If I love nothing else, I love you'.[58] Drugs may be some solace to her but usually she is in full control of all situations. She mercilessly manipulates Bashwood. An old man, he has fallen in love with her and, like a discontented wife, complains that she is not giving him enough attention. Gwilt explains how she manages him.

> "I pass over the wretched old creature's raptures and reproaches, and groans and tears, and weary long prosings about the lonely

months he has passed at Thorpe-Ambrose, brooding over my desertion of him. He was quite eloquent at times – but I don't want his eloquence here. It is needless to say that I put myself right with him, and consulted his feelings before I asked him for his news. What a blessing a woman's vanity is sometimes! I almost forgot my risks and responsibilities, in my anxiety to be charming. For a minute or two, I felt a warm little flutter of triumph. And it was a triumph – even with an old man! In a quarter of an hour, I had him smirking and smiling, hanging on my lightest words in an ecstacy, and answering all the questions I put to him, like a good little child.[59]

Miss Gwilt is in complete control and able to manipulate Bashwood to her every whim. She can delight in her power over him and is flattered by his attention. She is simultaneously the man manipulating his lover and the mother her child. She speaks rather than is spoken about, a substantial advance in the sexual arena. Bashwood is a good little child and on another occasion, in gratitude to her, he weeps 'womanish tears'.[60] Bashwood's is the submissive role in his relationship with the phallic woman. It is feminine to the extent that, just as women may be seen as innocent children, so Bashwood steps into this stereotype. This use of stereotypes is not an innocent or neutral activity. Normalcy, a sense of the real, is usually established through stereotypical representations and this sense of the real is that of the dominant opinion in society. It is part of a world view – a sensibility and an ideology which correspond to one particular value system. In his occasional pieces and his novels, Collins revamps these stereotypes and because he is simultaneously challenging accepted values, he often encounters hostile reaction.

Reading through a theory of phrenology, Jeanne Fahnestock suggests that Valeria Macallan's aquiline nose goes some way towards indicating how persistent she will be in her efforts to have her husband cleared of the charge of murder.[61] At the time of her marriage to him the Scottish jury had reached the verdict 'Not Proven'. Sue Lonoff also discusses Valeria Macallan and claims that she is representative of Collins' rendering of women, 'an uneasy blend of defiance and defensiveness, of feminism and traditional type-casting'.[62] Lonoff's appraisal is correct if rather impressionistic but she does not give any sustained attention to how her interpretations are structured in the text. *The Law and The Lady* deserves more attention than Lonoff's cursory treatment.

What is specifically at issue here is the representation of women and the proprietorship of these representations. Women are usually delineated in terms of male property; they are the objects of male desire and are assessed and given value in masculine terms. While Collins may not be a feminist, he certainly goes some way towards granting women a sense of their own subjectivity and lets them be free subjects rather than the objects of males. Admittedly, this subjectivity is ultimately subservient; Valeria Macallan is only forceful, for example, when she is operating in her husband's interests, but nevertheless she does operate as a subject for most of the novel. I want to extend the notion of propriety here to include our own most intimate sense of 'ownness' of owning ourselves, our own proper names and our own identity. This idea of propriety and names and a sense of ourselves is introduced in the opening of *The Law and The Lady* and is articulated alongside Valeria's discovery of herself. She has just got married, obviously involving a change of names, and this fact is spotlighted when Valeria signs her married rather than her maiden name in the marriage register. The whole notion of identity and names is brought to our attention. It is then that the reader is treated to a description of Valeria, but, significantly, Valeria describes herself as she looks in a mirror. Valeria is both subject and object of her own gaze – a marked change in the tradition of woman as object of the masculine gaze. Valeria's life has changed, she has changed her name and, when her aunt and uncle leave her, she looks at herself in the vestry mirror.

What does the glass show me?

The glass shows a tall and slender young woman of three and twenty years of age. She is not at all the sort of person who attracts attention in the street, seeing that she fails to exhibit the popular yellow hair and the popular painted cheeks. Her hair is black; dressed in these latter days (as it was dressed years since to please her father), in broad ripples drawn back from the forehead, and gathered into a simple knot behind (like the hair of the Venus de'Medici), so as to show the neck beneath. Her complexion is pale; except in moments of violent agitation there is no colour to be seen in her face. Her eyes are of so dark a blue that they are generally mistaken for black. Her eyebrows are well enough in form, but they are too dark, and too strongly marked. Her nose just inclines towards the aquiline bend, and is considered a little too large by persons difficult to please in matters of noses. The mouth, her best feature, is very delicately shaped, and is capable of presenting great varieties of expression. As to the face in general, it is too narrow and too long at the lower part; too broad and too low in the higher regions of the eyes and the head. The whole picture, as reflected in the glass, represents a woman of some elegance, rather too pale, and rather too sedate and serious in her moments of silence and repose – in short, a person who fails to strike the ordinary observer at first sight; but who gains in general estimation, on a second and sometimes even on a third, view. As for her dress it studiously conceals, instead of proclaiming, that she had been married that morning. She wears a grey Cashmere tunic trimmed with grey silk, and having a skirt of the same material and colour beneath it. On her head is a bonnet to match, relieved by a quilting of white muslin, with one deep red rose, as a morsel of positive colour, to complete the effect of the whole dress.[63]

Again it is apparent that Valeria is not a typical beauty – she does not conform to popular stereotypes and hence it is difficult to classify her or to predict her behaviour. If stereotyping can be seen as a mark of social control and an attempt to establish a social propriety, Valeria is obviously beyond this pale. She does not attract attention in the street. This is a reference to the male gaze which attempts to place women in objective positions. Rather Valeria has 'strongly marked' features as opposed to the 'popular yellow hair and popular painted cheeks'. But even, if Valeria is in many respects her own woman, with her sense of propriety and self-hood, it is still a sense of herself which is worked out in terms of the popular image. Such is the strength of the masculine definition that it even controls revolt against itself.

She gains a sense of her own self-hood from looking in a mirror. Rather than being the object of the masculine gaze, the look on the streets, she is both subject and object of her own gaze.[64] Her sense of herself is worked via her own image in a mirror rather than determined by men. Valeria has a greater autonomy than is usual for a woman and thus is able to challenge the verdict of 'Not Proven'. Her position contrasts with that of Miserrimus Dexter, a man but a man who is unable to identify his own self and significantly cannot control language. The representation of Dexter is discussed below.

While the novel opens with a marriage and its associated problems of identity, its closing pages deal with yet another marriage, that of Major Fitz David. The narrative is framed by matrimony and this latter marriage is important because it marks the limit of female emancipation. Valeria is a free subject, also the subjective narrator of the story, and allowed freedom traditionally associated with men in her attempts to prove her husband innocent. But it is important to stress that hers is a limited freedom, an independence which is only allowed within clearly defined, masculine controlled paradigms. Ultimately she is happy to return to a life of wedded bliss and subservience to her husband. Major Fitz David's marriage marks an extreme, a boundary which Valeria cannot cross. The Major had admitted to Valeria earlier that he was 'as weak as water in the hands of a pretty woman',[65] yet Valeria still sympathises with his fate. The Major's bride explains to Valeria her motives for marrying 'with a candour that was positively shameless'.

> "You see we are a large family at home, quite unprovided for!" this odious young woman whispered in my ear.
> ". . . between you and me, it was a great deal easier to get the money by marrying the old gentleman. Here I am provided for – and there's all my family provided for, too – and nothing to do but spend the money . . . I haven't played my cards badly, have I? It's a great advantage to marry an old man – you can twist him round your little finger."[66]

Valeria is aghast at this approach to marriage. She may well have reached a consciousness of herself which is of her own creation and other than that of women totally dependent on men, but Valeria is still willing to subjugate this aspect of her character in the best interests of her marriage. However, this cannot be seen as a complete defeat of the feminist impulse either. Valeria takes a cold and oblique look at the institution of marriage and when obviously willing to live with Eustace as man and wife is aware of the sordid nature of the contemporary marriage contract.

> When a woman sells herself to a man, that vile bargain is none the less infamous (to my mind), because it happens to be made under the sanction of the Church and the Law.[67]

The economic terminology is privileged. Valeria refuses the analogy of women with commodities and is well aware that the Church and the Law are mere ideological systems which give the appearance of respectability to woman's situation, while, what they do, in actual fact, is to conceal the covert economic exchange. Armed with this insight, it is difficult not to interpret her relationship with her husband as an entrapment in marriage.

But, up to this point, Valeria wins through because she has gained some autonomy and does not allow either the legal or the religious institution totally to control her sense of identity. These ideological systems or discourses normally fix women as objects but she wins for herself a certain limited amount of subjectivity. Again this contrasts with Miserrimus Dexter. Valeria is in control of her sense of self and there are certain connotations at play in her perseverance, courage, superior rationality, etc. which hint at a utilisation of the masculine preserve. She is also a victor, an empress as her name suggests. It is part of Dexter's tragedy that he is not in control of discourse and further he is described as having certain feminine qualities.

Gliding self-propelled in his chair on wheels, through the opening made for him among the crowd, a strange and startling creature – literally the half of a man – revealed himself to the general view. A coverlid, which had been thrown over his chair, had fallen off during his progress through the throng. The loss of it exposed to the public curiosity the head, the arms, and the trunk of a living human being; absolutely deprived of the lower limbs. To make this deformity all the more striking and all the more terrible, the victim of it was – as to his face and body – an unusually handsome, and an unusually well-made man. His long silky hair, of a bright and beautiful chestnut colour, fell over shoulders that were the perfection of strength and grace. His face was bright with vivacity and intelligence. His large clear blue eyes, and his long delicate white hands, were like the eyes and hands of a beautiful woman. He would have looked effeminate but for the manly proportion of his throat and chest; aided in their effect by his flowing beard and long moustache, of a lighter chestnut shade than the colour of his hair. Never had a magnificent head and body been more hopelessly ill-bestowed than in this instance! Never had Nature committed a more careless or a more cruel mistake than in the making of this man![68]

Dexter is a 'creature – literally half a man' because of his symbolic and literal lack of the phallus. While Valeria is endowed with a certain strength, Dexter is a representation of a weak man. In part, Valeria's strength is explained in terms of 'strongly marked eyebrows' whereas Dexter's weakness is epitomised by distinctly feminine characteristics: long silky hair, eyes and hands of a beautiful woman.

And while it has been established that Valeria is in control of discourse, Dexter cannot find himself in any of these ideological meaning systems. He is not a full man but a 'creature' and at another time is described as a 'Thing'.[69] Dexter is carried into Benjamin's study by his servant and the housekeeper explains that 'It' has been there all these hours.[70] Langauge does not have a pronoun which can accommodate Dexter. He is neither subject nor object but is totally other and exists on the margins of discourse and society. 'He' is neither masculine nor feminine, his sense of identity is problematised. And part of this fracturing of identity is made clear by the importance Dexter places on his name when giving evidence in court.

"People generally laugh when they first hear my strange Christian name," he said, in a low, clear, resonant voice, which penetrated the remotest corners of the Court. "I may inform the good people here that many names, still common among us, have their significance, and that mine is one of them."[71]

Another contradiction here may be the fact that his voice is not that of a castrato. His name means most wretched right-hand one. The left-hand, sinister, would indicate illegitimacy. So both he and Valeria have the idea of lineage inscribed in their names. In her narrative of events, Valeria draws attention to the connection between Dexter's physical appearance and his name when she refers to the 'deformed man, with the strange name'.[72] A motley collection of motifs is associated with Dexter. He has 'the eyes of a woman, clear as the eyes of a child' and he is fond of needle-work. He also dresses in the 'prettiest' clothes as he explains,

Except in this ignoble and material nineteenth century, men have always worn precious stuffs and beautiful colours as well as women. A hundred years ago, a gentleman in pink silk was a gentleman properly dressed.[73]

The contrast between Dexter and Valeria is most apparent in their use of language. Valeria is comfortable with language and able to articulate it to her advantage. Dexter's appropriation of language and convention is much more problematic. Valeria's mother-in-law is the first to explain about Dexter's tortured relationship with language. I have already mentioned his testimony in court and his explanation of the importance of names, but Mrs Macallan senior has an important qualification to make to Dexter's evidence.

> He began, fairly enough, with a modest explanation of his absurd Christian name, which at once checked the merriment of the audience. But as he went on, the mad side of him showed itself. He mixed up sense and nonsense in the strongest confusion; he was called to order over and over again; he was even threatened with a fine and imprisonment for contempt of Court. In short, he was just like himself – a mixture of the strangest and the most opposite qualities, at one time, perfectly clear and reasonable, as you said just now; at another breaking out into rhapsodies of the most outrageous kind, like a man in the state of delirium.[74]

Dexter has a tendency to lose control of language and ceases to make sense. His speech is a mixture of sense and nonsense, whereas Valeria's sense of her own propriety allows her to be in almost full control of language and it is this inability which contributes to her victory over Dexter. At a late point in the novel we have a dramatisation of Dexter's almost total inability with the language and its effect on him as a subject, as a person in control of his own identity.

Valeria and her mother-in-law visit Dexter in his home and find a notice outside his room claiming that:

> My immense imagination is at work. Visions of heroes unroll themselves before me. I re-animate in myself the spirits of the departed great. My brains are boiling in my head. Any persons who disturb me, under existing circumstances, will do at the peril of their lives, – DEXTER[75]

They approach tentatively and find their host in a darkened room, careering around furiously in his wheelchair. Dexter, the half-man, is fused in Valeria's consciousness with this chair, so that half-man and chair become one living body.

A high chair on wheels moved by, through the field of red light, carrying a shadowy figure with floating hair, and arms furiously raised and lowered, working the machinery that propelled the chair at its upmost rate of speed. "I am Napoleon, at the surprise of Austerlitz!" shouted the man in the chair as he swept past me, on his rumbling and whistling wheels, in the red glow of the firelight. . . . The chair rushed out of sight, and the shouting man in it became another hero. "I am Nelson!" the singing voice cried now. "I am leading the fleet at Trafalgar. I issue my commands, prophetically conscious of victory and death. I see my own apotheosis – my public funeral, my nation's tears, my burial in the glorious church . . .". The fantastic and frightful apparition, man and machinery blended in one – the new Centaur, half man, half chair – flew by me again in the dying light. "I am Shakespeare!" cried the fantastic creature now.[76]

Deprived of a clearly defined space in language, Dexter is free to become any subject he so desires. Here it is the masculine-heroic but his identity is unstable and therefore free to flow into what ever persona he wishes. And all this is connected with the fact that he is only half a man, a figure which cannot be described or contained in language. This is reinforced by Valeria's horror on seeing him. His physical inadequacy is emphasised.

For one moment we saw a head and body in the air, absolutely deprived of the lower limbs. The moment after, the terrible creature touched the floor as lightly as a monkey, on his hands.[77]

Without lower limbs, Dexter is a thing, a creature and a monkey. He is neither in control of his sexuality as a man nor of langauge, a language which deprives him of full identity, and can only supply metaphorical approximations to describe his condition. 'My imagination runs away with me and I say and do strange things'.[78] He is also feeble and uncontrolled sexually as is made clear when he attacks Valeria.[79]

Dexter disrupts the dialectic between gender and the rules of language, grammar. This is also true of his musical compositions. He composes a song for Valeria, which because it does not comply with musical notation, she is unable to appreciate.

Was it good music? or bad? I cannot decide whether it was music at all. It was a wild barbaric succession of sounds; utterly unlike any modern composition. Sometimes it suggested a slow and undulating Oriental dance. Sometimes it modulated into tones which reminded me of the severer harmonies of the old Gregorian chants. The words when they followed the prelude, were as wild, as recklessly free from all restraints of critical rules, as the music.[80]

Dexter is surrounded by his servants who appear to have similar problems in their relationship with protocol and convention. This is the case with his devoted maid and housekeeper, the improbably named Ariel. Ariel is female but has a 'coarse masculine voice . . . the Caliban's, rather than the Ariel's voice'.[81] Valeria is struck by this incongruous figure.

I could now see the girl's round, fleshy, inexpressive face, her rayless and colourless eyes, her coarse nose and heavy chin. A creature half alive; an imperfectly developed animal in shapeless form, clad in a man's pilot jacket and treading in a man's heavy laced boots; with nothing but an old red flannel petticoat, and a broken comb in her frousy flaxen hair, to tell us that she was a woman.[82]

Even his associates challenge the expectations of the times. Ariel's impropriety exists in the fact that she is a woman who dresses and speaks like a man. Dexter's impropriety is based on his unique condition, his lack of a sense of his own propriety or self-hood. Rather than have a clearly defined persona and personality, he is an unstable subject – 'I am the man I fancy myself to be'.[83]

There are further repercussions in the representation of Valeria which problematise the relationship of Fate and chance in the novel. Collins' tight plot could be seen to minimise the question of chance, but rather, it is chance which is the ultimate victor in the text. A lot depends on Valeria's efforts but she herself admits that it was only by chance that she managed to interpret the full importance of Dexter's fanciful meanderings.

It was all my doing – as the lawyer had said. And yet, what I had done, I had, so to speak, done blindfold. The merest accident might have altered the whole course of later events. I had over and over again interfered to check Ariel, when she entreated the Master "to tell a story." If she had not succeeded, in spite of my opposition, Miserrimus Dexter's last efforts of memory might never have been directed to the tragedy of Gleninch. And again, if I had only remembered to move my chair, and so to give Benjamin the signal to move off, he would never have written down the apparently senseless words which have led us to the discovery of the truth.[84]

This is an important point because it stresses that the verdict of the Scottish jury was proved to be wrong as a result of chance. Chance was just as important as Valeria's gallant detective work and this obviously detracts from her victory as a successful woman in a man's world. Collins has undermined the entire narrative by this move. The thrust of the novel implies that it is via Valeria's investigations that the Scottish verdict will be rescinded. But, then at the close of the work, it is explained that Valeria's victory is purely fortuitous. Even in this very densely plotted novel there is a place for chance.

This dilutes the feminist theme even more. Not only is Valeria acting in this positive masculine fashion for the sake of her marriage but all her efforts also come to nothing and it is only by chance that she is ultimately victorious. It is worth dwelling on this point a little longer before any composite conclusions are drawn about Collins' presentation of women in the novel. As ever with Collins, it is difficult to make definitive statements. And while it is suspect to quote Dexter on this subject, he is allowed a considerable speech on the situation of women.

> The one obstacle, Mrs. Valeria, to your rising equal to the men in the various industrial processes of life is not raised, as the women vainly suppose, by the defective institutions of the age they live in. No! the obstacle is in themselves. No institution that can be devised to encourage them will ever be strong enough to contend successfully with the sweetheart and the new bonnet. . . . There is the whole difference between the mental constitution of the sexes, which no legislation will ever alter as long as the world lasts! What does it matter? Women are infinitely superior to men in the moral qualities which are the true adornments of humanity. Be content – oh, my mistaken sisters, be content with that![85]

It is obviously of significance that this is Dexter's view of the 'woman problem' and it would be dangerous to confuse Collins and Dexter.

As it is Dexter who argues in this way it is possible that Collins is satirising this whole line of debate and so actually making female emancipation a matter of the plainest common sense. Valeria certainly answers Dexter with silence, and rather than debate with him, describes his strange and bizarre taste in ornament; casts of the head of famous murderers, a woman's skeleton with the inscription 'Behold the scaffolding on which beauty is built', and the skin of a French Marquis tanned in the Revolution of 93. The effect is to convince the reader that his taste in conversation pieces, like his views on women, contributes as evidence of his insanity. A sane person could not agree with his line on women.

Dexter believes that women are morally superior to men. However, it is an argument which Collins rehearses in a much less equivocal way in *The Evil Genius*. Some sympathy is shown towards women, particularly on the question of the custody of children after divorce and the law is condemned for its heartless treatment of women.

"Do you mean that the law takes my child away from me?"

"I am ashamed, Madam, to think that I live by the law; but that I must own, is exactly what it is capable of doing in the present case. Compose yourself, I beg and pray. A time will come when women will remind men that the mother bears the child and feeds the child, and will insist that the mother's rights is the best rights of the two."[86]

All very commendable, but Collins' feminist sympathies seem to stop short when he writes further of divorce and the grounds for annulling a marriage. Rather than defend the rights of women, he seems intent on protecting the family at all costs.

When there is absolute cruelty, or where there is deliberate desertion, on the husband's part, I seek the use and reason for Divorce. If the unhappy wife can find an honourable man who will protect her, or an honourable man who will offer her a home, Society and Law which are responsible for the institution of marriage, are bound to allow a woman outraged under the shelter of their institution to marry again. But, where the husband's fault is sexual frailty, I say that the English law which refuses Divorce on that ground alone is right, and that the Scotch law which grants it is wrong.[87]

This is a strange statement and comes in the novel with all the weight of authorial approval. It suggests that masculine moral failure should be legally codified. Women are morally superior, less likely to wander sexually and this should be recognised by the law of the land. It also sees the roles within marriage in fixed terms, man the provider etc.

But this reading of the law is complicated in *The Evil Genius*. Little trust is put in the legal domain as an arbiter of human justice. The legal aspects of marriage may be very important, but, in the last analysis, it is chance which determines happiness in marriage as in so much of life. In *The Evil Genius* the lawyer, himself involved in the divorce proceedings, has no great faith in the law anyway. Ultimately human destiny is decided on an altogether different plane.

"Do you really believe in luck?"

"Devoutly. A lawyer must believe in something. He knows the law too well to put any faith in that; and his clients present to him (if he is a man of any feeling) a hideous view of human nature. The poor devil believes in luck – rather than believe in nothing."[88]

Here Collins appears to be suggesting via the lawyer that our destinies are not subject to our control and our institutions provide but feeble defence against the working of chance. The active struggle for female emancipation has little importance, it is suggested, in a world dominated not by men after all, but by a much more nebulous force – the workings of chance.

Conclusion

My final chapter concludes with an important qualification which problematises Collins' entire approach and underlines the importance he places on chance as opposed to Providence or Fate. He goes a long way towards illustrating and illuminating how society, supported by the legal system, subordinates women in its own interests. However, the discussion of luck, taken from *The Evil Genius* (1886), one of his very last novels, tends to diverge from this view. Here I must introduce a final, but important modification to the argument; if so much in life is the result of random sequences of events, benign or otherwise, this, finally, may be seen as a dilution of the view that the organization of society is the result of a particular set of political and economic conditions, since it suggests that the world may not be susceptible to change by human agency. If everything is a matter of chance there is little we can do about it. Collins, I am claiming, goes much further, and is more consistent in his social and political analysis than has generally been recognised; but to see this is not to impose upon him, with retrospective hindsight, a neat form of modern political attitude or an unambivalently urged social programme. Collins' scepticism is both a political strength and a weakness. At every point in the *oeuvre*, there is a fascinating and difficult interaction between his formal innovation and the varying depth of his social and political analysis of the society in which he lived. Such an interaction can no more be 'solved' in the aesthetic sphere by the imposition of genre stereotyping, than it can in the political and social spheres, by the imposition of short-sighted topicality.

It is the representation of women which again crystallises this problem or paradox in Collins. The novels demonstrate how the position of women is socially and historically coded by the dominant patriarchal values of society and, yet, within this very critique, there is an emphasis on the functionings of chance which seems to deny that any social or human agency is responsible for the plight of women. Women's position is shown to be manufactured in the interests of property at one point, while at another, the entire organization of society is explained away in terms of luck and chance. The cultural specificity of gender is demonstrated in many novels but then masculinity is valorised in *The Evil Genius* and it is suggested that some masculine traits are innate to the sex and women must learn to live with them.

A similar ambiance surrounds Collins' use of propriety in the novels. When this concept is unpacked and explored in various novels, it becomes clear that the author is not advocating the unambiguous rejection of propriety. Propriety is a set of lived practices which, it is shown, serves the interests of the dominant order, but it would be wrong to condemn it absolutely out of hand. While it is factional, it is not completely negative and there is also a propriety, based on a more amorphous regime of sincere human feeling, which is a positive and necessary social attribute. Rather than condemn propriety completely, Collins is more interested in asking 'Whose propriety?' and in whose interests propriety works.

There is also a contradiction in the very form of Collins' novels. With Dickens, for example, the plot which, ultimately, creates order out of chaos is seen as evidence of the working of a Providential order and Dickens, despite the overtly negative treatment of evangelical Christians in many of his novels is proved, by one critic at least, to be writing in a tradition which connects him with Hannah More and Sydney Smith.[1] Collins is, of course, the master of the tightly plotted novel and it is often suggested that Collins' main contribution to Dickens' writing is this increased awareness of the importance of plot. However, while the revised Dickensian use of plot foregrounds Providence, Collins, reworking the same tradition emphasises chance. Despite similarities in form there is little common ground between Collins and Dickens on this point.

All literary works are not equally appropriate and well suited to all times. It is possible that, after initial success, works may fall into neglect and then become relevant again at a future date. I think the time is right for a reconsideration of Collins and not only because the publishing industry can play on the fact that it is the centenary of his death in 1989. Rather it is the history of our own period which makes these novels relevant to us. There are two major reasons for this. In recent years the growth of the women's movement and the increasing attention given to feminist theory encourages a new look at the representation and positioning of women within the literary text and in society as a whole. Collins' unique treatment of women is worthy of comment. There is also a second reason to now reread Collins with new insight, a second reason not unrelated to the development of feminism. This is the amplification of interest in that branch of literary and cultural criticism which focuses on the fraught relationship between literature and ideology and the ways in which the literary text reworks available ideologies to give us a mediated picture of reality.

Notes

INTRODUCTION

1. 'Wilkie Collins's Marginalia on His Copy of Forster's *Life of Dickens*', *The World* (2 Oct. 1889).
2. Reprinted in *Selected Essays*, T. S. Eliot (Faber, London, 1976), pp. 460–471.
3. Ibid., p. 460.
4. Ibid., pp. 460–1.
5. Ibid., p. 461.
6. Ibid., p. 469.
7. Ibid., p. 465.
8. Ibid., p. 469.
9. Ibid., p. 464.
10. G. K. Chesterton, *The Victorian Age in Literature* (Williams & Norgate Ltd., London, 1925). First published in the Home University Library series, 1912.
11. Dorothy L. Sayers, *The Omnibus of Crime* (Garden City Publishing Co., New York, 1929).
12. Dorothy L. Sayers, *The Moonstone* (Dent, London, 1944).
13. Unsigned review, *Westminster Review* (Oct. 1866), lxxxvi (n.s. xxx), pp. 269–71. Quoted in Page, Norman (ed.), *Wilkie Collins* (Routledge & Kegan Paul, London 1974), p. 158.
14. Mrs Oliphant, 'Sensation Novels', *Blackwood's Magazine* (May 1862), xci, 565–74. Quote in Page, op. cit., p. 113.
15. Ibid., p. 120.

CHAPTER 1: *THE MOONSTONE* AND *ARMADALE*

1. *The Dead Secret*, Wilkie Collins (Dover Publications Inc., New York), p. 223.
2. *The Moonstone*, Wilkie Collins (Penguin, 1979), p. 436.
3. Ibid., p. 437.
4. Ibid., p. 438.
5. Ibid., p. 346.
6. Ibid., p. 345.
7. Ibid., p. 122.
8. Ibid., p. 122.
9. Ibid., p. 109.
10. Ibid., p. 76.
11. Ibid., p. 222.
12. Ibid., p. 72.
13. Ibid., p. 69.
14. Ibid., p. 75.

15. Ibid., p. 208.
16. Ibid., pp. 214–15.
17. Ibid., p. 221.
18. Ibid., p. 506.
19. Ibid., p. 129.
20. Ibid., p. 120.
21. Ibid., p. 133.
22. Sue Lonoff neatly summarises this approach to *The Moonstone* in *Wilkie Collins and His Victorian Readers* (AMS Press, Inc., New York, 1982).
23. *The Moonstone*, pp. 417, 372.
24. Ibid., pp. 370–1.
25. Ibid., p. 457.
26. Ibid., p. 421.
27. Ibid., p. 420.
28. Ibid., p. 430.
29. Ibid., p. 422.
30. Ibid., p. 444.
31. A. D. Hutter, 'Dreams, Transformations and Literature: the Implications of Detective Fiction', *Victorian Studies*, 19 (Dec. 1975), pp. 197–8.
32. Wilkie Collins, *Armadale* (Dover Publications, New York, 1977), Appendix.
33. Ibid., Appendix.
34. Ibid., Appendix.
35. Ibid., Appendix.
36. Ibid., p. 123.
37. Ibid., p. 123.
38. Ibid., p. 129. Note the extraordinary syntax in the final sentence which implies the autonomy of conviction.
39. Ibid., p. 130.
40. Ibid., p. 145.
41. Ibid., p. 154.
42. Ibid., p. 155.
43. Ibid., pp. 153–4.
44. Ibid., p. 300.
45. Ibid., p. 161.
46. Ibid., p. 86.
47. Ibid., p. 233.
48. Ibid., p. 258.
49. Ibid., p. 259.
50. Ibid., pp. 252–3.
51. Ibid., p. 376.
52. Ibid., p. 250.
53. Ibid., p. 292.
54. Ibid., p. 323.
55. Ibid., p. 369.
56. Ibid., p. 479.
57. Ibid., p. 299.

58. Ibid., p. 516.
59. Ibid., p. 172.
60. Ibid., pp. 459–60.
61. Ibid., p. 539.
62. Ibid., p. 591.
63. Ibid., p. 591.

CHAPTER 2: *THE FALLEN LEAVES*

1. William H. Marshall, *Wilkie Collins* (Twayne Publishers, 1970), p. 102.
2. Norman Page (ed.), *Wilkie Collins: the Critical Heritage* (Routledge & Kegan Paul, 1974), p. 27.
3. Ibid., p. 27.
4. Robert Ashley, 'Wilkie Collins Revisited' in *Nineteenth Century Fiction* 4 (1950), p. 266.
5. Quoted in Page, p. 27.
6. Wilkie Collins, *Jezabel's Daughter*, Preface (Chatto & Windus, London, 1887).
7. Unsigned Review. Quoted in Page, p. 206.
8. Wilkie Collins, *The Fallen Leaves*, Preface (Chatto & Windus, London, 1890).
9. Wilkie Collins, 'The Unknown Public', rep. in *My Miscellanies*, pp. 249–63.
10. Wilkie Collins, *Jezabel's Daughter*, Dedication (Chatto & Windus, London, 1887).
11. Quoted in Page, pp. 205–6.
12. Thackeray quoted in Richard Stang, *The Theory of the Novel in England: 1850–1870* (Columbia University Press, 1959).
13. Bulwer-Lytton quoted in Stang, p. 195.
14. His essay on Balzac is also of interest in this trajection. He condemns those who see Balzac as coarse. See 'Portrait of an Artist' in *My Miscellanies*.
15. Wilkie Collins, Dedication to *Jezabel's Daughter*.
16. Ibid., pp. III–IV.
17. Charles Reade. Quoted in Stang, p. 201.
18. Ibid., p. 201.
19. Collins, *My Miscellanies*, p. 267.
20. Quoted in Stang, p. 217.
21. For more comment on this see Collins' marginalia on Forster's biography of Dickens.
22. Wilkie Collins, Dedication to *Jezabel's Daughter*.
23. For further discussion of Collins' treatment and representation of Christianity see Lonoff, pp. 100–1, 216–17, 218–24. Also Marshall, pp. 124–6 and Davis, pp. 211–12.
24. Karl Marx and Friedrich Engels, *The Communist Manifesto* (Penguin, London, 1967), p. 108.
25. Quoted in Robinson pp. 269–70.

26. Solomon built the city of Tadmor in the wilderness. See II Chronicles VIII 4.
27. *The Fallen Leaves*, pp. 17–18.
28. Maurice. Quoted in Christensen, *Origins and History Christian Socialism 1848–54*, p. 295.
29. See Frederick, Peter J., *Knights of the Golden Rule* (The University of Kentucky Press, 1976).
30. Wilkie Collins, *The Fallen Leaves*, p. 26.
31. Ibid., p. 28.
32. From my research I have been able to identify no one community at the time in Illinois which could be an accurate model for Tadmor. The closest approximation in Illinois is Cabet's community Nauvoo. See Holloway, *Heavens on Earth* (1966).
33. *The Fallen Leaves*, pp. 29–30.
34. Christensen, *History of Christian Socialism*, p. 26.
35. *The Fallen Leaves*, p. 33.
36. Ibid., p. 33.
37. Peter d'A. Jones, *The Christian Socialist Revival 1877–1914* (Princeton University Press 1968), p. 6.
38. *The Fallen Leaves*, p. 32.
39. Ibid., p. 159.
40. Maurice. Quoted in Peter d'A. Jones, *The Christian Socialist Revival*, p. 27.
41. *The Fallen Leaves*, pp. 153–4.
42. Ibid., pp. 154–5.
43. Peter d'A. Jones, *The Christian Socialist Revival 1877–1914*, p. 26.
44. *The Fallen Leaves*, p. 155.
45. Ibid., pp. 155–6.
46. Stephen Mayor, *The Churches and the Labour Movement* (Independent Press Ltd, 1967), p. 167.
47. *The Fallen Leaves*, p. 157.
48. Maurice. Quoted in Peter d'A. Jones, *The Christian Socialist Revival*, p. 23.
49. *The Fallen Leaves*, pp. 157–8.
50. Ibid., pp. 158–9.
51. Ibid., p. 159.
52. Ibid., pp. 39–40.
53. Ibid., p. 42.
54. Ibid., p. 43.
55. See Mark Holloway, *Heavens on Earth*, p. 204.
56. *The Fallen Leaves*, pp. 44–45.
57. Nordhoff, *The Communistic Societies of the United States*, p. 35.
58. Ibid., pp. 165–6.
59. Ibid., pp. 271–2.
60. *The Fallen Leaves*, pp. 319–30.
61. Ibid., p. 57.
62. Ibid., pp. 58–9.
63. Ibid., pp. 80–1.

64. This passage from *Man and Wife* is printed as a frontpiece to this book.
65. *The Fallen Leaves*, p. 93.
66. Ibid., pp. 119–20.
67. Ibid., p. 73.
68. Ibid., p. 104.
69. Ibid., pp. 183, 185.
70. Ibid., pp. 185–6.
71. Ibid., p. 188.
72. There is a precedence for this vision of the working class in *Culture and Anarchy*. See Chapter III.
73. *The Fallen Leaves*, p. 303.
74. Ibid., p. 200.
75. Ibid., p. 225.
76. Ibid., p. 225.
77. Ibid., p. 234.
78. Ibid., p. 232.
79. Ibid., pp. 235–6.
80. Ibid., p. 237.
81. Ibid., p. 240.
82. Ibid., pp. 240–1.
83. Ibid., p. 242.
84. Ibid., p. 245.
85. Ibid., p. 247.
86. J. H. Noyes, *History of American Socialism* (J. B. Lippincolt & Co., 1870), p. 631.
87. *The Fallen Leaves*, pp. 252–3.
88. Ibid., p. 255.
89. This is a misinterpretation of the novel which I found in Roger W. Dennis, *Wilkie Collins and the Conventions of the Thesis Novel*, dissertation, University of Alabama, 1973.
90. *The Fallen Leaves*, p. 327.
91. Ibid., p. 315.
92. Ibid., p. 317.
93. Ibid., p. 318.
94. Ibid., p. 318.
95. J. H. Noyes, *History of American Socialism*, p. 633.

CHAPTER 3: *BASIL*

1. Quoted in Page, *Wilkie Collins* (Routledge & Kegan Paul, London and Boston, 1974), p. 52.
2. Quoted in Page, pp. 47–8.
3. Richard Stang, *The Theory of the Novel in England 1850–1870* (Routledge & Kegan Paul, London, 1959).
4. Quoted in Page, pp. 52–3.
5. Quoted in Page, p. 49.
6. Page, p. 48.

7. Wilkie Collins, *Basil* (Dover Publications Inc., New York, 1980), p. iv.
8. Ibid., p. v.
9. Kenneth Robinson, *Wilkie Collins* (The Bodley Head, London, 1951), p. 309.
10. *Basil*, p. iv.
11. Ibid., p. v.
12. Ibid., p. v.
13. Ibid., pp. vi–vii.
14. Kenneth Robinson, *Wilkie Collins* (The Bodley Head, London, 1951), pp. 69–70.
15. Nuel Pharr Davis, *The Life of Wilkie Collins* (University of Illinois Press, Urbana, 1956), p. 116.
16. *Basil*, p. 10.
17. First published in *Household Words*, 1858. Reprinted in *My Miscellanies* (Samson and Low, London, 1863).
18. *My Miscellanies*, p. 18.
19. *Basil*, p. 192.
20. First published in *Household Words* (1856). Reprinted in *My Miscellanies*, op. cit.
21. *Basil*, pp. 18–19.
22. Ibid., pp. 19–20.
23. Ibid., p. 20.
24. Ibid., p. 20.
25. Ibid., p. 30.
26. Ibid., p. 39.
27. Ibid., p. 106.
28. Ibid., pp. 106–7.
29. Ibid., pp. 341–2.
30. Ibid., pp. 14–15.
31. Ibid., pp. 6–7.
32. Ibid., p. 7.
33. Ibid., p. 77.
34. Ibid., p. 237.
35. Ibid., p. 109.
36. Ibid., p. 110.
37. Ibid., p. 120.
38. Ibid., p. 61.
39. Ibid., p. 120.
40. Ibid., p. 130.
41. Ibid., p. 110.
42. Ibid., p. 110–11.
43. Ibid., p. 111.
44. Ibid., p. 295.
45. Ibid., pp. 242–3.
46. Ibid., p. 183.
47. Ibid., p. 186.
48. For a discussion of this, see Stang, pp. 191–206.
49. *Basil*, p. 199.
50. Ibid., p. 199.

51. Ibid., p. 48.
52. Ibid., p. 293.
53. Ibid., p. 339.
54. Ibid., p. vii.
55. Ibid., p. vii.

CHAPTER 4: *THE WOMAN IN WHITE*

1. Wilkie Collins, *The Woman in White* (Oxford University Press, 1980) p. xxx.
2. Ibid., p. 1.
3. Ibid., p. 1.
4. Ibid., p. 578.
5. Ibid., pp. 43–4.
6. Ibid., p. 3.
7. Ibid., p. 5.
8. Ibid., p. 7.
9. Walter E. Houghton, *The Victorian Frame of Mind* (Yale University Press, 1957) p. 156.
10. *The Woman in White*, pp. 365–6.
11. Winifred Hughes, *The Maniac in the Cellar* (Princeton University Press, 1980) p. 140.
12. *The Woman in White*, p. 27.
13. Ibid., p. 117.
14. Ibid., p. 150.
15. Ibid., p. 166.
16. Ibid., pp. 177–8.
17. Karl Marx, *The 18th Brumaire of Louis Bonaparte* (Progress Publishers, Moscow, 1977), p. 10.
18. *The Woman in White*, p. 259.
19. Ibid., p. 308.
20. Ibid., p. 312.
21. Ibid., p. 322.
22. Ibid., p. 325.
23. Ibid., p. 327.
24. Ibid., p. 331.
25. Ibid., p. 338.
26. Ibid., p. 348.
27. Ibid., p. 329.
28. Ibid., p. 434.
29. Ibid., pp. 45–6.
30. Ibid., p. 93.
31. Ibid., p. 95.
32. Ibid., p. 101.
33. Ibid., p. 104.
34. Ibid., p. 115.
35. Ibid., p. 117.
36. Ibid., p. 117.

37. Ibid., p. 122.
38. Ibid., p. 1.
39. Ibid., p. 124.
40. Ibid., p. 169.
41. Ibid., p. 169.
42. Ibid., pp. 190 and 268.
43. Ibid., p. 450.
44. Ibid., p. 187.
45. Ibid., p. 254.
46. Ibid., pp. 406–7.
47. Ibid., p. 408.
48. Ibid., p. 435.
49. Ibid., p. 465.
50. Ibid., p. 209.
51. Ibid., p. 209.
52. Ibid., p. 209.
53. Ibid., p. 211.
54. Ibid., p. 211.
55. Ibid., p. 212.
56. Ibid., p. 213. The theatrical resonance is also worthy of note and is reminiscent of *A Rogue's Life*.
57. Ibid., p. 299.
58. Ibid., p. 300.
59. Ibid., pp. 314, 329.
60. Ibid., p. 329.
61. Ibid., p. 379.
62. Ibid., p. 508.
63. Ibid., p. 508.
64. Ibid., p. 549.
65. Ibid., p. 25.
66. Ibid., p. 25.
67. Ibid., p. 25.
68. Ibid., p. 110.
69. Ibid., p. 208.
70. Ibid., p. 147.
71. Ibid., p. 191.
72. Ibid., p. 194.
73. Ibid., p. 200.
74. Ibid., p. 292.
75. Ibid., p. 404.
76. Ibid., p. 296.
77. Ibid., p. 296.
78. Walter E. Houghton, *The Victorian Frame of Mind* (Yale University Press, 1957), pp. 341–92.
79. *The Woman in White*, p. 26.
80. Ibid., p. 54.
81. Ibid., p. 88.
82. Ibid., p. 147.
83. Ibid., p. 167.

84. Ibid., p. 403.
85. Ibid., p. 441.
86. Ibid., p. 88.
87. Ibid., p. 68.
88. Ibid., p. 32.
89. Ibid., p. 32.
90. Ibid., p. 263.
91. Ibid., p. 326.
92. Ibid., p. 200.
93. Ibid., pp. 33–4.
94. Ibid., p. 34.
95. Ibid., p. 88.
96. Ibid., p. 97.
97. Ibid., p. 231.
98. Ibid., p. 322.
99. Ibid., p. 323.
100. Ibid., p. 354.
101. Ibid., p. 366.
102. Ibid., p. 376.
103. Ibid., pp. 393–4.
104. Ibid., p. 410.
105. Ibid., p. 465.
106. Ibid., pp. 581–2.

CHAPTER 5: *MAN AND WIFE*

1. Wilkie Collins, *Man and Wife* (Dover Publications, New York, 1983), Preface.
2. Matthew Arnold, *Culture and Anarchy* (Cambridge University Press, London, 1979), pp. 104–9.
3. *Man and Wife*, Preface.
4. *Man and Wife*, p. 9.
5. Ibid., p. 11.
6. Ibid., p. 11.
7. Ibid., p. 12.
8. Ibid., p. 18.
9. Ibid., p. 18.
10. Ibid., p. 00.
11. Étienne Balibar, 'The Elements of the Structure and their History' in *Reading Capital*, Louis Athusser and Étienne Balibar (New Left Books, London, 1975), p. 229.
12. *Man and Wife*, p. 23.
13. Ibid., p. 23.
14. This problem is at the centre of Collins' previous novel, *The Moonstone*. See John R. Reed, 'English Imperialism and the Unacknowledged Crime of the Moonstone', *Clio*, 1973.
15. *Man and Wife*, pp. 23–4.
16. Ibid., p. 221.

17. Ibid., p. 24.
18. Ibid., p. 24.
19. Ibid., p. 25.
20. Ibid., p. 25.
21. Ibid., p. 28.
22. Ibid., p. 28.
23. Ibid., pp. 26–7.
24. Ibid., p. 31.
25. Ibid., p. 33.
26. Ibid., p. 34.
27. Ibid., p. 38.
28. Ibid., p. 116.
29. Ibid., p. 150.
30. Ibid., p. 57.
31. Ibid., p. 57.
32. ibid., p. 70.
33. Ibid., p. 73.
34. Ibid., p. 75. There are similarities here with *Culture and Anarchy*. Arnold sees some good in the cult of Athleticism in so far as the future of the country is concerned – 'the result of all the games and sports which occupy the passing generation of boys and girls may be the establishment of a better and sounder physical type for the future to work with', but in the meantime the passing generation is 'culturally' sacrificed, p. 61.
35. Ibid., p. 75.
36. Ibid., p. 76.
37. Ibid., p. 80.
38. Ibid., p. 84.
39. Ibid., p. 85.
40. Ibid., p. 86.
41. Ibid., p. 88.
42. Ibid., p. 90.
43. Ibid., p. 98.
44. Ibid., p. 121.
45. Ibid., p. 124.
46. Ibid., pp. 128–9. Collins' attitudes to stereotypical representation of women is discussed elsewhere in this book.
47. Ibid., p. 128.
48. Ibid., p. 132.
49. Ibid., p. 143.
50. Ibid., p. 143.
51. Ibid., p. 164.
52. Ibid., p. 170.
53. Ibid., p. 167.
54. Ibid., p. 184.
55. Ibid., p. 185.
56. Ibid., p. 188.
57. Ibid., p. 191.
58. Ibid., p. 195.

59. Ibid., p. 195. Arnold and Blanche married in Kent.
60. Ibid., p. 195.
61. Ibid., p. 200.
62. Ibid., p. 200.
63. Ibid., p. 207.
64. Ibid., p. 209.
65. Cf. Charlotte Bronte's image of living burial in *Villette*.
66. *Man and Wife*, p. 209.
67. Ibid., p. 212.
68. Ibid., p. 217.
69. Ibid., p. 218.
70. Ibid., p. 218.
71. Ibid., p. 220.
72. Ibid., p. 220.
73. Ibid., p. 220.
74. Ibid., p. 220.
75. Ibid., p. 220.
76. Ibid., p. 221.
77. Ibid., p. 229.
78. Ibid., p. 232.

CHAPTER 6: *NO NAME*

1. Wilkie Collins, *No Name* (Dover Publications, New York 1978), p. 17.
2. Ibid., p. 11.
3. Ibid., p. 12.
4. Ibid., p. 13.
5. Ibid., p. 16.
6. Ibid., p. 17.
7. Ibid., p. 18.
8. Ibid., p. 22.
9. Ibid., p. 22.
10. Ibid., p. 25.
11. Ibid., p. 10.
12. Ibid., p. 34.
13. Ibid., p. 155.
14. Louis Althusser, 'Ideology and Ideological State Apparatuses', *Lenin and Philosophy* (Monthly Review Press, New York and London), p. 171.
15. Ibid., p. 156.
16. *No Name*, p. 173.
17. Ibid., p. 204.
18. Ibid., p. 517.
19. Ibid., p. 555.
20. Ibid., p. 40.
21. Ibid., p. 88.
22. Ibid., p. 492.
23. Ibid., p. 181.
24. Ibid., p. 182.

25. Ibid., p. 590.
26. Ibid., p. 586.
27. Ibid., p. 586.
28. Ibid., p. 269.
29. Ibid., p. 586.
30. Ibid., p. 184.
31. Ibid., p. 207.
32. Wragge is discussed in connection with Protestant conscience in *Horror Fiction in the Protestant Tradition*, V. R. L. Sage (Macmillan, forthcoming).
33. *No Name*, p. 203.
34. Ibid., p. 358.
35. Ibid., p. 270.
36. Ibid., p. 160.
37. Ibid., p. 55.
38. Ibid., pp. 250, 276.
39. Ibid., p. 446.
40. Ibid., p. 218.
41. Ibid., p. 121.
42. Ibid., p. 496.
43. Ibid., p. 147.
44. Ibid., p. 39.
45. Ibid., p. 70.
46. Ibid., p. 237.
47. Ibid., p. 119.
48. Ibid., p. 36.
49. Ibid., p. 65.
50. Ibid., p. 262.
51. Ibid., p. 248.
52. Ibid., p. 295.
53. Ibid., p. 307.
54. Ibid., p. 313.
55. Ibid., p. 319.
56. Ibid., p. 427.
57. Ibid., p. 41.
58. Ibid., pp. 417–18.
59. Ibid., p. 579.

CHAPTER 7: WOMEN IN COLLINS

1. Gail Cunningham, *The New Woman and the Victorian Novel* (Macmillan, London, 1978).
2. Ibid., pp. 27–8.
3. Ibid., p. 28.
4. 'A Petition to the Novel Writers' (1856) and 'A Shockingly Rude Article' (1858). Both republished in *My Miscellanies* (repr. A. M. S. Press, New York, 1970).
5. *My Miscellanies*, p. 107.

6. Ibid., pp. 113–114.

7. Ibid., p. 114.

8. Ibid., p. 115.

9. Ibid., p. 116.

10. Ibid., p. 117.

11. Ibid., p. 115.

12. Ibid., pp. 111–16.

13. Ibid., p. 117.

14. J. S. Mill, *The Subjection of Women* (Everyman, London, 1965), p. 232.

15. Ibid., p. 273.

16. E. Lynn Linton, 'The Girl of the Period', *Saturday Review* (14 Mar. 1868), pp. 339–40.

17. Mrs Lynn Linton, 'The Epicene Sex', quoted in John Goode, 'Women and the Literary Text' in *The Rights and Wrongs of Women*, eds Juliet Mitchell and Ann Oakley (Penguin, London, 1976), pp. 220–1.

18. *My Miscellanies*, pp. 18–19.

19. *The Evil Genius* (Chatto & Windus, London, 1907), pp. 45–6.

20. Ibid., p. 145.

21. *Basil*, p. 5.

22. Ibid., p. 21.

23. Ibid., p. 193.

24. Ibid., p. 30.

25. Collins is to repeat this equation of mouth with vagina. Marian Halcombe's 'moustache', as Harvey Peter Sucksmith argues, marks 'that nether face of sexuality with other lips and other cheeks, which is secretly displaced upwards in Marian's form'. Sucksmith, introduction to *The Woman in White* (Oxford University Press, 1980), p. xvi.

26. Ibid., pp. 168–69.

27. *Basil*, pp. 45–7.

28. Ibid., p. 75.

29. Ibid., p. 104.

30. Ibid., p. 172.

31. Ibid., p. 294.

32. *Armadale*, p. 87.

33. Gail Cunningham, op. cit., p. 29.

34. *Armadale*, pp. 254, 321, 334.

35. Ibid., p. 342.

36. Quoted in Page, p. 150.

37. *Armadale*, p. 56.

38. Ibid., p. 334.

39. Ibid., p. 335.

40. Ibid., p. 335.

41. Ibid., pp. 337–8.

42. Ibid., p. 283.

43. Ibid., p. 143. In *Wilkie Collins, Le Fanu and Others* (London, Constable and Company, 1931), S. M. Ellis argues that Mrs Oldershaw 'was suggested by the case of the notorious Madame Rachel, who at her Beauty Parlour, 47A New Bond Street, professed to make "beautiful for

ever" foolish women who were prepared to pay Madame's exorbitant prices for baths, perfumes and unguents'.

44. Ibid., pp. 148–9.
45. Jeanne Fahnestock, 'The Heroine of Irregular Features: Physignomy and Conventions of Heroine Description', *Victorian Studies* 24 (spring 1981), pp. 325–50.
46. *Armadale*, p. 245.
47. Ibid., p. 381.
48. Ibid., p. 380–1.
49. Ibid., p. 320.
50. Ibid., p. 193.
51. Ibid., p. 254.
52. Ibid., p. 254.
53. Ibid., p. 254.
54. Ibid., p. 254.
55. See above, p. 34.
56. Ibid., p. 488.
57. Ibid., p. 488.
58. Ibid., p. 377.
59. Ibid., p. 528.
60. Ibid., p. 576.
61. Jeanne Fahnestock, op. cit.
62. Sue Lonoff, *Wilkie Collins and His Victorian Readers*, p. 155.
63. *The Law and the Lady* (Chatto & Windus, London, 1913), pp. 4–5.
64. This metaphor is discussed at length in *The Mad Woman in the Attic*, Sandra M. Gilbert and Susan Gubar (Yale University Press, New Haven, Conn. and London, 1979), pp. 3–45.
65. *The Law and the Lady*, p. 67.
66. Ibid., p. 425.
67. Ibid., p. 425.
68. Ibid., p. 175.
69. Ibid., p. 301.
70. Ibid., p. 301.
71. Ibid., p. 175–6.
72. Ibid., p. 186.
73. Ibid., p. 237.
74. Ibid., p. 203.
75. Ibid., p. 203.
76. Ibid., pp. 210–11.
77. Ibid., pp. 211–12.
78. Ibid., p. 213.
79. Ibid., p. 308.
80. Ibid., p. 224.
81. Ibid., p. 213.
82. Ibid., p. 214.
83. Ibid., p. 222.
84. Ibid., pp. 410–11.
85. Ibid., pp. 252–3.

86. *The Evil Genius*, pp. 145–6.
87. Ibid., p. 308.
88. Ibid., p. 169.

CONCLUSION

1. Harland S. Nelson, 'Dickens' Plots: "The Ways of Providence" Or The Influence of Collins?', *Victorian Newsletter*, no. 19 (spring 1961), pp. 11–14.

Bibliography

The following bibliography includes all the Collins novels I mention in my book. Under *Secondary Material* I list all the critical and scholarly works which have contributed to the evolution of my thought. More detailed bibliographies on Collins may be found in *Wilkie Collins: an Annotated Bibliography*, ed. Kirk H. Beetz, The Scarecrow Author Bibliographies, No. 35 (The Scarecrow Press, Inc., Metuchen, N.J. and London, 1978). This has been supplemented with more recent material published since 1978 in *Wilkie Collins and His Victorian Readers: a Study in the Rhetoric of Authorship*, Sue Lonoff (AMS Press Inc., New York, 1982).

EDITIONS OF COLLINS' NOVELS MENTIONED IN BOOK

The Dead Secret (Dover Publications Inc., New York, 1979).
The Moonstone (Penguin, London, 1979).
Armadale (Dover Publications Inc., New York, 1977).
A Rogue's Life (Modern Library Company, London, c. 1890).
The Fallen Leaves (Chatto & Windus, London, 1890).
The New Magdalen (Chatto & Windus, London, 1900).
Basil (Dover Publications Inc., New York, 1980).
The Woman in White (Oxford University Press, 1980).
Man and Wife (Dover Publications, New York, 1983).
No Name (Dover Publications Inc., New York, 1978).
'A Petition to the Novel Writers' and 'A Shockingly Rude Article' in *My Miscellanies* (repr. A.M.S. Press, New York, 1970).
The Evil Genius (Chatto & Windus, London, 1907).
The Law and The Lady (Chatto & Windus, London, 1913).

SECONDARY MATERIAL

Adelman, Paul, *Victorian Radicalism* (Longman, London and New York, 1984).

Althusser, Louis, *Lenin and Philosophy* (Monthly Review Press, New York and London, n.d.).

Althusser, Louis and Balibar, Étienne, *Reading Capital* (New Left Books, London, 1970).

Andrew, R. V., *Wilkie Collins: a Critical Study of His Prose Fiction, with a Bibliography* (Garland Press, New York, 1979).

Arnold, Matthew, *Culture and Anarchy* (Cambridge University Press, 1979).

Ashley, Robert P., 'Kenneth Robinson's *Wilkie Collins*', *Nineteenth Century Fiction* (7 Sept. 1952) pp. 124–31.

——, *Wilkie Collins* (Barker, London, 1952).

——, 'Wilkie Collins and the Detective Story', *Nineteenth Century Fiction*, 6 (June 1951) pp. 47–60.

——, 'Wilkie Collins Reconsidered', *Nineteenth Century Fiction*, 4 (Mar. 1950) pp. 265–73.

Austen, Jane, *Emma* (Penguin Books, London, 1980).

Backstrom, Philip N., *Christian Socialism and Cooperation in Victorian England* (Croom Helm, London, 1974).

Barthes, Roland, *S/Z* (Jonathan Cape, London, 1975).

——, *Mythologies* (Paladin, London, 1972).

Belsey, Catherine, *Critical Practice* (Methuen, London, 1980).

Blair, David, 'Wilkie Collins and the Crisis of Suspense' in *Reading the Victorian Novel: Detail into Form*, ed. Ian Gregor (Vision Press, London, 1980).

Booth, Bradford, A., 'Wilkie Collins and the Art of Fiction', *Nineteenth Century Fiction*, 6 (Sep. 1951) pp. 131–43.

Brannan, Robert Louis, 'Introduction' to *Under the Management of Mr. Charles Dickens: His Production of 'The Frozen Deep'* (Cornell University Press, Ithaca, New York, 1966).

Brantlinger, Patrick, 'What Is "Sensational" about the "Sensation Novel"?', *Nineteenth Century Fiction* (June, 1982) pp. 1–29.

Brontë, Emily, *Wuthering Heights* (Penguin, London, 1976).

Brontë, Charlotte, *Villette* (Penguin, London, 1983).

Buckley, Jerome H., *The Worlds of Victorian Fiction*, Harvard English Studies 6 (Harvard University Press, Cambridge, Mass., 1975).

Burgess, Anthony, 'Introduction' to *The Moonstone* (Pan, London, 1967).

Calder, Jenni, *Women and Marriage in Victorian Fiction* (Thames & Hudson, London, 1976).

Caracciolo, Peter L., 'Wilkie Collins' "Divine Comedy"; the Use of Dante in *The Woman in White*', *Nineteenth Century Fiction*, 25 (Mar. 1971) pp. 383–404.

Cassirer, Ernst, *Language and Myth* (Dover Publications Inc., New York, 1953).

Christensen, Torben, *Origins and History of Christian Socialism, 1848–1854* (Universitetforlaget 1, Aarhus, 1962).

Coleman, William Rollin, 'The University of Texas Collection of the Letters of Wilkie Collins, Victorian Novelist', dissertation, University of Texas at Austin, 1975.

Colloms, Brenda, *Victorian Visionaries* (Constable, London, 1982).

Coward, Rosalind and Ellis, John, *Language and Materialism* (Routledge & Kegan Paul, London, 1977).

Cunningham, Gail, *The New Woman and the Victorian Novel* (Macmillan, London, 1978).

Cunningham, Hugh, *Leisure and the Industrial Revolution* (Croom Helm, London, 1980).

Davis, Nuel Pharr, *The Life of Wilkie Collins* (University of Illinois Press, Urbana, 1956).

Dennis, Roger W., 'Wilkie Collins and the Conventions of the Thesis Novel', dissertation, University of Alabama, 1973.

Dickens, Charles, *Letters to Wilkie Collins, 1851–1870*, eds Laurence Hutton and Georgina Hogarth (J. R. Osgood, McIlvane & Co., London, 1892).

——, *Dombey and Son* (Penguin, London, 1975).

——, *Little Dorrit* (Penguin, London, 1981).

Eliot, T. S., 'Wilkie Collins and Dickens', *Selected Essays* (Faber & Faber, London, 1932).

Ellis, S. M., *Wilkie Collins, Le Fanu and Others* (Constable, London, 1931).

Fahnestock, Jeanne, 'The Heroine of Irregular Features: Physiognomy and Conventions of Heroine Description', *Victorian Studies*, 24 (spring 1981) pp. 325–50.

Foucault, Michel, *Discipline and Punish* (Allen Lane, London, 1977).

Frederick, Peter J., *Knights of The Golden Rule* (University Press of Kentucky, 1976).

Gaskell, Elizabeth, *Mary Barton* (Penguin, London, 1979).

Gilbert, Sandra M., and Gubar, Susan, *The Madwoman in The Attic* (Yale University Press, New Haven, Conn. and London, 1979).

Goode, John, 'Woman and the Literary Text', *The Rights and Wrongs of Women*, eds Mitchell, Juliet and Oakley, Ann (Penguin, London, 1976) pp. 217–56.

Hennelly, Mark M., Jr, 'Reading Detection in *The Woman in White*', *Texas Studies in Literature and Language*, 22 (winter 1980) pp. 449–67.

Holloway, Mark, *Heavens on Earth* (Dover Publications, New York, 1966).

Houghton, Walter E., *The Victorian Frame of Mind, 1830–1870* (Yale University Press, New Haven, Conn. and London, 1957).

Hughes, Thomas, *Rugby, Tenessee* (Macmillan, London, 1881).

Hughes, Winifred, *The Maniac in the Cellar: Sensation Novels of the 1860s* (Princeton University Press, 1980).

Hutter, Albert D., 'Dreams, Transformations and Literature: the Implications of Detective Fiction', *Victorian Studies*, 19 (Dec. 1975) pp. 181–209.

Hyder, Clyde K., 'Wilkie Collins and *The Woman in White*', *PMLA* 54 (Mar. 1939) pp. 297–303.

Jackson, Rosemary, *Fantasy: the Literature of Subversion* (Methuen, London and New York, 1981).

Jones, Peter d'A., *The Christian Socialist Revival 1877–1914* (Princeton University Press, 1968).

Kendrick, Walter M., 'The Sensationalism of *The Woman in White*', *Nineteenth Century Fiction*, 32 (June 1977) pp. 18–35.

Knoepflmacher, U. C., 'The Counterworld of Victorian Fiction and *The Woman in White*', *The Worlds of Victorian Fiction*, ed. Jerome H. Buckley (Harvard University Press, Cambridge Mass., 1975).

Laidlaw, R. P., ' "Awful Images and Associations": a Study of Wilkie Collins' *The Moonstone*', *Southern Review: an Australian Journal of Literary Studies* (University of Adelaide, 9 Nov. 1976) pp. 211–27.

Lambert, Gavin, *The Dangerous Edge* (Barrie & Jenkins, London, 1975).

Linton, E. Lynn, 'The Girl of the Period' and 'The Epicene Sex' quoted in Goode, John, 'Woman and the Literary Text'.

Lonoff, Sue, *Wilkie Collins and His Victorian Readers* (A.M.S. Press Inc., New York, 1982).

——, 'Charles Dickens and Wilkie Collins', *Nineteenth Century Fiction*, 35 (Sept. 1980) pp. 150–70.

MacEachen, Dougald, 'Wilkie Collins and British Law', *Nineteenth Century Fiction*, 5 (Sept. 1950) pp. 121–36.

Macherey, Pierre, *A Theory of Literary Production* (Routledge & Kegan Paul, London, 1978).

de la Mare, Walter, 'The Early Novels of Wilkie Collins', *The Eighteen-Sixties*, ed. John Drinkwater (Cambridge University Press, 1932).

Marshall, William H., *Wilkie Collins* (Twaine, New York, 1970).

Marx, Karl, *The Eighteenth Brumaire of Louis Bonaparte* (Progress Publishers, Moscow, 1977).

Marx, Karl and Engels, Frederick, *The Communist Manifesto* (Penguin, Harmondsworth, Middx, 1967).

Mayor, Stephen, *The Churches and the Labour Movement* (Independent Press, London, 1967).

Mill, John Stuart, *The Subjection of Women* (Everyman, London, 1965).

Miller, D. A., 'From *Roman Policier* to *Roman-Police*: Wilkie Collins's *The Moonstone*', *Novel* 13 (winter 1980) pp. 153–70.

Neale, Stephen, *Genre* (British Film Institute, London, 1980).

——, 'Stereotypes', *Screen Education*, 32/32 (1979/80).

Nelson, Harland S., 'Dickens' Plots: "The Ways of Providence" or The Influence of Collins?' *Victorian Newsletter*, no. 19 (spring 1961) pp. 11–14.

Nordhoff, Charles, *The Communistic Societies of the United States* (Hillary House Publications, New York, 1961).

Noyes, John H., *History of American Socialism* (J. B. Lippincott & Co., Philadelphia, 1870).

O'Neill, Philip G., 'A Benevolent Salieri: From Russian Formalism to Structuralism in Literary Scholarship', dissertation University of Essex, 1979.

——, 'Illusion and Reality in Wilkie Collins' *Armadale*', *Essays in Poetics*, 7, 1 (1982) pp. 42–61.

Ousby, Ian, *Bloodhounds of Heaven: the Detective in English Fiction from Godwin to Doyle* (Harvard University Press, Cambridge, Mass. 1976).

Page, Norman, (ed.), *Wilkie Collins* (Routledge & Kegan Paul, London and Boston, 1974).

Parrish, M. L. and Miller, Elizabeth V., *Wilkie Collins and Charles Reade* (Burt Franklin, New York, 1968).

Porter, Dennis, *The Pursuit of Crime* (Yale University Press, New Haven, Conn. and London, 1981).

Phillips, Walter C., *Dickens, Reade and Collins – Sensation Novelists* (Columbia University Press, New York, 1919, repr. Russell & Russell, New York, 1962).

Reed, John R., 'English Imperialism and the Unacknowledged Crime of *The Moonstone*', *Clio*, 1 (June 1973) pp. 281–90.

——, *Victorian Conventions* (Ohio University Press, 1975).

Robinson, Kenneth, *Wilkie Collins: a Biography* (Bodley Head, London, 1951).

Sage, V. R. L., *Horror Fiction in the Protestant Tradition* (Macmillan, forthcoming).

Sayers, Dorothy L., *Wilkie Collins: a Biographical and Critical Study*, ed., E. R. Gregory (Friends of the University of Toledo Libraries, Toledo, 1977).

——, Introduction to, *The Moonstone* (Dent, London, 1944).

——, *The Omnibus of Crime* (Garden City Publishing Co., New York, 1929).

Shelley, Mary, *Frankenstein* (Oxford University Press, 1980).

Stang, Richard, *The Theory of the Novel in England: 1850–1870* (Columbia University Press, New York, 1959).

Stewart, J. I. M., Introduction to *The Moonstone* (Penguin, London, 1979).

Sucksmith, Harvey Peter, Introduction to *The Woman in White* (Oxford University Press, 1980).

Sutherland, John A., 'Two Emergencies in the Writing of *The Woman in White*', *Yearbook of English Studies*, 7 (1977) pp. 148–56.

Symons, Julian, *Bloody Murder* (Faber & Faber, London, 1972).

——, Introduction to *The Woman in White* (Penguin, London, 1974).

Thomas, Keith, 'The Double Standard', *Journal of the History of Ideas*, 20 (1959) pp. 195–216.

Todorov, Tzvetan, *The Poetics of Prose* (Cornell University Press, Ithaca, New York, 1977).

Trodd, Anthea, Introduction to *The Moonstone* (Oxford University Press, 1982).

Vicinus, Martha, *Suffer and Be Still: Women in the Victorian Age* (Methuen, London, 1972).

——, *A Widening Sphere: Changing Roles of the Victorian Woman* (Methuen, London, 1977).

Volosinov, V. N., *Marxism and the Philosophy of Language* (Seminar Press, New York, 1973).

Waites, Bernard *et al.* (eds), *Popular Culture: Past and Present* (Croom Helm, London, 1982).

Index

237

PAN AMERICAN UNIVERSITY LIBRARY
BROWNSVILLE, TEXAS 78520